# Democracy and Revolution

# Democracy and Revolution

## Latin America and Socialism Today

D.L. RABY

Pluto Press
LONDON • ANN ARBOR, MI

and

Between the Lines
TORONTO

First published 2006 by Pluto Press
345 Archway Road, London N6 5AA
and 839 Greene Street, Ann Arbor, MI 48106
www.plutobooks.com

and

Between the Lines
720 Bathurst Street, Suite 404, Toronto, Ontario M5S 2R4, Canada
1-800-718-7201
www.btlbooks.com

British Library Cataloguing in Publication Data
A catalogue record for this book is available from the British Library

ISBN    0 7453 2436 3 hardback
ISBN    0 7453 2435 5 paperback

Library of Congress Cataloging in Publication Data applied for

Library and Archives Canada Cataloguing in Publication
Democracy and revolution : Latin America and socialism today / D.L. Raby.
Includes bibliographical references and index.
ISBN 1–897071–20–5
  1. Socialism—Cuba. 2. Socialism—Venezuela. 3. Cuba—History—Revolution, 1959.
4. Venezuela—History—1974–1999. 5. Venezuela—History—1999– . 6. Socialism—
Latin America. 7. Revolutions—Latin America. I. Title.
HX110.5.R33 2006                    320.53'15098              C2006–903132–0

Between the Lines gratefully acknowledges assistance for its publishing activities from
the Canada Council for the Arts, the Ontario Arts Council, and the Government of
Canada through the Book Publishing Industry Development Program.


10   9   8   7   6   5   4   3   2   1


Designed and produced for Pluto Press by
Chase Publishing Services Ltd, Fortescue, Sidmouth, EX10 9QG, England
Typeset from disk by Stanford DTP Services, Northampton, England
Printed and bound in the European Union by
Antony Rowe Ltd, Chippenham and Eastbourne, England

*This book is dedicated to*
*Presidents Fidel Castro Ruz, Hugo Chávez Frías*
*and popular movements throughout the world*

# Contents

# Acknowledgements

First and foremost I have to acknowledge the constant support and assistance of Luisa, whose love and encouragement were fundamental in keeping me going. Secondly I have to thank all my Cuban friends, beginning with the staff and former staff of the Instituto de Historia de Cuba, especially Luis Serrano, Luis Rosado, Manuel Rosado, Gladys Marel García and Amparo Hernández; José Tabares del Real, now sadly deceased, and Sergio Guerra Vilaboy of the Instituto de Altos Estudios Don Fernando Ortiz in Havana; María del Pilar Díaz Castañón; Manuel Mencía of the Oficina de Publicaciones del Consejo de Estado in Havana; Guillermo Santisteban, Juana María Meza, Sunia Santisteban and family of Havana. In Venezuela there are many friends and colleagues who have been extremely helpful, notably Dick Parker of the Universidad Central de Venezuela, Deputy Elvis Amoroso and his wife Melania, Carolus Wimmer, Freddy Gutiérrez, Silvio Villegas, Gilberto Giménez, Maximilien Arbeláiz, Alex Main, Aurelio Gil Beroes, Blanca Eekhout, Carlos Pino, Zuraima Martínez, Pedro Morejón, Maritza Mendoza and Reinaldo Quijada of Clase Media en Positivo, Francisco González and Eluz Paredes and others of the Coordinadora Popular de Caracas, Hans Lorenzo and family, Juan Romero of the Universidad del Zulia, and the staff or former staff of the Universidad Bolivariana, Ernesto Wong, Adrián Padilla and others, especially those who participated in my guest seminar in September 2004. In Portugal thanks are due to Iva Delgado, João Arsénio Nunes, Fernando Rosas, Mário Tomé, António Costa Pinto, João Mário Mascarenhas, António Reis, Boaventura de Sousa Santos, Alípio de Freitas, Miriam Halpern Pereira and the staff of the ISCTE, and many others. In Britain I have to thank Alistair Hennessy, Tony Kapcia, Ken Cole, James Dunkerley, Francisco Domínguez, Andy Higginbottom and other friends of the Colombia Solidarity Campaign, and the staff of the Institute of Latin American Studies at the University of Liverpool. In Canada I am also grateful to many friends and former colleagues, notably Carlos Torres, Luis Aravena, Liisa North, Peter Blanchard, Keith Ellis, Judith Teichman, Dieter Misgeld and Claude Morin, and many others at the University of Toronto, York University and elsewhere. In Colombia I have to thank Lilia Solano, Gloria Gaitán, Francisco Ramírez, Jairo Iván Peña, Amalfi Serpa and several others. A special word of thanks is due to Marta Harnecker and Michael Lebowitz, whether in Caracas, Havana or elsewhere. Recognition is also due to José Nun, Miguel Murmis and Naguy Marcilla in Argentina, and many others in Latin America, North America and Europe whom I cannot mention by name for lack of space. Finally, a word of recognition to my son Chris who has also shown constant interest in my work. Doubtless some of those mentioned will have radical disagreements with my conclusions, but if this were not the case the book would not have been worth writing.

D.L. Raby
Liverpool, February 2006

# Preface

This book brings together ideas which I had been working through for many years, but it is above all a response to a sense of the urgency of finding a way forward for the Left and progressive popular movements in today's 'globalised' neo-liberal world. The main focus is on Latin America, above all Cuba and Venezuela, but the theses put forward are of global significance. My interest in Latin America has always been not only professional or even cultural but also political; for a number of reasons it was and is the world region which has generated the most original and vigorous popular and revolutionary movements, and which continues to offer inspiration to those struggling for a better world in Europe, North America and elsewhere. In my view the Cuban revolution, for all its faults, continues to represent the most advanced attempt to build socialism anywhere in the world; but this makes it all the more important both to defend Cuba and to analyse it critically. It also makes it essential to understand just why this island nation has been able to achieve so much and why it survives, which most friends of Cuba do not. As for Venezuela, its prominence in the (limited) coverage granted by the British media to Latin America makes its relevance obvious, although those who rely on the mass media for their information will be more than a little surprised by my positive, indeed enthusiastic and passionate, view of current developments in that country. The brief attention given in Chapter 6 to Chile and Nicaragua is justified by the book's concern above all with successful revolutionary processes, although much can be learnt from these regrettably aborted processes; the same applies to Portugal, which is given somewhat more attention because it brings the argument home to Europe.

My conclusions are (guardedly) positive: a new, non-dogmatic, popular Left is emerging, with a clear political perspective. It can draw inspiration from all the experiences mentioned (and others), but above all from Cuba and Venezuela, which demonstrate that another world is indeed possible, but only if the enormous energy of popular resistance is ultimately directed to achieve political power. The state may have been weakened by capitalist globalisation, but it has not disappeared, and indeed part of the neo-liberal conjuring trick has been to create the illusion that it has.

One more preliminary remark: I have relied heavily on Latin American (and Portuguese) sources, both in order to let the protagonists speak for themselves and because I believe a great deal of creative theoretical work is being produced in these countries which tends to be ignored in the Anglo-Saxon world. In order to convey what I believe to be the correct meaning of these authors, all translations from Spanish, Portuguese or French are mine unless otherwise indicated.

D.L. Raby

# 1
# The Disinherited Left: From Dogmatic Orthodoxy to Romantic Anti-capitalism

Since the collapse of the Soviet Union, the Left has been in crisis. The orthodox Communist model was discredited even among its traditional supporters, and as the Eastern European countries were seduced one after another by the siren song of capitalist consumerism, it soon became clear that Western Social Democracy had also lost its way. The ideological victory of supply-side economics and monetarism paved the way for what we now know as neo-liberalism, and with Tony Blair and 'New Labour' leading the way, Social Democratic parties ceased to defend even a minimal degree of public ownership and became advocates of 'Thatcherism lite': the supremacy of the market with only a limited social safety net to protect the most vulnerable. Neo-liberal globalisation appeared to make the viability of any kind of socialism problematic: could any state, even the most powerful, resist or control market forces? With some transnational corporations being bigger than the GDPs of all but the largest countries, it was said that the state could no longer even regulate the economy, let alone control it.

In these conditions even traditional left-wing critics of Stalinism like the Trotskyists failed to benefit politically from the implosion of 'really existing socialism', and the neo-liberal consensus seemed to rule the roost in both East and West. The electoral defeat of the Sandinistas in Nicaragua early in 1990 seemed to confirm that even Latin America, with its vigorous independent revolutionary tradition, was not immune to the debacle of socialist values. Although Communist regimes survived in China and Vietnam, they appeared to be adopting capitalist market mechanisms with indecent haste, while the other case of East Asian socialism, North Korea, seemed to be locked in a Stalinist time-warp. It was in this context that Francis Fukuyama could write about 'The End of History' (Fukuyama 1992), presenting liberal capitalism as the final and universal goal of humanity, and in Latin America Jorge Castañeda could produce *Utopia Unarmed: The Latin American Left after the Cold War* (Castañeda 1994), which amounted to a repudiation of that continent's revolutionary

1

heritage in the name of Blairite Social Democracy (and perhaps not surprisingly, Castañeda later became a minister in the government of right-wing Mexican President Vicente Fox).

Of course, the triumphalism of the neo-liberal advocates of the 'New World Order' was soon tempered by the rise of vigorous mass movements in opposition to the negative impact of market reforms. In Latin America the ink was scarcely dry on Castañeda's book when in January 1994 the Zapatista uprising in Chiapas showed that the region's revolutionary heritage was not dead and that popular opposition to the neo-liberal consensus could take militant forms. In Europe and North America the anti-globalisation movement revealed the hostility of a significant minority to the new orthodoxy and their allegiance to collective, egalitarian and anti-capitalist values. The rise of the PT (Workers' Party) in Brazil and its innovative practices of local participatory democracy with such original initiatives as the 'participatory budget' was another hopeful sign, and within a few years the Brazilian city of Porto Alegre became the symbol of the convergence of the new Latin American popular movements with the anti-globalisation movement in the North, by hosting the first three World Social Forums. But none of these new movements presented a coherent alternative strategy: their strength was based on contestation and disruption of the neo-liberal consensus, and if they had a strategy it was almost anti-political or neo-anarchist, rejecting political parties and (as the Zapatistas explicitly proclaimed) repudiating the struggle for state power on principle, whether by armed or peaceful means. The spirit of the times is radically democratic and suspicious of self-proclaimed vanguards, or indeed of vanguards of any kind – but the apparent alternative favoured by many in the anti-globalisation, anti-war and anti-capitalist movements is a kind of idealistic anarchism, a conception which has not ceased to be profoundly problematic. Without a doubt the great strength of these movements, which have achieved such an impressive degree of support in Europe and North America, has been their loose, decentralised and flexible character. But such a structure (or lack thereof) may be very effective in an oppositional or contestational movement, yet thoroughly dysfunctional for a coherent political project, let alone a government exercising state power. Those who defend the actions and vision of Chávez in Venezuela or Lula in Brazil, or indeed of the Cuban government, are constantly greeted with the refrain that liberation, or socialism, or popular democracy, has to be the work of 'the people themselves' or 'the working class itself', begging the question of what kind of structure and leadership the Promethean people or working class might need in order to implement their sovereign will. Insistence on direct, unmediated popular protagonism is admirable, but it becomes a futile distraction if it is elevated to the status of absolute dogma, evading questions of representation, leadership, organisation and structure which are crucial to the success of any alternative movement. This romantic but ultimately defeatist approach has since been formulated in more elaborate philosophical form by John Holloway in *Change the World Without Taking Power* (Holloway 2002).

Today, 15 years after the fall of the Berlin Wall, the neo-liberal consensus is increasingly questioned and the 'End of History' thesis is thoroughly discredited. The new geo-political polarisation in the wake of the 9/11 attacks and the aggressive strategy of the Anglo-Saxon powers in the so-called 'War on Terror' has created a much more problematic situation not just for the Left but for the future of humanity as a whole. This has provoked the emergence of an unprecedented mass anti-war movement throughout the world, and particularly in Europe, which has merged with the anti-globalisation or anti-capitalist movement to produce the embryo of a real alternative. But it still lacks a political strategy, a strategy for taking power and an alternative socio-economic model. This book will attempt to address the problem of a political alternative for the Left and the popular movement, an alternative which is not limited to cosmetic reforms of neo-liberal capitalism. Such an alternative is scarcely likely to emerge from within existing Social Democratic parties, which are so thoroughly incorporated into the system as to be incapable of renewal. Equally, in those countries where Communist parties still retain a residual strength and adhere to a traditional anti-system line (the Portuguese party is a good example), they may constitute admirable bastions of resistance to neo-liberal hegemony, but their almost total lack of theoretical renovation shows that they have failed to come to terms with the lessons of the Soviet collapse and have nothing creative to offer. With some exceptions, this also applies to most of the Communist offshoots – the many varieties of Trotskyists and Marxist-Leninists – who are still wedded to variations on the theme of the democratic centralist party, the ideological monopoly of dialectical and historical materialism and the centralised model of state socialism. This does not by any means imply a complete rejection of Marxism or indeed of some aspects of Leninism, but it does mean that it is essential to recognise that no single ideology, much less a single partisan organisation, can any longer lay claim to a monopoly of wisdom. Marx's analysis of capitalism and of the dynamics of class struggle remains extraordinarily accurate, much of Lenin's analysis of the state and of the need for a political vanguard remains convincing, but they cannot provide exclusive formulae for political organisation, strategy and tactics in today's world, or for the alternative society to which we must still aspire.

It is here that many in the anti-globalisation and anti-war movements, and indeed in other social movements from the Zapatistas to the Argentine *piqueteros* or the Brazilian MST (Movement of the Landless), proclaim that a party or a vanguard is not necessary and that 'the movement is everything'. Leadership is not necessary, the movement will constantly throw up new leaders and rotate them at will, or will function on the basis of spontaneous unanimity: 'We are all Marcos!' as the Zapatistas and their sympathisers declared when the Mexican government claimed to have discovered the true identity of their semi-clandestine and media-conscious spokesperson. But a decade later, not only have they failed to undermine the Mexican state or to dissolve its power from below, they have achieved only very modest results in terms of autonomy or improved rights for the native people of Chiapas who continue to be their main social base. The Argentine *barrio* movement has been very impressive in its capacity for non-partisan mobilisation and has contributed to the downfall of five presidents, but when a serious political alternative finally emerged in that chronically divided country, it did so from a totally unexpected source: an establishment politician, Nestor Kirchner, who as President surprised almost everyone by adopting an independent foreign and financial policy and going some way to meet the demands of the *barrio* movement, which now gives him critical support while remaining suspicious of his ultimate intentions. The classic vanguard party and the Marxist-Leninist model of socialism may have produced unsatisfactory results, Social Democracy may have been completely assimilated by capitalism, but to proclaim the superiority of non-politics or Holloway's 'anti-power' is in practice to leave the power of corporations and the capitalist state untouched: myriad particular struggles and mass movements may come and go, and may in the best of cases achieve results on specific issues, but the power of the state – of the nearly two hundred nation-states around the world – and of the global economic system will continue as before. There is no alternative to the search for an alternative.

Another consequence of the fall of the Soviet bloc was the apparently universal conversion to 'democracy', and the conclusion of Communists and Marxists – again, with rare exceptions – that the road to power must henceforth be democratic. The Marxist critique of bourgeois democracy had too easily become an excuse for bureaucratic despotism in the name of socialism. But does this mean that the critique of bourgeois democracy has no relevance? Is the concept of revolution now to be consigned to the dustbin of history, now that the only revolutions that attract attention are those that overthrow bureaucratic state socialist regimes? We are all democrats now – advocates of democracy on the Western liberal model – and so revolution, or any political change that implies the use of force or direct action, is apparently out. In Latin America, with its rich revolutionary heritage of armed guerrilla struggle, where in the 1960s and '70s the debate over the armed or peaceful roads raged fiercely, the same is apparently now the case: with the failure of the Central American insurgencies, the defeat of *Sendero Luminoso* in Peru and the peaceful transitions to democracy in the Southern Cone, only the Colombian guerrillas (the FARC, ELN and others) still hold out – and they are now unmentionable in polite company (or else they are dismissed as 'narco-guerrillas', a convenient distortion which permits US interventionism to disguise itself as counter-narcotics policy). The universal assumption that democracy is the only valid regime – accepted even by most ex-Communist parties – obscures the question of what democracy really means, of whether Western liberalism is the only valid form of democracy, and of whether revolutionary change is possible by democratic means. These are also central questions which will have to be addressed in the search for a political alternative.

At this point we come to the binary pair of revolution and reform: revolutionaries have traditionally been scornful of reform as an instrument of the system, as a means of assimilating and neutralising popular struggle. Social Democrats are by definition reformist. But the violent seizure of power does not guarantee revolutionary change, and in most countries the technological capacity of the modern state makes defeat of the regular military an extremely costly, if not impossible proposition. But in countries with a vigorous revolutionary tradition, 'reform' is not necessarily seen as incompatible with revolution – and revolution is not necessarily equated with total armed struggle. In Cuba and Nicaragua – countries with a weak state, with corrupt personalist dictatorships – outright military victory was possible. But in most countries (even, in fact, in the two just mentioned) revolution has implied 'the combination of all forms of struggle', with an emphasis frequently on methods which are neither completely peaceful nor completely violent: militant demonstrations, political strikes, sabotage, occupations of landed estates, public offices and factories. Accumulation of reforms or of popular pressure may lead to a situation of rupture with revolutionary implications; rather than overt confrontation with the military there may be splits within the armed forces and sections of the military may identify with the reformist/revolutionary process. In Latin America, when an individual is described as revolutionary, it does not mean that he/she is hell-bent on taking up arms: it means that they are morally committed to the struggle for a better world, that they are prepared to accept any sacrifice necessary, that they will refuse to abandon the struggle. In this conception being revolutionary does not exclude negotiation and compromise; it does exclude acceptance of compromise as a permanent solution. Reforms are perfectly acceptable, indeed essential; reformism, on the other hand, means limiting the struggle to reforms within the system. On this basis, the debate on democracy and revolution acquires new meaning: democratic campaigns on specific issues have a validity of their own, and whether they become reformist or revolutionary depends on the broader strategic perspective. If a process of democratic change threatens to undermine the established system of power it will eventually lead to ruptures which imply at least some degree of violent confrontation, but the precise form this will take is unpredictable and cannot necessarily be determined by the movement or its leadership. Here, surely, closer attention to Gramsci and to his concepts of 'hegemony' and of the 'historical bloc' is in order (Golding 1992).

But the issue of democracy goes beyond this: it has also to address the question of direct and participatory democracy as opposed to liberal parliamentarism. In the nineteenth century democracy was not equated with liberalism: it was understood that liberalism was an elitist system of constitutional rule and division of powers, guaranteeing civil rights but not popular sovereignty as implied by democracy. One of the most telling aspects of the retreat of the Left in the past 30 years has been the way in which democracy has come to be seen as synonymous with parliamentary liberalism, and any idea of direct or participatory democracy is automatically dismissed as equivalent to the sham of the so-called 'popular democracies' of Eastern Europe. But if democracy does not include direct participation by workers, the poor, the marginalised and excluded of capitalist society, then it excludes all possibility of real change, of a genuine political alternative. As recently as the 1960s C.B. Macpherson could write his now classic *Political Theory of Possessive Individualism* (Macpherson 1962), demonstrating how from its seventeenth-century origins liberalism was based on a market society of individual proprietors, and arguing that this was no longer an adequate basis for a theory of political obligation. But in the last two decades, in all the now fashionable literature on 'democratic transition' and 'consolidation', it is as if Macpherson (not to mention Marx!) had never existed. In recent decades parliamentary liberalism has assimilated the Left in the name of democracy, when the real task is for the Left to reclaim democracy from liberalism.

It follows from this discussion that the collapse of the Soviet and Eastern European models should not be taken as proof of the failure or irrelevance of all socialist or revolutionary experiences. Few would want to defend the Stalinist rigidity of North Korea, and the apparent acceptance of many aspects of robber-baron capitalism by China and Vietnam is cause for grave doubts about their continuing socialist credentials (although it has to be recognised that the jury is still out on their long-term evolution). But Cuba is still widely admired for its social achievements and its valiant resistance to US hostility, and its former association with the Soviet Union should not be taken as proof that its social and political model is identical or that it will suffer a similar fate. If Cuba has survived, it is precisely because its socialism differs in important respects and its revolution had different origins and characteristics; indeed, it will be argued in Chapter 4 that the true originality of the Cuban revolution has yet to be appreciated, and that its political relevance for the Left today is much greater than is normally assumed.

Along with Cuba, what are arguably the most original and most successful revolutionary experiences of our times have occurred in Latin America: the Sandinista revolution in Nicaragua (until it was tragically destroyed by US sabotage), and today the Bolivarian revolution in Venezuela. Together with one European case – Portugal and the 'Revolution of the Carnations' of 1974–75 – they offer the most interesting and inspiring examples of popular revolutionary politics in the past half-century, and will constitute the empirical basis of this book. None of these revolutions was made by a Socialist or Communist party; two were led by guerrilla insurgents and two by rebels from within the military establishment; all were inspired by original and apparently eclectic ideologies; all have involved a great emphasis on direct democracy and popular power; and all have featured the prominent role of one or a few charismatic individual leaders. The fact that much of the Left rejects Cuba and Venezuela, dismisses Nicaragua as a defeat without considering its contemporary relevance, and regards Portugal as no more than a demonstration of the success of the liberal capitalist model, only confirms the poverty of contemporary Socialist and progressive thought. It will be argued here that Nicaragua and Portugal in their respective revolutionary phases offered examples of popular and democratic politics which are still relevant, and that Cuba and (especially) Venezuela represent the real revolutionary alternative for our times. One other Latin American process which will be briefly considered, the 'Popular Unity' under Allende in Chile, serves in many respects as a counter-example, since it was a coalition of traditional political parties of the Left, with a conventional Marxist ideology and a leader who, however admirable, was singularly lacking in charisma.

It is not accidental that all but one of these examples arose in Latin America: that region of creative ferment, with a longer experience of colonial rule than any other, the 'backyard' of US imperialism, far more of an ethnic and cultural 'melting pot' than North America, also has a long and intense history of popular revolutionary struggle which is less contaminated by political and ideological distortions than that of any other continent. The wealth of revolutionary history in Europe, particularly in certain countries such as France and Russia, is constrained as a source of inspiration by the continent's history of internecine strife and imperialist expansionism, and in recent times by the straitjacket of the Cold War. In most of Asia traditional cultures and social structures have remained too solid to permit the emergence of revolutionary movements transcending the nationalist and anti-colonialist phase, and the major East Asian exceptions are profoundly problematic. India is in the grip of right-wing Hindu nationalism, while other countries of South and West Asia appear torn between Islamic fundamentalism and Western neo-liberalism. In South Africa the African National Congress, once a totemic source of anti-imperialist inspiration, has embraced the free market, while the rest of the continent wallows in neo-colonial poverty, internecine strife and corruption, and progressive movements remain weak. Only in Latin America does the revolutionary impulse appear to flourish, so that in addition to Cuba and Venezuela we find the progressive governments of Lula in Brazil, Kirchner in Argentina, the *Frente*

*Amplio* (Broad Front) in Uruguay and powerful popular movements such as Pachakutic in Ecuador, Evo Morales and the MAS in Bolivia, the FARC and ELN as well as peaceful popular resistance in Colombia, the FMLN in El Salvador and in Mexico, the Zapatistas as well as the promising presidential campaign of Andrés López Obrador. Despite the defeat of the Sandinistas in Nicaragua and the neutralisation of the other Central American insurgencies, despite the apparent failure of the Zapatistas to achieve fundamental change in Mexico, popular and progressive movements in Latin America continue to show a vitality and creativity without parallel in today's cynical, unipolar and terrorist-obsessed world.

Recent advances in Latin America have not come without problems. Lula was elected President of Brazil at the fourth attempt, but lacks a clear majority in Congress and has to negotiate any legislative project with a bewildering variety of political forces, and his government has been weakened by corruption scandals. Chávez survived the April 2002 coup and the subsequent strike/lockout but faces continuing harassment by an intransigent and sometimes violent opposition, and ill-disguised US hostility. Lucio Gutiérrez, a former rebel colonel whose electoral victory in Ecuador led some to compare him to Chávez, proved a disappointment and was disowned by the popular indigenous Pachakutic movement. But what distinguishes the region in today's world is that the question of power for progressive movements is on the agenda, and has in fact been realised in some countries – something which on other continents is only a remote dream. Major problems remain for the Left in Venezuela, Brazil, Uruguay and Argentina – how to consolidate revolutionary power in Venezuela, how far Lula's reforms or those of the *Frente Amplio* can go in Brazil and Uruguay, whether or not Kirchner will really ally with the popular movement in Argentina – but the extraordinary and positive development is that for the first time since the defeat of the Sandinistas in 1990, these issues are once again on the table.

The Cuban revolution is clearly the starting-point for contemporary Latin American revolutionary movements, yet remarkably little attention has been devoted to its political originality. Accounts of the armed struggle and the events of the revolutionary transformation are legion, and Cuba has been much discussed in terms of armed struggle and the *foco* theory of guerrilla action, and also with reference to the Guevarist concept of the 'New Man' and socialist theory; but the actual political process which led first to revolutionary victory and then to socialist transition has not been adequately studied. In the enormous literature on Cuba there is general recognition that the old Communist Party, the *Partido Socialista Popular* (PSP), was incapable of making the revolution, both because it opposed armed struggle and because of its former compromises with Batista. It is also generally recognised that revolutionary victory was the work of Fidel Castro and the 26 July Movement, a broad, popular, nationalist and social-reformist movement which did not adopt a strictly defined ideological label and did not mention Socialism or Communism until more than two years after the victory of 1 January 1959. But the implications of this for revolutionary theory have never been adequately explored beyond vague references to the genius of Fidel (from admirers) or Castro's duplicity (from detractors), coupled with correct but inadequate observations about the radicalising effects of US hostility. Surely the fact that a broad national movement with individual charismatic leadership was capable of leading one of the most popular and radical revolutionary processes in history deserves careful analysis. It raises fundamental questions about the concept of a revolutionary vanguard, about the role of political parties and the relationship between leadership and mass. Perhaps today's distrust of political parties and of formulaic ideologies is neither so new nor so original, and the same questions (and possible answers to them) may have been raised in Cuba over 40 years ago – only to be lost in the rhetoric and the harsh realities of the Cold War.

A second crucial formative experience for the contemporary Latin American Left was Chile; the defeat of the Popular Unity, widely seen at the time as demonstrating the futility of the electoral road, offers other equally important lessons. It is currently fashionable to compare Venezuela under Chávez with Chile under Allende, but there are important differences. Certainly Pinochet's betrayal and the brutality of the Chilean coup (the original '9/11') confirmed the implacable hostility of imperialism and of local elites to any project of popular transformation, and the unreliability of the supposedly 'constitutionalist' Chilean military. The economic sabotage by Chilean business and the truckers' strike have parallels in the recent opposition strike in Venezuela, and CIA involvement in the Chilean coup seems to be mirrored by the overwhelming circumstantial evidence of US complicity in the short-lived 2002 coup against Chávez. In both cases reliance on elections and constitutionalism seems to be undermined by the refusal of hegemonic interests to accept a democracy which they do not control. But the Chilean experience also underlines the fateful consequences of partisan divisions (the rivalries of Socialists, Communists, MAPU and other parties), and the dangers of attempting a transformational project without a clear popular majority. It must never be forgotten that Allende was elected in a three-way race with only 36 per cent of the popular vote, and although his support increased somewhat in subsequent municipal and legislative elections, he never had a solid absolute majority. Opposition control of Parliament also made it impossible for Allende to impose his projected constitutional changes. By contrast, Chávez has won massive majorities in no less than ten elections and referenda and was able to begin his term with a Constituent Assembly that led to a sweeping institutional transformation of Venezuela. Finally, although the jury is still out on the ultimate fate of the *chavista* project, Chávez' own military origins and the less elitist characteristics of the Venezuelan military have so far guaranteed majority support in the armed forces for the Bolivarian process. If Chile demonstrated the hazards of the purely electoral road, that does not necessarily imply that armed insurgency is the only solution. The issue is much more complex, and cannot be reduced (as was often done in the 1960s and 1970s) to a matter of dogma, of being always and on principle 'for' or 'against' taking up arms.

Here it needs to be pointed out that Latin America has an outstanding tradition of popular armed struggle which long predates the Cuban revolution, having its roots in the Independence Wars of the early nineteenth century. It is based on a concept of popular collective insurgency which has nothing to do with militarism or with the 'individual right to bear arms' of the US Constitution. The idea of the people taking up arms to achieve liberation is central to Latin American political culture, and it by no means excludes other forms of struggle and participation. It embodies a distrust of institutionalised politics and a radical rejection of all forms of paternalism: rights are gained by struggle, whether armed or peaceful, and not granted by benevolent authority. It is intimately linked to the concept of popular sovereignty, that sovereignty really does reside in the people as a whole and not in the propertied classes or in any hereditary group or privileged institution. The people, moreover, constitute themselves as political actors by collective mobilisation, not merely by passive reception of media messages or individualised voting. The secret ballot is undoubtedly regarded as essential, but as inadequate unless accompanied by mass organisation and mobilisation; and this will ideally be peaceful but may encompass an entirely legitimate recourse to arms if faced with repression or arbitrary authority. Hence the resonance of the term 'revolutionary' tends to be positive, unlike in contemporary Europe or North America where it has come to be associated with irrational violence or dogmatic sectarianism. For the same reasons, 'democracy' in Latin America is popularly associated with collective rights and popular power, and not just representative institutions and liberal pluralism. The concept is also indissolubly linked with the rights and cultures of oppressed ethnic and social groups, with indigenous, black and mestizo empowerment.

The Cuban revolution brought with it a reaffirmation of this tradition of armed struggle, and even if for a while in the 1960s and '70s it became fetishised in the form of the isolated guerrilla *foco*, it also contributed to the rise of more substantial insurgent organisations organically linked to popular movements in several countries: Nicaragua, El Salvador, Guatemala, Colombia. The Central American insurgencies of the 1970s and '80s represented the internationalisation of the popular revolutionary movement, and precisely for this reason they were regarded as an intolerable threat by the United States. Victory in Nicaragua in 1979 revived the hope of continental liberation inspired by the Cuban revolution, and significantly it also came about in unorthodox form. As in Cuba it was a national uprising against a brutal dictatorship in a small and extremely dependent country, a client regime in a region which had suffered frequent US intervention. The Sandinista Front (FSLN, *Frente Sandinista de Liberación Nacional*) was a broad movement of national liberation with three constituent tendencies and with ideological influences ranging from Marxism-Leninism to Social Democracy and liberation theology. The Sandinistas were opposed throughout by the small Nicaraguan Communist Party, and as in Cuba, drew inspiration from national and Latin American revolutionary and anti-imperialist traditions. While expressing admiration for and gratitude to Cuba, they did not adopt the Cuban model (and much less the Soviet one), insisting on maintaining a 'mixed economy' and a pluralist electoral system combined with elements of direct democracy. The Nicaraguan agrarian reform and literacy campaign, and the rank-and-file organisational structure of the Sandinista Defence Committees (similar to the Cuban Committees for the Defence of the Revolution), clearly drew on Cuban experience, but were combined with efforts to work with the private sector and with a pluralist political system.

Sandinista defeat at the polls in 1990 was undoubtedly due above all to unrelenting US hostility and the devastating effects of the

Contra war, but there were other contributory factors, notably internal divisions and the abandonment after 1986 of popular participatory and welfare policies in favour of conventional liberal democracy and an IMF deflationary package. The subsequent defeat or neutralisation of the Salvadorean and Guatemalan insurgencies was more straightforward, consisting essentially of the application by the US of overwhelming pressure in order to forestall revolutionary victory. These reverses, coinciding as they did with the collapse of the Soviet bloc, led to profound demoralisation and disorientation among the Latin American Left and contributed to the worldwide crisis of progressive ideas from which we are only now beginning to emerge. If a victorious armed revolution could be defeated in little more than a decade and two other apparently solid insurgent movements could be neutralised, what hope was there for radical social change of any kind? And since the final Sandinista defeat came at the ballot box, hope of progress through elections was also undermined. Were free elections and multi-party systems incompatible with revolutionary power? If the Sandinistas were to win elections again, would they – indeed could they – reinitiate the revolutionary transformation of 1979–84? It is no accident that after the Sandinista defeat, any prospect of a liberal 'opening' in Cuba was closed off indefinitely: the message for Fidel and the Cubans was that if they permitted political liberalisation, Washington and the Miami mafia would subvert the country's institutions and buy the elections.

Further South, in the more socially and economically advanced 'Southern Cone' countries (Brazil, Argentina, Uruguay and Chile), this period was more optimistic since it brought the end of repressive militarism and the gradual process of 'democratic transition'. With the imposition of superficially democratic solutions in the Central American countries, and similar transitions occurring in Bolivia, Paraguay and even Mexico (with the PAN's electoral victory in 2000 heralding the end of the PRI's 71-year reign), the media and the dominant powers in North America and Europe were able to proclaim the universal triumph of liberal democracy in Latin America (the remaining Andean countries – Peru, Ecuador, Colombia and Venezuela – remained formally democratic throughout this period). This was Fukuyama's or Castañeda's vision triumphant. Of course there remained the inconvenient exception of Cuba, but it was assumed that this 'dinosaur' – dismissed as a kind of tropical Albania – would fall into line at any moment.

But the crucial questions, both for the newly liberalised countries and those which had observed liberal constitutional norms over a longer period, related to the nature of the 'democracy' which had now become the continent-wide norm. With the universal imposition of neo-liberalism and with the Left in disarray, liberal democracy seemed to be reduced to a formal electoral game with little relevance to the real conditions of existence for the popular classes. The one significant exception was Brazil, where the rise of the PT (Workers' Party) ushered in major progressive changes, first at municipal and state levels and then, with Lula's presidential victory, potentially at national level. What the PT has achieved, most notably in Porto Alegre, is of enormous significance for popular movements everywhere. The systematic practice of reporting back by elected representatives and the possibility of recall, and even more important, the participatory budget, together constitute a revolution in local government whose full consequences have yet to be worked out. While there is still no doubt some validity in the Marxist doctrine that true workers' power, or popular power, is only possible at national level, the extent of change in some PT-run municipalities is very impressive both in material terms and in popular empowerment. But Lula's achievements as President are so far very modest, as was to be expected given the lack of a majority in Congress and of any significant change in the judiciary, the armed forces or other institutions; the current Brazilian process is one of reform, not revolution.

In historical perspective it seems clear that Lula is subject to similar constraints to those faced by Allende – although it may be hoped that the final outcome will not be so tragic, both because Lula's apparent goals are more modest and because neither the international climate nor the attitude of the Brazilian armed forces is favourable to an unconstitutional solution. However, the possibility of a radicalisation of the popular movement, beyond the control of the PT government, could lead to a more complex situation. Both the MST (Movement of the Landless) and certain sectors of the PT have revolutionary positions which more truly represent the aspirations of the popular movement, but which also face violent hostility from the Brazilian oligarchy – and this could lead to a very dangerous confrontation with unpredictable consequences in the absence of a coherent unified strategy by the Government and its supporters. Given the lack of a serious transformative strategy on the part of Lula and the PT Government and the current corruption crisis, the prospects for Brazil are not encouraging.

If the Brazilian situation offers the prospect of no more than limited reform, it is in Venezuela that a revolutionary transformation is not only possible but is already well under way. It is also Venezuela which most clearly raises the theoretical issues formulated above: the relation of leadership and mass, the question of party versus movement, the problem of the true nature of democracy, and reform versus revolution. In Venezuela there has been a real (although still incomplete) change in the structure of power, with a new Constitution, a population which is mobilised and organised in a participatory democracy, a government of popular origin which is pushing forward an ongoing process of transformation, a political reorientation of the armed forces, and the beginnings of an economic restructuring with the effective renationalisation of the vital oil industry. An agrarian reform is under way, producer and consumer cooperatives are being promoted, and a reform of urban property is giving effective ownership and control to slum dwellers. 'Bolivarian schools' have brought education to over a million children previously excluded from the system, a literacy campaign has been initiated, and millions of people are organised in local land, water and electrical utility committees, 'Bolivarian Circles' and other grass-roots organisations of popular power. Yet this process was not initiated by a Socialist or Communist party, nor indeed by any party, but by a movement of military origin, the Bolivarian Revolutionary Movement (MBR-200) led by Lt-Col. (now President) Hugo Chávez Frías. Named for the bicentenary of liberator Simón Bolívar's birth in 1983, the MBR-200 was a clandestine military and civilian movement for social and political change in Venezuela. In February 1989, when in the *caracazo* the people of the shanty-towns rose up against the further impoverishment implied by an IMF economic package and were savagely massacred by troops on the orders of the corrupt Social Democratic President Carlos Andrés Pérez (CAP), Chávez' movement was not yet ready to act. But three years later, on 4 February 1992, it was the MBR-200 which took the initiative in launching a military/civilian uprising against CAP, and despite the movement's failure this action sounded the death-knell of the old Venezuelan pseudodemocracy. February 1989 and February 1992 between them set in motion a revolutionary dynamic which would lead, through Chávez' two-year imprisonment, his amnesty under popular pressure, his resignation from the armed forces in order to enter civilian politics and create a broad civilian movement, the Fifth Republic Movement (MVR), and his election as President in December 1998, to the process of transformation which has been under way since his inauguration in February 1999. The comparison of Chávez with Allende as leading a radical transformation by electoral means fails in part because it ignores the insurrectional origins of the process: December 1998 was the electoral ratification of the events of February 1989 and February 1992, popular and military revolts which were temporarily unsuccessful but from which the old political system never recovered.

Once again, as in Cuba, we are faced with an extremely unorthodox situation: a genuine popular revolution which is not led by a Socialist party, which does not have (or did not appear to have until recently) a Socialist programme or ideology, which is headed by a charismatic individual leading a broad and somewhat amorphous popular movement, and in which the leader is (of all things!) a former military officer. Not surprisingly, it is Chávez' military origins which have raised eyebrows, and initially provoked outright hostility, among many progressive observers in Latin America and elsewhere. In a continent with a long tradition of reactionary militarism, most recently manifested in the brutal dictatorships of the Southern Cone and Central America, the idea of a popular revolution led by the military seemed too absurd to contemplate. But there does exist a different military tradition in Latin America, a tradition of nationalist, democratic and anti-imperialist officers like Omar Torrijos in Panama, Velasco Alvarado in Peru or Francisco Caamaño Deno in the Dominican Republic. Indeed it is a tradition with deep roots, going back to the Socialist Republic of Col. Marmaduke Grove in Chile (1931), the Brazilian '*tenentes*' (lieutenants) of the 1920s, and all the way back to the early nineteenth century liberators. Also, in the specific case of Venezuela, officer recruitment is much less elitist than in Argentina or Chile – Chávez comes from a provincial lower-middle-class family of mixed race – and crucially, most of the officers of Chávez' generation were not trained in the notorious US 'School of the Americas' but in Venezuela, with political science courses taught by French-trained academics. The old stereotype has to be modified, and it has to be recognised that the military are not genetically reactionary; they are social beings subject to many of the same influences as civilians.

For me the issues raised by the Venezuelan process are less about the military as such and more about the character and leadership of revolutionary movements in general: the same issues raised by the Cuban experience. Once again, a successful popular revolution – at least, more successful to date than anything we have seen since

Nicaragua – has taken place in a manner that was totally unexpected. Once again, the organised Left was totally irrelevant to the process, and only gave its support (in the best of cases – because several left-wing parties have joined the reactionary opposition) when victory was already at hand. Once again, the people recognised the revolutionary leadership long before the politicians or the intellectuals. And once again, victory was achieved by a broad, democratic national movement, ideologically flexible but united in action, with an individual charismatic leader with remarkable oratorical gifts and capacity for decisive action. This type of movement and this type of leadership inevitably raise the issue of populism – a term which is anathema to the organised Left, and which both the leaders themselves and most of their followers would indignantly reject. But if populism is understood not as opportunism or demagogy, nor as a specific ideology or programme, but rather as a style of political action, a methodology, a phenomenon which arises at critical conjunctures and which can have completely different political orientations and consequences depending on the specific context and class character of the movement, then perhaps it is legitimate to describe these processes as populist – as a revolutionary form of populism (Laclau 1977; Raby 1983; Cammack 2000). This is also one of the central theses of this book, and its implications for progressive politics are no less revolutionary than the political processes herein analysed, from Cuba to Venezuela.

There is another important revolutionary process of the contemporary era in which the military played a central role, not in Latin America but in Latin Europe, namely the Portuguese revolution of 1974–75. Despite the very different context – a European colonial power, albeit small, peripheral and relatively poor – the Portuguese experience may be relevant to an analysis of the Venezuelan situation. Here also junior military officers, many of them of relatively humble origins, revolted against a discredited civilian regime (in this case a Fascist-oriented dictatorship) and identified with popular aspirations – both the aspirations of colonised African peoples for self-determination and the aspirations of the Portuguese people for democracy and social justice. The poetic moment of 25 April 1974 – when the people of Lisbon celebrated the liberating coup by placing red carnations in the soldiers' rifles – quickly turned into a genuinely revolutionary process as the frustrations of nearly 50 years of repression burst forth in mass demonstrations, factory occupations, purges of police informers, housing occupations by slum-dwellers and the homeless, land occupations by rural labourers, and protests of every kind. For 19 months, until 25 November 1975 when a moderate but nevertheless counter-revolutionary coup restored bourgeois order in Portugal, the country was in turmoil, in a process of creative ferment which was the first truly revolutionary process in Europe since the end of the Second World War.

During the 'hot summer' of 1975 Henry Kissinger, throwing up his hands in horror, declared that Portugal was 'the Cuba of Europe', but the Portuguese establishment, aided and abetted by European Social Democracy, the Catholic Church and the CIA, succeeded in putting the revolutionary genie back in the bottle. Throughout the process, the key events were played out in the popular movement and among the military, the Armed Forces Movement (MFA) as the rebel military movement became known. During the 19-month upheaval, six weak civilian provisional governments succeeded one another, but real power was in the street, among the people – and in the hands of the MFA. Many officers quickly became radicalised and identified with the popular movement, and by early 1975 the MFA was talking of 'popular power', socialism and the 'People–MFA Alliance', and proposing a revolutionary system of workers', peasants' and soldiers' committees, with a National Assembly of People's Power as the ultimate goal. Observers talked of the 'populism' of the MFA, and with good reason: the personal leadership, charisma and oratorical capacity of Col. Vasco Gonçalves, Prime Minister of four of the six provisional governments, was rivalled by that of Major Otelo Saraiva de Carvalho, operational commander of the 25 April coup. But the MFA was divided between a dominant pro-Communist sector around Gonçalves, a 'moderate' sector which was gaining in strength, and a radical sector personified by Otelo and aligned with the revolutionary Left. Conservative forces led by the Catholic Church dominated the North of the country, and allied with the political Right, the Socialist party and the MFA 'moderates' to confront the Provisional Government and the military radicals. The standoff led to a growing threat of civil war, which was resolved with the 25 November coup by the Centre Right. The military Left and the Communist Party decided not to resist in order to avert open war, and were rewarded with guarantees of political rights within a newly consolidated bourgeois state. Leftist officers were purged from the military; the popular movement, now effectively leaderless, was subjected to limited but effective repression; liberal norms were preserved and Portugal became a conventional parliamentary democracy, entering the

European Union a few years later. But the real Portuguese revolution was destroyed, and the victors expunged from the official record the memory of the mass movement for popular power and socialism – now subject to ironic ridicule as the 'PREC', *Processo Revolucionário em Curso* or Revolutionary Process under Way – and replaced it with the myth of the heroic resistance of the democratic forces against the Communist threat. They cannot, however, destroy the folk memory of how, for a brief period at least, the Portuguese people in alliance with the radical military took matters into their own hands and created a vision of popular power and socialism which is without parallel in contemporary Europe.

These four revolutionary experiences – the Cuban, Nicaraguan, Venezuelan and Portuguese – all point in the direction of a broad, popular and democratic movement with a bold, charismatic and non-partisan leadership, ideologically flexible and inspired by national popular culture and traditions as well as different strands of international progressive thought, as the essential components of successful revolution. But this raises major questions about the role of political parties, the relevance of Marxism or any kind of socialist ideology, the relationship between revolution and democracy and the nature of the new revolutionary society. What are the implications of these processes for the future of the international Left? What relevance do they have to the Left in Britain or other advanced countries? Is Socialism still the ultimate goal, and if so, what does Socialism mean in today's globalised world? The attempt to answer these questions may produce some surprising, but ultimately inspiring, conclusions.

# 2
# Democracy, Formal or Substantive: When Liberalism Becomes Counter-Revolutionary

For the revolutionary Left the clearest lesson of the collapse of the Soviet bloc was the importance of democracy: Socialism could not be imposed by authoritarian means. We are all democrats now: gone are the days when hard-line Stalinists would dismiss elections as an irrelevance and exalt 'the dictatorship of the proletariat' not merely as a metaphor for working-class control of state power but as a literal apology for despotism.

So far, so good: it had long been apparent that in 'democratic centralism' the noun was everything and the adjective purely decorative. The defence of self-perpetuating party bureaucrats had become a millstone round the neck of the Communist movement, and non-Soviet alternatives, whether Trotskyist or Maoist, had failed to differentiate themselves effectively from the Stalinist model in this respect. Even Democratic Socialists were affected since the Cold War polarisation made it virtually impossible for any non-capitalist model to flourish without being assimilated either by the Communist bloc or by Social Democratic reformism. The connection between bureaucratic centralism and ideological dogmatism also stultified Socialist thought and made a mockery of the liberating aspirations of revolutionaries.

It is scarcely surprising, then, that the collapse of the Berlin Wall and then of the so-called 'popular democracies', culminating with that of the Soviet Union itself, was greeted with rejoicing by some sectors of the Western Left. But those who imagined that the removal of the bureaucratic carapace would release an explosion of grass-roots Socialist democracy in the East were quickly disillusioned as the ex-Communist countries rushed headlong into the embrace of Western liberalism and robber-baron capitalism. The stifling of popular initiative in the name of Socialism had been far too thorough and prolonged for a truly revolutionary alternative to emerge in the short- or even medium-term, and the propaganda of Western consumer society and 'liberal democracy' was overwhelmingly effective.

Rather more surprising was the impact of Soviet collapse in the West: rather than opening the way to a rebirth of independent Socialism and radical energies unhindered by the spectre of Stalinism, it led – at least in the short-term – to the capitulation of Social Democracy before the triumphal advance of neo-liberalism and the Thatcherite 'there are no alternatives' dogma. Liberalism, both economic and political, reigned supreme, as Francis Fukuyama trumpeted 'The End of History'. Although as we have seen alternative voices soon re-emerged in the form of the anti-globalisation and anti-war movements, the ideological bases of these alternatives remained weak in terms of both political economy – what would non-Stalinist Socialism look like? – and political philosophy: what was the political vehicle for change if not a Marxist-Leninist party, and what kind of political system would permit the true expression of popular interests?

## THE RECEIVED WISDOM: 'LIBERAL DEMOCRACY' AS TAUTOLOGY

This is where the victory of neo-liberalism was perhaps most complete, because if the economic nostrums of free-market dogma soon encountered resistance and began to reveal their practical deficiencies, political liberalism was accepted with scarcely a murmur of protest and is still, 15 years later, only timidly questioned. Citizens of the former Soviet bloc, including most of the ex-Communist parties, have now accepted 'democracy'; but they have done so in most cases uncritically, without questioning the Western liberal model which is presented as the only viable democratic system. For Eastern Europeans this was perhaps an understandable reaction to the sham 'popular democracies' to which they had been subjected; but what is even more striking is that the Western Left, including most Western Communist or Marxist parties, has also capitulated more than ever before to the liberal model as the quintessence of democracy. Political pluralism, regular elections, freedom of speech and organisation: these principles are accepted as universal and sufficient without any questioning of why countries governed in this manner have so singularly failed to achieve more than a minimum level of social justice or popular empowerment. Why has the United States, home of liberalism par excellence, become the most unequal society in the developed world? Why has Britain, birthplace of parliamentary democracy, moved more and more towards the US pattern of social exclusion and low electoral participation? Liberals would say that this is what the people voted for with Reagan and Thatcher, Bush and

Blair; but Socialists and revolutionaries cannot accept such a facile and complacent interpretation.

A political critique of the hegemonic system in the Western world has to start from the observation that 'liberal democracy' is *the preferred political expression of advanced capitalism*, and it would be absurd to assume that such a political regime poses no problems for those who advocate an alternative social and economic system. For opponents of capitalism it should at the very least arouse suspicion that the invariable agenda of the West for any country it 'liberates' or threatens to liberate is 'free elections and a market economy': Eastern Europe, Russia, Afghanistan, Iraq, Cuba ... 'Democracy' and 'a market economy' are assumed to be linked, and if free elections produce a majority opposed to neo-liberal market economics, then there are dark mutterings about 'populism' and 'the problem of governability'. Political commentators are concerned above all about the 'competence' of party leaders to manage the system, and their ability to win popular support for 'viable' policies; any idea of real popular sovereignty or direct popular involvement in decision-making is regarded as dangerous and irresponsible. Referenda may occasionally be necessary on ethical matters or to rally support on a contentious issue, but in general (except at election time, and even then only in a carefully controlled and manipulated manner) politics is assumed to be a matter for party elites and unelected civil servants.

The exclusive identification of democracy with liberalism is quite recent; or to be more accurate, although the ruling-class desire to limit democracy to the liberal variety has deep historical roots, until relatively recently it was always challenged by those who advocated a more profound, direct or participatory democracy in which the word's literal meaning – 'rule by the people' – would be taken seriously. The seventeenth- and eighteenth-century founders of liberalism such as Locke and Montesquieu were quite explicit in connecting liberal constitutional government with private property, a point which was brilliantly brought home for modern readers by the Canadian political philosopher C.B. Macpherson in his *Political Theory of Possessive Individualism*, published over 40 years ago. In Macpherson's view this was the fundamental flaw of liberalism as a system of government for the twentieth century: 'the continued existence of liberal-democratic states in possessive market societies ... has been due to the ability of a possessing class to keep the effective political power in its hands in spite of universal suffrage' (Macpherson 1962, 274).

The desire to avoid what were seen as the dangers of 'rule by the mob' also prevailed among the Founding Fathers of the United States. Although the US Constitution was a milestone in the establishment of representative and responsible government (in other words, liberalism), its authors were wary of 'the turbulence and follies of democracy': in the words of Argentine political scientist José Nun, 'This constitution ... is concerned with property rights at least as much as it is with political freedoms, and it is evident that it fears "the abuses of freedom" more than "the abuses of power"' (Nun 2003, 111). It was for this reason that they were concerned to establish such institutions as the Senate and the Electoral College, to restrict the unmediated expression of the popular will (even by the all-male and white electorate of those times); this was due to the influence of the more conservative figures in the independence movement such as James Madison and Alexander Hamilton. This view of democracy as distinct from liberalism, and as potentially dangerous, continued through the nineteenth century, and it was only in the mid-twentieth century that the phrase 'liberal democracy' came to prevail and to become, in the discourse of the Western establishment, virtually a tautology.

The restricted liberal view of democracy was perhaps most explicitly formulated by Joseph Schumpeter, the Austrian political economist, writing during the Second World War (Schumpeter 1942). For Schumpeter democracy was only a constitutional procedure for choosing political leaders, and the leaders were the only ones capable of making decisions on public issues. The role of the electorate was limited to resolving potential conflict among rival political elites by periodically choosing which politicians would hold office for the next few years; and even this very limited popular intervention in politics could only be trusted if the society had achieved a certain level of economic and social development, if there existed a well-trained bureaucracy, if sensitive matters like justice and finance were left to experts, and if the people had the necessary self-discipline and respect for the law. As Nun points out, Schumpeter's opinion of the common people was so poor that it is difficult to see why he believed them capable even of choosing the politicians who would govern in their name (Nun 2003, 14–15).

Although few liberal apologists are quite so explicit as Schumpeter in justifying elitist control of the political process, their assumptions

*[handwritten margin note: liberalism = representative and responsible government]*

are essentially the same. Any suggestion that MPs should be subject to the express will of their electors is rejected by reference to the sacrosanct rule of liberal parliamentarism, that MPs are sovereign representatives, not delegates directly controlled by their constituents; when challenged they will insist that they refuse to be 'dictated to' by their electors, that at the polls the people choose 'the best man [or occasionally woman] for the job', but that they as representatives will vote according to their individual consciences. Of course, except on minor matters like fox-hunting or possibly ethical issues like abortion, their individual consciences tend to coincide remarkably with the party line imposed by the whips, a type of pressure which is somehow regarded as much more legitimate than that of their constituents. Some of them may pride themselves on being good 'local MPs', taking up specific local issues; but when it comes to matters of national policy they will generally fall into line. In doing so, they effectively cease to represent the voters, as was pointed out 60 years ago by an author who could scarcely be accused of extremism, Hans Kelsen:

The formula that the member of parliament is not the representative of his electors but of the whole people, or, as some writers say, of the whole State, and that therefore he is not bound by any instructions of his electors and cannot be recalled by them, is a political fiction. Legal independence of the elected from the electors is incompatible with legal representation. (Kelsen, quoted in Colletti 1972, 187)

To suggest that this deficiency is remedied by the need for representatives to present themselves for election again is to ignore the fact that several years may go by in the meantime, often making the issues moot (a decision to go to war cannot be undone two years later), and also that many controversial policies may be at stake and cannot adequately be condensed into a single vote to choose a member of parliament. Again, liberal theorists do not really deny this, in effect reducing the political input of the electors to a minimal choice between two or three packaged manifestos which they know will only be very partially applied.

In normal circumstances, moreover, the electoral process is very effectively controlled by the two or three dominant parties, and party machines are organised in a strictly oligarchic manner. Policy formulation and candidate selection are normally tightly controlled by the party elite, and even in parties which hold internal elections or where local branches nominate candidates, these procedures are generally subject to mechanisms designed to ensure central control.

On policy, even if the grass roots succeed in imposing orientations which are at variance with the desires of the leadership, elite control of party strategy will normally ensure that such policies are ignored or distorted in practice. A party in which such elite control breaks down – like the British Labour Party in the late 1970s and early 1980s, or the German Green Party in its early years – will tend to suffer from internal factionalism and even if united, will be marginalised by the media as 'irrelevant' or 'unfit to govern'. If despite this it is elected to office, it will be confronted by enormous domestic and international pressures to modify its policies, and should it refuse to give way it will be faced with capital flight and threats of destabilisation.

None of this ought to be surprising: on the contrary, it would be surprising if fundamental issues of the distribution of wealth and power in society, affecting entrenched class interests, could be resolved by the simple act of voting once every four or five years. But the problem is that 'liberal democracy' bases its legitimacy on the illusion that it permits such radical change; that multi-party elections are the ultimate expression of popular sovereignty and that if the people vote for Socialism, for example, they can have it. Down to the 1970s critics of the Schumpeterian or procedural view of democracy, such as Macpherson, were quite common and indeed respected in Western establishment circles. But since the neo-liberal revolution of the 1980s and '90s such critics have been pushed to the margins: establishment discourse, whether in the media or in academia, assumes that democracy is summed up in free elections, freedom of speech and organisation and political pluralism, but says nothing about social and economic rights or the distribution of power and wealth; and frequently a 'market economy' is also added as a necessary criterion, implicitly excluding any kind of socialism as an option. Franz Hinkelammert, an outstanding liberation theologian and political theorist based in Costa Rica, points out that late capitalism has produced a theory of democracy corresponding to its economic model, based on treating the voters as consumers whose political choices amount to superficial whims in response to marketing techniques (Hinkelammert 1990, 6).

To appreciate the sleight-of-hand which has made 'liberal democracy' the hegemonic formula in the West, it is necessary to remind oneself that liberalism, whose great virtue when compared to feudalism or absolutism was to establish constitutional and responsible government with respect for civil rights, was the instrument of the rising bourgeoisie – the 'Third Estate' in French terms – against aristocratic and ecclesiastical privilege. It was this, but nothing more than this; as was made clear by the conflicts between Parliamentarians and Levellers or Diggers in seventeenth-century England, or between the Girondins, the Jacobins and the Enragés in the French Revolution, the bourgeois leaders of the Third Estate never intended that the mass of commoners should have an equal right to govern. Liberalism was democratised in the nineteenth and twentieth centuries only under pressure from below, and with great reluctance (witness the dramatic struggles over the Great Reform Bill of 1832 in Britain or the extension of the suffrage to women early in the twentieth century). In reality, the essence of most Western political systems today is liberalism, in the sense of civil constitutional government by elites, and the democratic component is a superficial adornment. Once again Nun expresses it elegantly:

> ... when people refer today to 'liberal democracies', a deliberate rhetorical distortion occurs that puts the adjective in place of the noun. We are actually dealing with 'democratic liberalisms', *within which there are scarce concrete expressions of the idea of a self-governed community, while this idea operates as their main ideological attraction.* To put it in different terms, today's most successful democracies were not initially the consummation of the idea of democracy, but embraced it later and in a very partial way. (Nun 2003, 112–13; emphasis in original)

In my view even Nun's phrase 'democratic liberalisms' is too generous with regard to most Western systems; a more accurate term to describe them would be 'liberal pluralism', which recognises their genuine virtues – of being relatively open systems with plurality of political expression and respect for civil rights – without pretending that they are democratic in the sense of empowering the people, except to a very limited extent.

The true virtues and profound limitations of liberalism will become clearer from a critical examination of two of its key concepts: the 'rule of law' and the 'division of powers'. The 'rule of law' essentially means an absence of arbitrary measures: that executive and judicial decisions, and administrative actions, must be sanctioned by constitutional or traditional legal norms. As a reaction against feudal particularism or absolutist fiat this was obviously desirable, and no-one would dispute its value in the abstract as a safeguard against arbitrary measures in general. But the problem in societies governed in the typical liberal manner is that the actual laws whose rule is guaranteed are conceived and enacted by the privileged sectors of society, who are also those who have easiest access to the police and judicial institutions which enforce those laws. Similarly the classic concept of the 'division of powers' between legislative, executive and judicial branches of government, with the corresponding 'checks and balances' between them, originated in the US Constitution and was inspired by a particular reading of Montesquieu on the part of its authors; it was intended above all as a check on an overweening executive. In this it was successful for well over a century, but in the process it vested enormous political power in the hands of an entrenched judiciary. From a working-class or popular-democratic perspective the problem with this conception is that it provides checks and balances between different privileged institutions, or to be more accurate, institutions of the privileged: a parliament elected on a basis in which candidate selection has a strong class bias combined with top-down party elite control; an executive (president or prime minister) normally of similar background; and a judiciary which is both socially and professionally highly elitist. In such circumstances checks and balances do not serve to make the system any more democratic or accessible to the poor majority, and indeed when what is at stake is class conflict – if, for instance, there is a progressive president or parliamentary majority which actually does try to pass Socialist measures – then these checks and balances may well become an obstacle, with the judicial power being used to prevent change. This was the case with Allende in Chile and again with Chávez in Venezuela, to mention only two examples.

This does not mean that liberal 'checks and balances' as such are undesirable; it means that they do nothing to promote true democracy unless the institutions being 'checked' and those doing the checking are themselves democratised. Unless the legislature is made truly democratic and accountable, unless the executive is also subject to effective popular control, and unless the judiciary is democratised (not by the demagogic US system of electing judges but by making the legal profession less elitist in recruitment, training and mode of operation), then checks and balances between them are of limited use. Moreover, in order to really democratise the system what are needed are checks and balances of a different kind, to subject all state institutions to popular control: the obligation to report back, the right of recall, referenda and popular initiatives, and the institutionalisation of popular participation in all areas of public life. In the absence of these the liberal-pluralist system will inevitably tend to work in favour of the rich and privileged, and the more unequal the society the more it will tend to do so; only the emergence of a really powerful mass movement may force it to work for the poor majority, and this typically leads to enormous tension so that either the liberal system or the mass movement has to change.

Apart from the inherent limitations of liberal pluralism, recent years have witnessed a series of developments in the 'advanced democracies' which have further restricted the citizenship rights of which they are so proud. In the UK especially, but also in a number of other countries, measures have been introduced which strengthen the executive at the expense of the legislature, the prime minister at the expense of the cabinet, the cabinet at the expense of the backbenchers and so on. Since the notorious 9/11 attacks in the US, and on the pretext of the 'War on Terror', a whole range of arbitrary measures has been introduced which seriously undermine civil liberties. The situation has now reached the point where one has to turn to a critical concept developed to analyse the abuse of presidential power by some Latin American leaders: 'delegative democracy'. This formulation was invented by Guillermo O'Donnell, a prominent Argentine political theorist now based in the US, to criticise the practice of such rulers as Alberto Fujimori of Peru and Carlos Menem of Argentina: 'Delegative democracies rest on the premise that whoever wins election to the presidency is thereby entitled to govern as he or she sees fit, constrained only by the hard facts of existing power relations and by a constitutionally limited term of office' (O'Donnell 1994, quoted in Norden 2003, 93–4). Apart from its relevance to some Latin American cases, this sounds like a fair description of the actions of George W. Bush in Washington and Tony Blair at Westminster, and is suggestive of the degeneration of the liberal system in its classic heartlands. The growth of executive power, the emasculation of parliament and the destruction of inner-party democracy and civil liberties have contributed powerfully to voter disillusionment in the very countries which like to present themselves as democratic models for the world, but which no longer even live up to their own liberal principles. Hinkelammert in 1990 criticised the newly emerging liberal regimes of Latin America as 'National Security democracies' still subject to military supervision, and perceptively suggested that this restricted liberal model was also beginning to take hold in the advanced Western countries (Hinkelammert 1990, 215–16). Anathema though it may be for the Anglo-Saxon powers, there is a strong case for the suggestion that they should take lessons in democracy from Brazil or Venezuela. More than ever we are forcibly reminded of Rousseau's scathing comment: 'The people of England regards itself as free; but it is grossly mistaken; it is free only during the election of members of parliament. As soon as they are elected, slavery overtakes it, and it is nothing' (quoted in Colletti 1972, 183).

## AN ALTERNATIVE VIEW OF DEMOCRACY

It was indeed Rousseau who first clearly elaborated the alternative view of democracy, as rule by the people in the fullest sense. Regarded by most of his eighteenth-century contemporaries as something of a maverick, Rousseau considered the issue of political participation as a collective matter which was intimately connected with the functioning of society as a whole. The crucial issue was not the individual's right to choose so much as the emergence of the 'general will' as the expression of popular sovereignty. Society – social life in the broad sense – should not be separated from government; rather, as far as possible the people themselves should govern directly, thus eliminating politics as a specialised field of action and also nullifying the 'division of powers' theorised by liberalism. In Rousseau's words,

... the basis of government [is] often wrongly confused with the sovereign, whose minister it is ... It is simply and solely a commission, an employment, in which the rulers, mere officials of the sovereign, exercise in their own name the power of which it makes them depositories. This power it can limit, modify or recover at pleasure. (in Colletti 1972, 183)

Here it should be emphasised that for Rousseau 'the sovereign' is the people.

Politicians as a professional group should not exist; instead, the people would choose delegates to represent them directly, delegates who would be instructed to carry out the will of their constituents, would report back to them regularly and would be subject to recall. Rousseau stressed the need 'for the representatives to be mingled with the body of the people' (Roman 2003, 13), and for them to carry out the work of government in specialised commissions dealing with each particular field of administration, work which would be regarded just like any other kind of socially necessary labour, without enjoying any special powers or privileges. They would either be unpaid or would have the wage of an average labourer.

Such a view of democracy as the direct rule of the people, subject to as little mediation as possible, also had its advocates in the early United States, the most notable of them being Thomas Jefferson who declared that 'My most earnest wish is to see the republican element of popular control pushed to the maximum of its practicable exercise.' Although he accepted the necessity of representation, he insisted that as far as possible government should be by the citizens 'acting directly and personally, according to rules established by the majority' (in Vanden and Prevost 1993, 8). With time Jefferson's approach was distorted more and more by defenders of the rights of property such as Hamilton and Madison, and eventually all that would remain would be an exaggerated individualism serving primarily the plutocratic interests of a tiny minority who use democratic rhetoric to attack 'big government' while conferring all the privileges of citizenship on private corporations.

Rousseau's concept of direct democracy with responsible mandated delegates subject to strict popular control was taken up by Marx in his essay 'The Civil War in France', the source of his famous remark that bourgeois democracy enabled the voters to decide 'once in three or six years which member of the ruling class was to misrepresent the people in parliament' (Marx and Engels 1968, 292). Inspired by the example of the great Paris Commune of 1871, Marx explained that 'While the merely repressive organs of the old governmental power were to be amputated, its legitimate functions were to be wrested from an authority usurping pre-eminence over society itself, and restored to the responsible agents of society' (ibid.). The people constituted in communes would hire and fire employees to carry out necessary governmental functions just as an employer hires workers and managers and dismisses them at will.

But Marx, of course, also went beyond Rousseau in analysing the capitalist basis of liberal representative government and arguing that true popular democracy could not exist without socialism. The true secret of the Commune, he declared, was that 'It was essentially a working-class government ... the political form at last discovered under which to work out the economic emancipation of labour'; and 'Except on this last condition, the Communal Constitution would have been an impossibility and a delusion. The political rule of the producer cannot coexist with the perpetuation of his social slavery' (Marx and Engels 1968, 294). This analysis in turn would lead to Engels' conclusion in *Socialism: Utopian and Scientific* that 'State interference in social relations becomes, in one domain after another, superfluous, and then dies out of itself; the government of persons is replaced by the administration of things, and by the conduct of processes of production. The state is not "abolished". *It dies out ...* ' (ibid., 430, emphasis in original). This was the Marxist way of expressing Rousseau's concept of the disappearance of politics as a profession and the resumption by society of the functions which liberalism had relegated to the political sphere. To what extent it is possible to introduce direct popular rule in a society in which class divisions remain and in which capitalist relations have not yet been completely replaced, is a crucial issue to bear in mind in analysis of actual experiences and projects of participatory democracy.

This formula of the *mandat impératif*, of delegates subject to strict instructions and recall, was applied briefly by the Jacobin Commune of Paris in 1792 and again in the great Paris Commune of 1871; it would appear in the Russian Soviets of 1905 and 1917 and would continue for two to three years after the Bolshevik Revolution, only to be stifled under the pressures of civil war and foreign invasion and the centralism imposed by the Party. It has re-emerged, at least briefly, in virtually all popular revolutions, with slight variations: in the anarchist communes of Catalonia during the Spanish Civil War and in the Portuguese neighbourhood committees of 1974–75, for example. But the most ambitious attempts to institutionalise it on a permanent basis have occurred in Cuba since the Revolution and in Nicaragua during the early years of the Sandinistas, and now in Venezuela under the Bolivarian Constitution, all of which will be examined in detail in later chapters.

Popular direct democracy of this kind may be exercised at local level by neighbourhood or municipal governments, or by popular commissions with specific functions: housing committees, agrarian committees, food or water committees, and so on. At national or even regional level application of these principles becomes more complex, as direct popular administration and constant consultation and reporting back become less practicable. But liberal critics of direct democracy have been too quick to dismiss it as unworkable, and it does not follow that the only solution is that of professional politicians independent from popular control except in occasional elections. Referenda and popular legislative initiatives can provide input; reporting back can still take place, especially with modern communications technology; and large-scale consultation of popular views on specific proposals can take place through mechanisms like the Cuban 'workers' parliaments' of 1994 (tens of thousands of workplace assemblies to debate the government's economic reform proposals before their final adoption).

Of course, consultation does sometimes take place in liberal-pluralist systems as well, but it is vitiated by two fundamental flaws: the lack of effective mechanisms to hold representatives (MPs, deputies) responsible, and the preference given to privileged social sectors and organisations in the consultation process. Consultation which gives priority to business associations, chambers of commerce, specialised professional bodies, established religious hierarchies or elite-dominated quangos is very different from that which favours working-class and popular organisations, unions, neighbourhood associations and the like. Genuine participatory democracy cannot avoid this implicit class issue: to be truly democratic representatives must not only be systematically answerable for their decisions but must be answerable primarily to the vast majority, in other words to working people in the broad sense. Popular democracy – a term unfortunately discredited by the Eastern European bureaucratic regimes – does not require the absurdity of referring all national decisions to local mass meetings, but it does require institutionalising access to the decision-making process by the underprivileged, by workers, peasants, small farmers, women, indigenous people, ethnic minorities, in other words all those marginalised by the entrenched structures of capitalist society which include the mechanisms of 'liberal democracy'. The crucial point is not just that citizens should participate – neo-liberal rhetoric is full of talk about participation – but *who* participates and what influence their participation has on important decisions.

Western political establishments are keenly aware of this fundamental issue, which is why they are so insistent on 'the sovereignty of parliament' or its equivalent in congressional systems: to preserve the independence of the legislators from popular control except during the (carefully managed) electoral process, and to ensure that consultation, influence and lobbying are dominated by 'respectable' organisations while expressions of mass popular interests are marginalised. The true 'general will', the interest of the poor majority, thus rarely finds expression as it is individualised and atomised by the liberal-pluralist electoral process and subordinated to the criteria of 'responsible' elites which control the institutions of capitalist 'democracy'. By contrast, direct participatory democracy ensures popular control or at any rate input into decision-making, and political accountability, at least at local level (and institutionalisation of the role of democratic mass organisations such as unions, women's and peasant associations can facilitate both input and accountability at national level also).

Another crucial and closely related issue is that of the media. The way in which the classic liberal right to freedom of expression has been hijacked by capitalist interests is now a cliché, but it is no less scandalous for that. This is not the place for a discussion of TRIPS (Trade-Related Intellectual Property Rights, an outrageous distortion of the original concept of author's or artist's copyright), but the question of expression and communication of social and political discourse is absolutely fundamental to any discussion of democracy, and the notion that such powerful instruments of communication as newspapers, radio or TV stations should be the private property of individuals or commercial enterprises would be laughable if it were not already established practice.

The standard liberal defence of this state of affairs is, first, the implausible claim that proprietors do not control the editorial line of their media, and second, to attack state control as the great enemy of free expression. Now it should go without saying that state control of the media is unacceptable and is just as bad as private monopoly, but the real issues go far beyond this. Even the question of editorial control is no more than the beginning of a much more profound problem, namely that of popular access to the media in all forms. The technology of modern communications has to be made accessible to all, not merely as consumers but as participants and creators. The internet has become a powerful instrument of such participation, and it is instructive how alternative movements of all kinds – anti-globalisation, environmental, indigenous, anti-capitalist and so on – have made use of it to great effect. But already commercial and state interests are trying to restrict and control internet access, and the battle for popular democratic rights is present here too.

The fundamental problem is to facilitate popular participation in all modes of media communication, at local, regional, national and international levels. This means supporting community media, not in the traditional sense of local newspapers and radio stations which are controlled by commercial interests and local elites, but local media of any kind produced by neighbourhood associations, tenants' groups, unions, ethnic community centres, women's and youth organisations and the like. The alternative local radio and TV stations which are proliferating in Venezuela, Brazil and other Latin American countries provide the example, equipping working people and poor and marginalised communities with the technological skills and financial means to create their own media. But at national level also, it is necessary to press for media laws which do not merely guarantee 'free expression' in the abstract, but institutionalise access to all national media – newspapers, magazines, radio and TV and other technologies – by independent popular organisations. Technological sophistication and professional production skills should not serve as excuses to justify capitalist or elite establishment control of the means of mass communication and information. The crucial issue here has been well identified by Hilary Wainwright in *Reclaim the State* as the popular gestation of knowledge through praxis, the democratisation of knowledge through collective enterprise (Wainwright 2003, 14–29).

Ultimately, the whole of society, including all social institutions, has to be democratised. It is not only the formal institutions of government, or even other public institutions like the judiciary and the civil service, which must be at the service of the people, but also all institutions which exercise authority, including workplaces. The key issue is well formulated by Norberto Bobbio, as quoted by Ana Irene Méndez:

The index of the degree of democratic development is not the number of people with the right to vote but the number of areas other than the political in which the right to vote is exercised; what matters then is not 'who votes' but 'where they vote'. (Méndez 2004, 15, quoting Bobbio 1996, 63, translation mine)

It is for this reason that real participatory democracy is tendentially Socialist: a society which takes seriously the idea that all have an equal right to participate can scarcely accept an arrangement by which some have control and ownership of economic resources to the exclusion of others. This is why that great innovation of the Brazilian Workers' Party, the participatory budget, is so important and has attracted so much attention; but so long as the same democratic principles are not applied to national finances and to the workplace, the transformation of Brazilian society will remain severely limited. The democratisation of economic life does not necessarily imply the total socialisation of all enterprises, large and small, and certainly not along classic state-socialist lines; but it does imply extending democratic and participatory principles to all workplaces, including community input and not just that of the workers in each enterprise. The political implications of this are indeed revolutionary, which is why true participatory democracy has only flourished in revolutionary societies like Cuba, Sandinista Nicaragua and present-day Venezuela.

The actual development of popular participatory democracy in a given society must inevitably be a process of trial and error and of constant political debate and struggle. Thus in relation to the Cuban experience, for example, even sympathetic critics have pointed to the absence of real political and ideological debate as a serious weakness (Roman 2003, 143–4, 160). The quest for unanimity or at least consensus, as expressed in the concept of the 'general will', works fine in the direct administration of local affairs, especially in a relatively classless society. But in more complex societies where divisions of class and interest are real – and even in a relatively classless society when major issues of national policy are at stake – alternative policies such as are presented in liberal systems by rival political parties are bound to arise. It is not impossible for such debates to take place in a one-party or a non-party system, but as appears to be the case in the Cuban National Assembly, the pressure for consensus tends to stifle or at least mute the expression of differences. It is therefore necessary to ask whether some elements of liberal pluralism, such as multi-party elections, cannot be combined with direct participatory democracy.

The conventional answer to this question has been that the two systems are incompatible because to hold both types of elections will lead to a conflict of powers in which one or another source of legitimacy will have to prevail. But this does not prevent liberal systems from having two-chamber legislatures in which the second chamber is elected on a different basis; and there is certainly no inherent reason why MPs elected on a multi-party basis should not be subject to obligations of report-back and possible recall. If, as was the case in the early years of Sandinista Nicaragua, in Cuba and now in Venezuela, mass organisations such as trade unions, neighbourhood associations and women's associations share in the direct exercise of power, there is likewise no inherent reason why the executive bodies of these organisations should not include delegates elected on party political platforms (although subject always to rules designed to prevent partisan factionalism from usurping total control to the exclusion of broad rank-and-file interests). The real reason why the two systems have been regarded as incompatible may simply be because liberals have always insisted on the exclusive or overriding legitimacy of pluralist elections, refusing to countenance any sharing of power with other expressions of the popular will, while attempts to institutionalise direct democracy have generally taken place in one-party states which have rejected political pluralism.

To achieve a genuine direct and participatory democracy with ideological pluralism in any country will require a thoroughgoing revolutionary transformation, but it also requires a completely new constitutional paradigm. One of the greatest defects of liberal pluralism is the convention that a party winning a national majority has a mandate to implement its entire political platform, affecting every aspect of national life, when it is perfectly clear that many electors may have voted for its general programme while disagreeing strongly with some of its specific policies. A party proposing to combat bureaucracy and excessive centralisation may well win over a majority of the electorate despite reservations about its proposals to begin privatisation of social services, for example. Even more preposterous is the established practice whereby a party may simply abandon or even directly contravene major aspects of its platform without being held to account until the next election. It may indeed be the case that circumstances sometimes require such policy changes, but this surely further underlines the need for accountability. Such anti-democratic practices could be overcome by a constitutional requirement that major legislative initiatives in specific policy areas must be submitted to referendum, or by referral to a second chamber of delegates of mass organisations elected on a non-partisan basis. Institutionalising the right of recall, as has now been done in Venezuela, would also limit the arbitrary exercise of party-political power. Political parties may indeed have a legitimate function as vehicles for the formulation and expression of different ideological options, but this should not be confused with the exclusive right to govern; and an authentic democracy would require parties to win popular consent for any specific policy and to submit at all times to the sovereign will of the people.

Mainstream political commentators typically respond to such proposals by proclaiming that they would make a country 'ungovernable', but there is good reason to believe that this objection only reflects the vested interests of professional politicians and elite distrust of the popular classes. 'Governability' all too often means the prerogative of governments to eliminate the pension rights of tens of thousands of workers, to allow a foreign corporation to introduce GM foods, or to declare war without any meaningful consultation whatsoever. Democratisation should, on the contrary, mean bringing more and more areas of social and economic life under democratic control. Mass education and modern information and communications technology (ICT) make this more feasible than ever before, and there is good reason to argue that the time has come when Rousseau's ideal of direct popular sovereignty in all spheres of life (with the consequent disappearance of the political class) can finally be put into practice. The time has come to reclaim democracy from the liberal elites and to make it the instrument of the people, of the great majority; to show that another world is possible, not only in terms of economics and social justice but also in terms of democratic participation and control.

## THE SIREN SONG OF LIBERALISM

If we are to transcend liberalism and develop a conscious movement for real participatory democracy, we have first to recognise why liberal ideology has such a hold on the popular mind. There can be no doubt that despite widespread disillusionment with politics and politicians, the majority of the population in the West continues to regard 'liberal democracy' as desirable; they simply find its actual performance to be profoundly disappointing. Similarly there can be no doubt that liberal-pluralist elections serve as an attractive alternative to an arbitrary regime, as in many Latin American countries in the 1980s and in Eastern Europe since 1989. The attraction of liberal pluralism in these circumstances is simple: it offers the opportunity to complete the overthrow of a repressive system and to have at least a minimal say in choosing the politicians who will run things. It provides no possibility of real popular participation, but for those who have been denied any say at all for decades and may also have been subject to brutal repression, its appeal is obvious. This is why Western propaganda has such a powerful impact, despite the harsh economic effects of neo-liberalism and the blatant hypocrisy of Western leaders: as witnessed in one Eastern European country after another, culminating recently in the Ukraine, the chance to throw out an arbitrary regime mattered more in the short-term than social services and protection from the vagaries of the market. While it is true, as was pointed out by several critics, that Ukraine's so-called 'Orange Revolution' benefitted from considerable Western financing and pressure (Laughland 2004; Steele 2004; Traynor 2004), the evident corruption and dirty tricks of the previous Kuchma Government made it impossible to defend on any kind of democratic or popular basis. Once pluralist elections are firmly established and the futility of the political choices on offer becomes apparent, together with the negative consequences of unbridled capitalism, then disillusionment sets in; but even so few seek a return to the state-Socialist system.

This minimal but real possibility of choice, of at any rate selecting from time to time the least bad set of politicians on offer, is also one source of the residual legitimacy of liberal pluralism for the majority of the population in the West. Most people have few illusions about 'liberal democracy', they do not believe that politicians really represent them except in a very limited sense and are aware that their influence over political decisions is minimal. Hence the widespread and frequently expressed contempt for politicians and the view that 'they are all the same'. But people still value basic civil liberties, the absence of arbitrary rule and the limitations on state power consequent on the possibility of choice, however limited, between rival governmental teams. They are aware that with rare historical exceptions – exceptions of which most of them know almost nothing – the alternatives have been even worse: absolute monarchy, military dictatorship, fascism or authoritarian socialism (which some saw as an alternative while it lasted, but which has lost all credibility since the fall of the Soviet bloc). The quest for a viable alternative is fundamental if popular interest in politics is to be revived and if the Hobson's choice of liberal pluralism is to be transcended.

But there is another factor which is crucial to understanding the legitimacy of the liberal system in the central Western countries, and that is the welfare state. Indeed, given the deficiencies of liberal-pluralist electoral arrangements and the lack of accountability of politicians, it would be impossible to account for the continuing strength of the liberal system in these countries were it not for this major concession to popular demands. Beginning in the late nineteenth century and reaching a peak in the three decades following the Second World War, a whole range of social rights and benefits was conceded which transformed the life of the great majority of people in these countries: 'the most lasting political compromise known thus far between capitalism and democracy in times of peace' (Nun 2003, 55). This was also, as Nun recognises, an acceptance of the argument made by the Cambridge economist T.H. Marshall, 'that any genuine commitment to freedom also required a commitment to the conditions that would make it feasible for all citizens, and that establishing such conditions was a foremost obligation of the state' (ibid., 46) – a notion which would be summarily rejected by the neo-liberals.

The welfare state was only achieved through the pressure of working-class organisations (above all the trade unions) and political action by Social Democratic/Socialist and other left-wing parties, and also because of capitalist fear of the alternative represented by the Soviet Union and other Socialist states. But its impact can scarcely be overestimated: it is the welfare state which has done more than anything else to give working people the feeling that they have real, if limited, influence on the political process. There is much to be said for the Leninist argument that these material concessions to the working class were only possible because of the resources derived from colonialism and imperialism, which would account for the inability of liberal reformists in Latin America (for example) to create effective welfare states there; but in Western Europe and North America (and other developed countries: Japan, Australia, New Zealand) this has been fundamental for their entire social and political development. For this very reason the threat to the welfare state posed by neo-liberalism is the most important factor tending to undermine the legitimacy of the liberal system in recent times.

In Eastern Europe and the Third World, the siren song of liberalism will continue to exert an attraction wherever arbitrary regimes hold sway, leading to so-called 'democratic transitions' in yet more countries. Of course, such transitions will only take place if the previous regime is already beginning to break down under either internal or external pressures or a combination of the two, and it is no accident that many such transitions have taken place due to massive Western pressure or direct intervention. But this only occurs when the international context is favourable, in other words when such transitions coincide with the interests of the dominant Western powers. In other cases all kinds of electoral irregularities are ignored by the West, as happened in Mexico for many years or as continues to be the case in Colombia, where the two-party Liberal-Conservative hegemony is preserved by blatant fraud and state-sponsored terrorism against any serious opposition; and if it suits Western interests, open despotism continues to be tolerated as in Saudi Arabia, Pakistan or Uzbekistan. On the other hand, if free elections produce victory for a popular anti-imperialist movement or one which opposes neo-liberal orthodoxy, as in Nicaragua in 1984, Haiti with Aristide or Venezuela with Chávez, then their legitimacy is immediately questioned and they are subjected to immense pressures (including violence and sabotage) to hold fresh elections under 'international supervision', a term which all too often means interference to favour pro-Western candidates.

Even where 'regime change' of a democratic character is promoted, once it has occurred the popular will ceases to be of interest either to the West or to the new elites who have taken over, and measures are taken to contain democratic impulses within acceptable limits. Nowhere was this clearer than in Chile after 1989: the constitutional restrictions imposed by Pinochet remained in effect, and transition was rendered manageable by the Christian Democrat/Socialist Party *Concertación* which maintained the dictatorship's economic model. Similarly in Eastern Europe, the revolutionary overtones of the popular mobilisations against the bureaucratic establishment were quickly suppressed or diverted into acceptable channels as privatisation was imposed. But it would take several years for disillusionment to set in, and in the meantime the euphoria of 'freedom' gave legitimacy to the new dispensation.

Once the real agenda of the West and the profound limitations of the new 'democracy' become apparent, apathy and abstention tend to be the initial responses. But then alternative movements begin to emerge: in some Eastern European cases a resurgence of the ex-Communist parties, in others neo-Fascist movements, and in Latin America, anti-globalisation, indigenous and revolutionary movements. In most cases these movements lack a clear political programme and strategy and are defined more by opposition to the neo-liberal agenda than by support for a clear alternative, and this has led 'mainstream' scholars to dismiss them as transitory protest movements doomed to disappear as 'democratic consolidation' proceeds. In this respect the 'mainstream' is once again profoundly mistaken; but before we examine why, it is first necessary to review the received wisdom on 'democratic transition'.

## 'TRANSITOLOGY' AND THE NEW ORTHODOXY

The rise of neo-liberalism since the early 1980s is generally viewed in economic terms, as the imposition of 'free trade' and monetarist fundamentalism as the only economically acceptable policy. But the neo-liberal strategy also has a specifically political agenda, which is the concerted attempt to impose liberal pluralism as the only acceptable form of government (with the convenient exception of a number of pro-Western dictatorships). In keeping with this approach, and with the collapse of both the Soviet bloc and the

Latin American military regimes of the 1960s–1980s, a vast academic literature has sprung up on 'democratic transition'. Starting with serious analysis of 'regime change' in a few Southern and Eastern European and Latin American countries, 'transitology' has become a growth industry, so that we now have discussion of Middle Eastern and Islamic transitions, Chinese transition, African transition, and so on: virtually all countries outside the North Atlantic core are assumed to be 'in transition', and the transition can have only one goal, or rather two which are intimately connected: 'liberal democracy' and 'a market economy'. One of the first authors to attempt a serious academic analysis of the process, the conservative US theorist Samuel Huntington, described these developments as the 'Third Wave' of democratisation (Huntington 1991).

To evaluate the progress of 'new democracies', standard criteria are applied such as regular elections, freedom of speech and assembly and absence of electoral fraud, and if these criteria are satisfied then the goal becomes 'democratic consolidation'. Usually 'respect for private property' and the 'free market' are thrown in as well, and the notion that the democratic will of the people might prefer to place restrictions on the unfettered rule of the market is scarcely even considered. The 'transitology' literature is very revealing as to the true significance of neo-liberal orthodoxy on the issue of democracy. A classic of the genre, Linz and Stepan's *Problems of Democratic Transition and Consolidation*, provided a summary of what they saw as the necessary conditions for the liberal system to flourish. They identified 'five interacting arenas' of democratic consolidation: first, the development of a 'free and lively civil society'; second, a 'relatively autonomous and valued political society'; third, the rule of law; fourth, an effective state bureaucracy which is usable by democratic governments; and finally, an 'economic society' which protects property rights and allows markets to function with a degree of public regulation (Linz and Stepan 1996, 7). It was also Linz and Stepan who produced the succinct definition of democratic consolidation as having occurred when democracy became 'the only game in town' (ibid., 5).

This is undoubtedly a good description of the ideal characteristics of the liberal system as it functions in the central capitalist countries. Particularly striking is the emphasis on markets and property rights and the absence of any mention of social justice or popular participation. The authors would object that the latter, at least, is implicit in 'civil society', but as Rousseau argued this concept means in practice the plethora of non-state actors, dominated by the propertied and the privileged, who take the stage once the sovereign people has been deprived of power. What the transitologists are talking about is really the establishment and consolidation of civil constitutional government, which in most cases is no doubt preferable to the previous arbitrary regimes but which has little to do with popular participation or empowerment. During the crucial stages of transition there may well be mass popular mobilisations or even revolutions of a limited kind, heralded with great fanfare in the Western media; but these soon subside, indeed it is assumed that they must subside for 'consolidation' to take place. If popular mobilisation continues and takes the form of a political movement for real participation and social justice, then both academic transitologists and the media become concerned about 'populism' and 'unconsolidated democracy'.

To be fair, it has to be recognised that some of the most articulate and sophisticated transitologists do recognise the limitations of the 'democracy' which is assumed as the norm. Thus Linz and Stepan recognise in their conclusion that 'to create an economic society supportive of democracy requires more than just markets and private property. It is time to problematize and transcend "illiberal liberalism" … ' (Linz and Stepan 1996, 457). Even more interesting is the position of the Polish-American scholar Adam Przeworski, who although using a Schumpeterian definition of democracy as 'a particular system of processing and terminating intergroup conflicts' (Przeworski 1986, 56), goes on to admit that 'what we need, and do not have, is a more comprehensive, integral, ideological project of antiauthoritarianism that would encompass the totality of social life' (ibid., 63). But what is striking is that in the prevailing discourse, whether in academia or in establishment politics and the media, such caveats have disappeared and all discussion of 'democratic transition' and 'consolidation' now assumes a narrow Schumpeterian definition. A good example is a recent text entitled *Democracy in Latin America* by a respected British scholar, George Philip. Philip begins by quoting Schumpeter approvingly (Philip 2003, 2–3), and then proceeds to summarise the recent democratic performance of different Latin American countries on the basis of the indicators proposed by Freedom House, a right-wing Washington think-tank (ibid., 8–11). But it was Freedom House which, on the basis of its 'free market' criterion, classified Sandinista Nicaragua as less democratic than El Salvador in 1984, when Nicaragua had institutionalised popular participation at all levels and held multi-party elections which were approved by numerous European and Canadian observers, whereas the Salvadorean military were conducting a 'dirty war' with massive human rights violations (Méndez 2004, 42).

The problem here is not only the insistence on capitalist values (the 'free market') but also the restriction of the debate to purely formal criteria. Thus in a discussion of what he calls 'unbalanced presidentialism', Philip refers to Juan Linz who argues that lack of parliamentary control over the presidency can lead to democratic breakdown, as with 'the Allende government in Chile (1970–73), which could not be removed constitutionally by a congressional vote of no confidence despite its unpopularity among the majority of Chileans', and that this deadlock precipitated Pinochet's coup (Philip 2003, 28). Quite apart from the fact that most Chilean democrats would be horrified by this assertion of the 'unpopularity' of Allende, the analysis effectively attributes the coup to technical constitutional problems rather than to the intense class struggle being waged in Chile at the time and the well-documented intervention of US imperialism.

Formal criteria are also the basis of most liberal critiques of Hugo Chávez and the Bolivarian revolution in Venezuela. Unable to dispute Chávez' popularity (he has now won no less than ten elections and referenda with large majorities, with international observers approving the results), they accuse him of carrying out a 'constitutional coup' (Norden 2003, 93) and of running a 'delegative democracy' in O'Donnell's terms. Philip laments the decline of the traditional parties in Venezuela 'with their emphasis on negotiated solutions to problems' (Philip 2003, 135), overlooking the fact that the fundamental problems of maldistribution of wealth, corruption and state repression were simply ignored in these 'negotiated solutions', which is why the excluded majority turned to Chávez. But in an unguarded moment Philip recognises the essence of the problem, which relates directly to the issue of the limits of liberalism: 'The argument that Venezuela has a democratic culture but not a liberal or pluralist one seems plausible indeed' (ibid.). For Philip this is a criticism, but for those of us who regard true democracy as transcending liberalism, this only confirms the significance of the Venezuelan process.

I have focussed on Philip here only because he writes on my own field of specialisation, Latin America; but he is in good academic (and non-academic) company. Contemporary discussion of poverty in Africa or South Asia or Latin America tends to recognise the paucity of results of 'democracy' and market liberalisation for the poor, but offers no solution other than more of the same, perhaps adding a critique of 'weak states' and political corruption. The probability that massive privatisation, especially in impoverished countries, will necessarily weaken the state and will also tend to favour corruption, is conveniently ignored. Progressive critiques focus on the economic ills of globalisation and the imposition of neo-liberal policies by the IMF, the World Bank and the Western powers, but have few suggestions as to how governments in the global South are to resist such policies. When radical governments such as those of Cuba, Venezuela or Malaysia take effective measures to promote independent development, they may be admired by anti-globalisation activists who will nevertheless criticise them for being 'undemocratic'. But the reality is that only a strong state can assert a measure of independence in the face of global capital, and if strength is not to come from authoritarianism it can only derive from mass popular support, the legitimacy that comes from true democratic mobilisation; in other words, not the formality of liberal pluralism but the mass participation of real popular democracy.

The reality of many of the new liberal regimes in the Third World and Eastern Europe was well summed up in the title of a critical study published more than a decade ago: *Low Intensity Democracy* (Gills, Rocamora and Wilson 1993). The authors were referring particularly to certain countries which the transitologists would have regarded as 'non-consolidated democracies' (Guatemala, Argentina under Menem, the Philippines and South Korea), with elements inherited from an authoritarian past, but their critique of 'formal democracy' without 'progressive social reform' can be applied to most of the regimes emerging from Huntington's 'Third Wave', whether or not 'consolidated'. Indeed, as we have seen, under neo-liberal hegemony and anti-terrorist hysteria, even many of the so-called advanced democracies could be regarded as 'low-intensity'.

## NEO-LIBERALISM AND THE EMERGING CRISIS
## OF CONSENSUS POLITICS IN THE WEST

If liberal pluralism is on transparently shaky ground in the global South, it still appears to be hegemonic in the North. But as we have seen, even here the concentration of executive power and the growing restrictions on civil liberties have begun to undermine it, and there is another recent development which threatens to destroy its legitimacy completely: the retreat from the welfare state and the imposition of monetarist free-trade policies brought about by neo-liberalism. Of course the retreat is far from complete – to withdraw all social benefits would be suicidal – but certainly many state-provided benefits which were once regarded as irreversible have been reduced, made contingent on income or transferred to schemes run by private agencies, undermining the entire philosophy of universal rights and public service and with it the sense of collective empowerment that was the foundation of (for instance) Labour Party strength in Britain.

The neo-liberal victory was only possible because of the deficiencies and contradictions of social democracy: undemocratic and bureaucratic decision-making, inefficiency, uniformity and conformism. In terms of political economy it is no doubt true, as argued in numerous studies, that the welfare state and the accumulation of union power were undermining capital accumulation. By emphasising these points and by appealing to individual self-interest the political establishment and the media were able to sell the new dispensation to the electorate, although the degree of resistance encountered was still considerable and led to recourse to methods which made the issues brutally clear: Thatcher's confrontation with the coal miners, the poll tax, the destruction of independent (and popular) metropolitan governments, Reagan's attack on the air traffic controllers in the States, and the drastic reversal of a long-established welfare state in New Zealand.

If the right-wing populism of Thatcher aroused working-class indignation, it could still be seen by some as a temporary phenomenon, a 'swing of the pendulum' to be followed by a revival of progressive social democracy with the reassertion of workers' rights and public services. Real disillusionment would come with Blair (and with Clinton in the US and the Social Democratic governments of Jospin in France, Schroeder in Germany, or the 'Olive Branch' coalition in Italy). As it became clear that Social Democracy, never revolutionary but at least traditionally the guardian of basic welfare rights and public services, had sold out to the neo-liberal doctrine of market efficiency and individualism, the political system began to suffer a crisis of credibility not seen for generations, arguably not since the 1930s. The system is still far from collapse, but as the abandonment by Social Democracy of any pretence of commitment to socialism or working-class interests becomes clearer, popular cynicism about politics and politicians reaches new heights and electoral abstentionism grows apace. The scale of indifference has long been apparent in the US, reaching a new peak (or trough) with the first election of George W.

Bush when barely 51 per cent of an electorate from which many poor citizens are anyway excluded bothered to vote, and this was followed by the second election of Blair in the UK, with turnout at 59 per cent being the lowest since the introduction of universal suffrage.

It is surely no accident that electoral participation remains high where, despite the rise of more conservative parties, inroads on the welfare state have been limited: the Scandinavian countries, Germany and the Netherlands, for example. It could be objected that some more recent elections have shown increased participation even in countries where neo-liberalism has had greater impact: in France, where around 80 per cent turned out in the second round of the presidential elections to vote for Jacques Chirac; in Spain, where voters rallied to support the PSOE of Zapatero against Aznar; in the February 2005 Portuguese general election; and in the US where George W's re-election benefitted from an increased turnout of about 60 per cent. But in all four cases special circumstances were at work and voter motivation seems to have been less an expression of faith in the liberal system than a desire to protest or to veto the worst alternatives.

The French case is paradigmatic: mediocre turnout in the first round, with large protest votes for three Trotskyist candidates demonstrating working-class disillusionment with the neo-liberal policies of the Socialists and the irrelevance of the Communists, but thereby permitting the neo-Fascist LePen to reach the run-off election against Chirac. The massive vote for the latter in the second round was therefore in no way a show of confidence either in him or in the system, but a panic-stricken rejection of Fascism. In Spain the electoral dynamic was similar: it was the Aznar government's blatant manipulation of the 11 March terrorist bombings in Madrid, trying to gain electoral advantage by blaming ETA in order to divert attention from its own responsibility for embroiling Spain in Bush's 'War on Terror', which provoked a decisive swing against Aznar and the Partido Popular (PP) at the last minute. Again, it was not enthusiasm for the PSOE but revulsion at the deceitful cynicism of the PP and its neo-Francoist sympathies which motivated Spanish voters. In Portugal it was also the extreme unpopularity of the right-wing PSD–PP coalition and its egocentric leader Santana Lopes which provoked the biggest victory for the Left since the 1974 revolution: a parliamentary majority for the Socialists, the first increase in years for the Communists (up from 12 to 14 seats) and a big increase for the Left bloc (from three to eight seats). But here also, the increase in turnout was quite modest (from 63 to 67 per cent) and many voters declared that they had little faith in the Socialists but wanted to reject the Right. Moreover the strong vote for the Communists and the Left bloc, which together with two small extraparliamentary Marxist parties won 16 per cent of the popular vote, was essentially an anti-system vote indicating that a sizeable minority of the electorate is consciously seeking a non-liberal alternative.

In the US a similar dynamic was at work, but only up to a point: progressives mobilised in large numbers, despite having no illusions about Kerry, just to get rid of Bush; but the disturbing reality is that Bush still won with an increased turnout, essentially because the 'Christian Right' was able to mobilise more effectively than the Left. In other words, the political dynamic in the States is no longer just one of voter disillusionment with the fraudulent democracy of liberal pluralism, but the rise of a right-wing populism with Fascist overtones.

Recent trends in the central capitalist countries thus suggest that the legitimacy of the liberal-pluralist system is increasingly questioned, with electorates using the vote to prevent further deterioration in their rights and living standards but having little hope of real improvement. Even in those European countries where the adoption of neo-liberal policies has been more cautious, such as Germany and the Scandinavian countries, disillusionment is growing: in the words of the outstanding German intellectual Gunter Grass,

[p]arliament is no longer sovereign in its decisions. It depends on powerful pressure groups – the banks and multinationals – which are not subject to any democratic control. Democracy has become a pawn to the dictates of globally volatile capital ... Questions asked as to the reasons for the growing gap between rich and poor are dismissed as 'the politics of envy'. The desire for justice is ridiculed as utopian. The concept of 'solidarity' is relegated to the dictionary's list of 'foreign words'. (Grass 2005)

Popular discontent in Germany was clearly manifested in the recent general elections which produced a stalemate with a diminished vote for both major parties and significant support (nearly 9 per cent) for the new Left Party.

This brings us back to the 'minimalist' legitimacy of liberalism: people are well aware that it is only minimally democratic, essentially only at election time and even then only in allowing them to veto the worst alternatives on offer, but they see little possibility of creating a better system and hence continue to participate, although with growing reluctance. This is the opportunity, but also the challenge, for those of us who really believe that 'another world is possible', and as part of that world 'another democracy is possible'. To build an alternative will requires working through the existing liberal parliamentary system, but also outside it, to build a new broad movement for popular democracy and social justice which will transcend all left-wing parties and groups to achieve unity and strength. It will require developing a vigorous popular democratic consciousness which will not be satisfied with token participatory gestures, and a sense of community and collective rights such as has not been seen in the West for at least 30 years.

## THE EMERGENCE OF DEMOCRATIC ALTERNATIVES IN LATIN AMERICA

In contrast to this, it is in Latin America that the failure of the liberal model has provoked the most interesting and indeed revolutionary response. Since here the background was one of brutal right-wing militarism, pro-capitalist and supported by the US, and of previous corrupt liberal regimes, neo-liberalism had very limited credibility whether in economic or political terms. Unlike Eastern Europe, in most Latin American countries there was little euphoria about the new liberal arrangements, which in most cases emerged as a compromise imposed by the US and the military in order to avert more radical alternatives. It therefore did not take long for the economic failures of neo-liberalism to translate into political terms with the re-emergence of popular revolutionary movements, albeit movements working mainly through peaceful and institutional channels. This is why Latin America has become the main source of inspiration for those who seek a more profound and participatory democracy and an alternative to neo-liberal globalisation; it is also the source of headaches for the 'transitologists', as many of the new Latin American democracies fail to become 'consolidated' in keeping with the standard liberal formula.

The reasons for this become apparent when we look at the actual results of liberal pluralism in Latin America, whether before or after the recent 'transitions'. The example of Venezuela is paradigmatic: a 'liberal democracy' for 40 years before the first election of Hugo Chávez in 1998, it was frequently held up (especially by the US) as a model for the region, yet by the 1990s its political system had lost all credibility in the eyes of the poor. The main reason for this was not, as some have argued, any defect in the electoral system which favoured the two-party domination of Acción Democrática (AD, Social Democratic) and COPEI (Christian Democrat) and excluded the Left: in this respect it was less exclusionary than the US or British systems, and electoral reforms in 1988 actually facilitated the rise of alternative parties, in particular La Causa R (the Radical Cause) which might have brought about a popular transformation. Similarly, the appointment of state governors by the national authorities, often pointed to as a defect, was replaced by direct election in 1988. The Venezuelan system had its peculiarities, but this is true of all liberal systems; no two constitutions are exactly the same. The fundamental cause of popular disillusionment with 'liberal democracy' in Venezuela was not any peculiar defect of *puntofijismo* (as the system was known from its foundation in the 1958 Pact of Punto Fijo) but the fact that all parties (including after 1994 the Radical Cause) pursued IMF-style neo-liberal policies despite repeatedly manifested popular hostility to them. In typical liberal fashion, the system produced a 'consensus politics' which was both exclusionary and repressive towards the poor.

The Venezuelan welfare state created during the oil boom from the 1940s to the 1970s was always inadequate, but with the 1980s debt crisis it fell apart and successive governments put the burden of austerity on the poor and the lower middle class. The process reached crisis point in February 1989 when AD President Carlos Andrés Pérez, elected on a populist platform promising to oppose international financial pressures and introduce new welfare measures, turned round and did precisely the opposite, introducing an IMF deflationary package. The resultant price rises and in particular the increase in bus fares provoked massive popular riots which the Government repressed by sending in the military, leading to hundreds, indeed probably thousands, of deaths. This episode, subsequently labelled the *Caracazo,* was a turning-point: in the words of Fernando Coronil and Julie Skurski –

'El pueblo tiene hambre' (the people are hungry), the slogan widely painted on walls, was the explanation most frequently offered by participants for the uprising ... Hunger was regarded as a national cause for revolt, but it was a shorthand expression referring, through the image of food, to what was regarded as unnecessary deprivation and insult in a country that had both wealth and democracy ... . (Coronil and Skurski 2004, 95–6)

The state's response to spontaneous riots and looting was indiscriminate repression: 'Mass killings were thus a way of constructing the pueblo as irrational and the government as the sole defender of reason' (Coronil and Skurski 2004, 102).

The harsh reality dissected by Coronil and Skurski is taken up by Michael Derham in a controversial article, 'Undemocratic democracy', in which he concludes that in many ways the record of the 1950s dictator Marcos Pérez Jiménez was better than that of the *puntofijista* democrats: 'On the evidence available to Venezuelans, dictatorship and military rule might be considered a force for civilisation while the reality of democracy brings barbarism' (Derham 2002, 286). Not surprisingly, Derham's comments provoked an indignant response from a mainstream Venezuela specialist, Daniel Levine (Levine 2003); but other than correcting some unfortunate exaggerations in Derham's article, Levine fails to deal with the fundamental issue of social exclusion and state repression under the Punto Fijo system, which despite improving its liberal-democratic procedures after 1988 actually became more socially and economically exclusionary.

Moreover, these defects of a conventional liberal-democratic regime in a socially polarised society are not confined to Venezuela: another article in the same volume as the Coronil and Skurski article, a brilliant essay on Ecuador by Liisa North, argues the same case for that country's experience during most of the past century:

[s]ince the July Revolution of 1925, military dictatorships rather than elected civilian governments have most consistently pursued inclusionary policies that could have led to domestic market development and social progress. In fact, the country's dominant political-economic elites repeatedly blocked the military's efforts to, for better or worse, engage in nation-building ... (North 2004, 1992)

Furthermore, in North's view, when these civilian elites won power through elections, they were often more repressive than the military, 'and almost always more rapacious, corrupt, and shortsighted' (North 2004, 204). Of course, neither North nor Derham is advocating dictatorship or military rule, but they are concerned to demonstrate that in the polarised societies of Latin America, 'liberal democracy' in its pure form leads only to further polarisation and social exclusion. The reason for this, as argued above, is that liberal institutions – the judiciary, political parties, the media, 'civil society' – are controlled by these same 'elites' (the dependent bourgeoisie) which have no interest in national development or social justice but rather in maintaining the neo-liberal status quo, to their own benefit and that of transnational capital. This vicious circle can only be overcome by alternative political models which guarantee effective participation by the poor majority, and which are therefore more democratic but less liberal; and the most impressive current attempt to build such an alternative is that of Hugo Chávez and the Bolivarian revolution in Venezuela (which will be examined in detail in Chapter 5).

Another recent demonstration of the anti-popular character of the liberal-democratic system is offered by Bolivia, where the poor indigenous majority has repeatedly shown its opposition to the neo-liberal agenda of privatisation of water and natural gas, only to see such policies imposed by elected governments controlled by the country's white ruling elite and by transnational capital. The massive protests provoked by such policies met with violent repression (causing some 70 deaths) by the government of President Sánchez de Losada who was then forced to resign by what amounted to revolutionary popular pressure; but his successor, former Vice-President Carlos Meza, having reverted to similar policies, faced months of militant contestation until he also was forced to resign in June 2005. At the same time the most popular man in the country, the indigenous peasant leader Evo Morales, who as head of the MAS or Movement to Socialism party won the December 2005 elections, has been demonised by the elite and the US as a 'narcoterrorist' and subversive ally of Chávez.

Liberals could object here that this only demonstrates the failure of the Bolivian bourgeoisie and their US masters to play by their own liberal rules, and that what the popular sectors have to do is insist on the strict fulfilment of those rules. But this is only true up to a point. The root of the problem is that the liberal system, which until recently functioned as intended to preserve elite privilege, was unable to contain the growth of a mass popular movement based on non-liberal indigenous principles of communal participation and economic collectivism, and it is this which has the dominant groups, both national and international, running scared. As in Venezuela under *puntofijismo*, so also in Bolivia, the persistent failure of the liberal electoral system to produce a government responsive to the needs of the poor majority led to the emergence of a counter-hegemonic movement which has finally won electoral victory, but only after having to confront repeated violence and fraud by the dominant elites. In such circumstances it is indeed tactically advisable for the popular movement to demand fulfilment of the liberal principle of free and fair elections; but its success has come despite the limitations of liberalism; and in order to implement its programme, which includes nationalisation and land reform, it will undoubtedly have to transcend liberal institutions and create a direct and participatory democracy more responsive to popular needs. Whether this can be done by predominantly peaceful means remains to be seen.

Finally we have the case of Brazil, the giant of Latin America and the country which until recently seemed to offer the best prospect of social justice and democratic renewal in the region. With the emergence in the early 1980s of the PT (Partido dos Trabalhadores or Workers' Party) and the MST (Movimento dos Trabalhadores Rurais Sem Terra or Movement of the Landless) the Brazilian popular movement embarked on a process which had enormous significance for the renovation of the Latin American Left. Under the leadership of Lula (Luis Inácio 'Lula' da Silva, a union activist of the São Paulo metallurgical workers), the PT was the first major labour-based political party to have been created anywhere in the world in the previous 50 years. Ideologically pluralist, with tendencies ranging from Social Democratic to Marxist-Leninist and radical Christian, it appeared to offer an alternative independent of both the Communist and Social Democratic traditions. By the 1990s, as the PT won control of several important municipalities such as Porto Alegre, its innovative practices, including the participatory budget and other mechanisms of direct democracy, attracted international attention (Branford and Kucinski 2003; Wainwright 2003). Then with Lula's victory in the 2002 presidential elections and his inauguration early in 2003, there was enormous hope of radical social and political change in Brazil. But two years later that hope had been replaced by frustration and disillusionment: Lula looks less like a Brazilian Hugo Chávez than a tropical Tony Blair (or perhaps it would be fairer to say a Latin Gerhard Schroeder, since he has not indulged in the same degree of neo-liberal arrogance as Blair). Adhering to a strict IMF-approved monetary and fiscal policy, the PT Government has severely limited its social programmes and has done nothing to attack the entrenched privileges of the landed and commercial oligarchy in Brazil. Its achievements in agrarian reform are no better than those of the previous neo-liberal Cardoso presidency, and its social policies such as *Fome Zero* (Zero Hunger) are little more than welfare hand-outs (in contrast to the Venezuelan 'Missions' which are accompanied by systematic efforts to promote the organisation and empowerment of the poor). Not surprisingly, a left schism – albeit a small one – has now taken place from the PT bloc in Congress, and Lula's relations with the MST and other social movements are seriously strained. It is no accident that at the World Social Forum in Porto Alegre in January 2005 Lula was booed while Chávez was given a hero's welcome. A veteran Luso-Brazilian activist, Alípio de Freitas, summed up the mood of many when he said to me at a meeting in Lisbon in February 2005 that the PT, once viewed as the main expression of people's power in Brazil, is now just a party like any other.

If there is one lesson to be drawn from the Brazilian experience it is once again that, as in Venezuela and Bolivia, electoral victory for a mass popular movement within a liberal system is only a first step, an initial basis for undertaking a thoroughgoing transformation. Like Chávez in 1998, Lula in 2002 had a massive popular mandate, with 60 per cent of the vote and a recognition even by most of the opposition that radical change was on the agenda. Several key institutions such as the Catholic Church and the armed forces were prepared to give Lula the benefit of the doubt, and decisive action to begin redistribution of wealth and income and to reassert national economic priorities against neo-liberal globalisation would surely have strengthened his hand: would the IMF, which tolerated independent financial policies by Venezuela and more recently by Argentina, want to bankrupt the eighth largest industrial economy in the world? But Social Democratic technocrats had already surrounded Lula and taken control of the PT, and caution dictated the new government's line. Now, four years later, there are some hints that Lula wants to take the offensive, but it is almost certainly too late: the bourgeois oligarchy has recovered from the initial shock of his victory, and the social movements are either too demoralised or too distrustful of government to provide the required momentum.

It follows from this that wherever a party or movement representing the excluded masses wins a clear mandate at the polls for radical change, it must immediately take bold action to meet popular expectations and to begin the transformation of all public institutions: not just the formal government but the judiciary, the civil service, the police and armed forces, the media and so on, which must all be democratised and made to serve popular interests. This does not mean imposing 'totalitarian' control, as many liberals will immediately object; it is not the government or a party which must take over these institutions, but the people themselves, supported by a progressive government but acting through myriad forms of grass-roots organisation and participation. This necessity flows from the recognition that the institutions of the liberal state, from top to bottom, are capitalist institutions, designed to maintain the hegemony of capital, and true popular democracy will never be possible if they are left untouched. The task of a working-class or popular government is to create mechanisms which permit mass initiative and participation, and to stimulate and protect popular power in all areas of public life.

In relation to these recent positive developments in Latin America, the outstanding Cuban theorist Aurelio Alonso refers to 'the signs of recovery of the capacity to make use of the electoral apparatus in favour of the interests of the majority' (Alonso 2004, 11; translation mine). He goes on to declare that

It seems paradoxical that we should still have to regard as exceptional in the Third World those situations in which the democratic system – by which I mean, the system based on the liberal formula – has begun to work for the purpose for which it was supposedly created in the first place: so that the will of the majority may decide who will govern and in what manner ... (Alfonso 2004, 11).

Indeed, as in the observation by José Nun quoted earlier, the paradox is that the liberal system offers few examples of what it claims to provide and which is its main ideological attraction: the concept of a freely self-governing community. Moreover, if as Alonso says Latin America has recently witnessed a 'recovery of the capacity to make use of the electoral apparatus in favour of the interests of the majority', this is only as the result of a critical social and economic situation, and this very capacity to make elections serve true popular interests has produced a crisis of the liberal political system in the region. But it is also this mass consciousness of the need to create a truly democratic system serving the interests of the great majority which makes Latin America the most exciting and inspiring region of the world today. The practice of participatory budgetting in Brazil, the reclaiming of indigenous traditions of collective decision-making in Chiapas, Ecuador and Bolivia, the implementation of workers' control and community self-government by the *barrio* movement in Argentina, the local democracy of People's Power in Cuba, and above all the creative ferment of the Bolivarian revolution in Venezuela: these are the examples of popular democratic renewal which can provide inspiration for the disillusioned and jaded working-class electorates of the so-called advanced countries. Latin America is the centre of the popular democratic revolution of our times, and if the transformation there can be consolidated and developed, it has the potential to inspire similar transformations in Europe and elsewhere. To take democracy out of the hands of the liberal elites and reclaim it for the people is the crucial task of our times, without which socialism or any other conceivable alternative social order is completely illusory.

# 3
## Socialism or Popular Power: Revolutionary Reality in a Globalised World

For many in the new social movements around the world, in the anti-globalisation and anti-capitalist movements, the ultimate goal of their activities remains vague, even obscure: a better world, a different world, an alternative society, social justice, ecological balance. There is a general feeling that the alternative must be democratic, participatory, communitarian; but the distrust of politics and politicians is such that few are willing to engage in organised politics except in an oppositional stance, or to formulate a global alternative. Socialism remains attractive as an abstract concept, but following the Soviet debacle and the degeneration of Social Democracy, there is no consensus on the characteristics of a future socialism or on the strategy for its realisation. A vague anarchism pervades the movements, although without in general the theoretical perspective of Bakunin, Kropotkin, Malatesta or other classics of anarchist thought.

For many the failure of familiar political strategies and models implied, if not acceptance of neo-liberal capitalism, at least the reduction of progressive politics to particular struggles without any broader perspective. There was an apparent inability to refute the 'End of History' rhetoric of the neo-liberals; when establishment politicians proclaimed that 'The idea of revolution ceases to make sense', and poured scorn on any notion of 'the "leap outside capitalism", or magic and tragic "liberation", or an idealistic search for a "third way"' (Valdés 1995, 130), the Left seemed to have no clear answer except voluntarism. Confronted with capitalism triumphant it was essential to reassert the belief in a just society, but in the absence of a new strategy or theoretical model both the dogmatic Marxist-Leninist or Trotskyist reaffirmation of proletarian revolution, and the new social movements' insistence that 'another world is possible', were voluntarist assertions of wishful thinking.

The Zapatista rebellion of 1994 and the anti-globalisation rallies of Birmingham, Seattle, Genoa and Prague showed that mass resistance had not died and that the search for an alternative continued, but they provided few clues as to where that alternative might be found. And more than a decade after the eruption of the Zapatista uprising, few in the 'advanced countries' believe that they have found it: many would agree with the former Marxist Martin Jacques, that 'The left, as history knew it, is dead – and it will not be reborn' (Jacques 2004). Jacques identifies two fundamental reasons for this state of affairs: 'The first is the loss of agency, the decline of the industrial working class and its consequent erosion as a meaningful and effective political force' (ibid.), and the second is the collapse of communism. In the 'First World' at least, most observers see little sign of this changing, and hence political disorientation continues to prevail.

It is this disorientation and distrust which have spawned the ultimate theoretical formulation of negativism, John Holloway's *Change the World Without Taking Power*, a pretentious critique not merely of orthodox Marxist-Leninism but of virtually any political strategy whatsoever except spontaneous resistance (Holloway 2002). Apparently inspired by the Zapatistas, but much less circumspect and more dogmatic than they, Holloway has produced a manifesto for the 'scream' of horror and revolt against an unjust world, but one which ends as it begins – after 215 dense pages of neo-marxian philosophising – with a self-indulgent proclamation of political agnosticism: 'How then do we change the world without taking power? At the end of the book, as at the beginning, we do not know ...' (Holloway 2002, 215). For Holloway, there is no point in taking power, whether by revolution, elections or any other means, because power itself is oppressive and the only solution is 'anti-power'; the state, even a revolutionary state, is an instrument of capitalism.

Now it is one thing to recognise that revolutionary state power has all too often lost its popular democratic foundations, and quite another to deny the importance of state power as such and the possibility of constructing a non-capitalist power structure based on social justice. To ignore state power altogether and, in the name of popular autonomy, to rely exclusively on grass-roots organisation and resistance, is to leave the essence of capitalism untouched and to condemn the people to an endless cycle of circumscribed struggles, frustration and disillusionment. As Atilio Boron points out, the capitalist state is the principal organiser of bourgeois domination and the principal 'disorganiser' of the subordinate classes:

... the state is precisely where the correlation of forces is condensed. It is not the only place, but it is by far the most important one. It is the only one from which, for example, the victors can transform their interests into laws, and create a normative and institutional framework that guarantees the stability of their conquests. (Boron 2005, 37)

This is why, despite the fact that the Soviet state had long since ceased to express popular power in any meaningful sense, health care and education remained free and universal in the USSR until its collapse and unemployment was virtually unknown: a legal and institutional structure existed which was fundamentally inimical to capitalism. Of course, since that structure had become completely divorced from its popular and democratic origins, it collapsed like a house of cards as soon as the iron hand of the central Soviet authority was relaxed, and there was no independent popular movement with the strength to salvage socialised health care, education or other benefits. But Boron's point holds: it was the original revolutionary conquest of power 70 years before which had institutionalised fundamental benefits for the common people, benefits which long outlived the exhaustion of this particular revolutionary model. The lesson surely is not to ignore state power, but to insist more than ever on its importance while searching for the means to avoid the expropriation of revolutionary state power from the people by a self-selected party bureaucracy.

Imperialist policy-makers are only too well aware of the crucial importance of the state: this is why, for instance, the first priorities for Washington in a hypothetical reconquest of Cuba are to dismantle the Revolutionary Armed Forces and the Communist Party and to hold 'free elections' from which the Castro brothers would be excluded: privatisation, Coca-Cola and McDonald's can wait, the key issue is state power. In the same perspective, the contrast in the US attitude to Brazil and Venezuela is instructive: they have no great problem with a left-wing president like Lula holding office for a few years since he has done nothing to challenge the basic power structure in Brazil, but Chávez is a totally different matter since from the very beginning he has sought to transform electoral victory into a revolutionary reconstruction of the entire Venezuelan state. To deny the issue of power, or to assert that it can simply be 'dissolved' from below by discrete and uncoordinated struggles – which is Holloway's perspective – is to deny reality and to abandon all hope of effective change.

None of this should be taken to imply that the *specific characteristics* of revolutionary state power, and by extension of revolutionary parties and movements, are not problematic. It is with very good reason that most of the Left has turned its back on the Soviet and Eastern European models and also on the Chinese and other East Asian variants. The Cuban experience is more positive and will be discussed in detail later, but it should be clear that any new revolutionary strategy must look beyond all existing models and must address the reasons for popular scepticism with regard to both political parties and power structures of any kind. The repeated failures of both revolutionary regimes and progressive governments of different kinds, whether due to 'betrayal', to underestimation of the structural resilience of capitalism, or to an anti-democratic and oligarchic bias in the structures of progressive and revolutionary parties, demand critical assessment if a viable new alternative is to be developed. But critical reassessment should not mean total rejection of past experiences or cavalier dismissal of real and even historic achievements: veteran militants of Communist, Social Democratic or populist parties have good reason to resent the facile condemnation of their efforts by young neo-anarchist idealists with little experience and less understanding.

The search for a new alternative, then, has to start with an acute yet balanced critique of past experiences; and one of the crucial lessons is that, in the words of a very perceptive Cuban author, Aurelio Alonso, 'it is not possible to speak of an alternative without also talking about power' (Alonso 2004, 12). While accepting the need to place limitations on the authority of the centralised state, to give priority to local community action, to recognise the validity of social movements without explicit political goals and to promote grass-roots participatory democracy, Alonso insists that he cannot view these ideas as a reason to ignore the importance of power but rather 'as another means of seeking it which is more in accordance with the complexity of the political spectrum and with a socialist perspective, as part of which the construction of a different kind of democracy is indispensable' (ibid.). Moreover – and in direct contradiction to the neo-liberals who see democracy as predicated on capitalism – Alonso proclaims that 'History has shown that capitalism can reproduce itself without democracy, but socialism cannot.'

If the term 'Socialism' continues for many to express the ideal of an alternative society, of 'a better world', it is far from clear just what Socialism means in our times. Today the classic Soviet state-Socialist model has few defenders, and with good reason; even Communist

Party members generally now prefer a more open and democratic version thereof, or else simply advocate state-Socialist policies within a liberal-pluralist system (a position which is surely unviable given the realities of power under a liberal-capitalist state). But there are still a handful of ultra-orthodox doctrinaires like the veteran Portuguese leader Álvaro Cunhal (recently deceased) who show little inclination to abandon the Soviet model: Cunhal astonished many with an article in November 2003 specifying China, North Korea, Vietnam, Laos and Cuba as the bastions of progressive and anti-capitalist politics in today's world, and pointedly omitting Venezuela or any other new alternative (Cunhal 2003). Given the record of Cunhal and his ilk – before 1989 he was a totally uncritical defender of the USSR and shared typical Soviet reservations about China – it is difficult to see this as anything other than a desperate desire to salvage what remains of the old Stalinist paradigm with a wilful blindness to any kind of change. Neo-liberals like to label Socialists of any kind as dinosaurs; for the Cunhals of this world, a better comparison might be with the ostrich.

Before moving on to more interesting issues, it is necessary briefly to confront Cunhal's position. It should be obvious why the rigid Stalinism of North Korea, or even the Chinese combination of centralist authoritarianism with large enclaves of state-supervised robber-baron capitalism, can have little attraction for those who seek a genuinely popular and participatory alternative; there is good reason to suspect that the 'Democratic People's Republic of Korea' will eventually suffer a similar fate to the Soviet Union or – perhaps a better parallel – Albania, having maintained a rigid state-Socialist model by force and left no democratic space whatsoever for popular forces to introduce democratic change from within. China is more complicated and may yet produce interesting surprises, but it is difficult to see how the extreme inequality and exploitation in the booming coastal zones can ever revert to Socialist standards of equality and collective values without another revolution; and the limitations on any kind of democratic participation in both party and state also makes progressive internal reform extremely difficult. Vietnam seems to present a slightly less extreme version of the Chinese model, and as for Laos, detailed information is hard to come by. Cuba remains the only case of genuine popular and participatory Socialism to have emerged from the former Communist bloc, for reasons which will be examined in detail in Chapter 4: the Cuban revolution always had different characteristics which fortunately survived its partial adoption of the Soviet model.

Cuba does offer an extraordinary, indeed priceless, example for all those who seek an alternative to genocidal and ecocidal neo-liberal capitalism. Without Cuba, the disorientation and despair of the last 15 years would have been much worse. Cuba has shown in practice that another world, however imperfect, *is* possible; it is no accident that so many activists of all generations, not just from the Old Left and not just from Latin America, have looked to Cuba for inspiration. But Cuba alone does not provide all the answers; indeed, to be fair, the Cubans themselves have never suggested that it does. Not only do the Cubans recognise that the Left can no longer afford the mistake of trying to copy a fixed model of any kind, but they accept that the peculiar circumstances of the US blockade and their geographical situation on the doorstep of the imperial hegemony have conditioned and limited their own Socialist democracy.

It is here that Venezuela becomes crucially important. Again, it is not that the Bolivarian revolution (which in any case is still very much a work in progress) should be taken as a model to copy. But as the first successful popular and anti-capitalist revolution since the fall of the Soviet bloc, and one which is also profoundly democratic, open and original, it offers hope to a degree unimaginable even five or six years ago. Moreover since December 2004 President Chávez has surprised many observers (although not this writer) by beginning to talk of Socialism: of the need to re-evaluate the legacy of Socialism, to consider how to build 'the Socialism of the twenty-first century', and so on. At the World Social Forum in Porto Alegre in January 2005 Chávez declared that he could not find any other term to describe the new non-capitalist social system now beginning to be developed in Venezuela. This raises directly the difficult question of the meaning of Socialism in this post-Soviet, globalised world. If the Cuban example cannot be copied or reproduced – and in any case, although the Cubans claim that they are in the process of adapting and strengthening their form of socialism for today's world, they have so far failed to produce a theoretical formulation of their strategy – then the entire issue has to be re-examined.

Returning to the classics, 'Socialism' (for Lenin) or 'the lower stage of Communism' (for Marx) was supposed to be a transitional phase on the road to the classless, stateless Communist society. The 'Socialism in one country' of the USSR was a response to the absence of revolution in the other major capitalist countries and the reality of coexistence with a capitalist world. Without necessarily accepting the Trotskyist analysis of the impossibility of building Socialism in one country, the notion that the 'Socialist camp' with its own ruling class and state structures could exist indefinitely as the embryo of a new mode of production was always questionable. If Socialism was intended to be a transitional phase in which the working class exercised state power in order to repress the remnants of the bourgeoisie and of capitalist structures, after which the state would 'wither away' and Communist society would blossom, then it is very difficult to conceive of a stable, long-lasting Socialist system with its own distinct economic laws of motion. Certainly, following the collapse of the 'really existing Socialism' of the Soviet bloc, this whole debate needs to be revisited.

To return to the basics, in the *Manifesto* Marx proclaims that 'the first step in the revolution by the working class, is to raise the proletariat to the position of ruling class, *to win the battle for democracy*' (Marx and Engels 1968, 52, emphasis mine). In other words, despite the metaphor of the 'dictatorship of the proletariat' to express the idea of the domination of one class being replaced by that of another, it was understood that this domination would be exercised in a democratic manner. Secondly, Marx says that the proletariat will wrest all capital from the hands of the bourgeoisie and 'centralise all instruments of production in the hands of the State, i.e. of the proletariat organised as the ruling class' (ibid.). But he says nothing about just *how* that rule will be organised; and despite the use of the term 'centralise', if the instruments of production are to be in the hands of *the proletariat organised as the ruling class*, it is possible to imagine many different forms in which proletarian control of production could be organised within the framework of an overall centralised coordination. Again, Marx talks of 'despotic inroads on the rights of property', but this is surely no more than his penchant for vivid rhetoric, and a way of formulating the idea that decisive action against bourgeois property will indeed be necessary, action which the propertied classes will always see as arbitrary no matter how democratically it is decided. Furthermore, if we move from the abstract principles of the *Manifesto* to Marx's comments on a specific historical process – the Paris Commune – we find a more nuanced vision of the revolutionary order. Marx comments on the acceptance by intelligent members of the ruling class of the concept of cooperative enterprise; and

If co-operative production is not to remain a sham and a snare; if it is to supersede the Capitalist system; if united cooperative societies are to regulate national production upon a common plan, thus taking it under their own control, and putting an end to the constant anarchy and periodical convulsions which are the fatality of Capitalist production – what else, gentlemen, would it be but Communism, 'possible' Communism? (Marx and Engels 1968, 294)

Even more significant for our purposes are Marx's comments in the next paragraph:

The working class did not expect miracles from the Commune. They have no ready-made utopias to introduce *par decret du peuple*. They know that in order to work out their own emancipation, and along with it that higher form to which present society is irresistibly tending by its own economical agencies, they will have to pass through long struggles, through a series of historic processes, transforming circumstances and men. (Marx and Engels 1968, 294–5)

Moreover as we have seen in the discussion of democracy, Marx's endorsement of the Commune's application of the principles of direct democracy and the *mandat impératif* scarcely suggests that he would favour literal despotism in the name of proletarian rule.

If we turn to Lenin, despite his frequently dogmatic tone and his eventual resort to centralised bureaucratic rule on grounds of expediency in the critical situation of invasion and civil war, we find in *The State and Revolution* that in principle he was also prepared to recognise that the revolutionary Socialist state might take many different forms:

The forms of bourgeois states are extremely varied, but their essence is the same: all these states, whatever their form, in the final analysis are inevitably the *dictatorship of the bourgeoisie*. The transition from capitalism to Communism certainly cannot but yield a tremendous abundance and variety of political forms, but the essence will inevitably be the same: *the dictatorship of the proletariat*. (Lenin 1965, 41; emphasis in original)

So apart from the insistence on the need for revolutionary overthrow of the bourgeois state and on the general character of the Socialist state as the expression of class domination by the formerly exploited class, we have here no exclusive political formula. So much for the rigid reproduction of 'democratic centralist' single-party bureaucratic rule from Moscow to Beijing and Tirana to Pyongyang! Elsewhere in the same text Lenin repeats that proletarian rule will mean 'democracy for the vast majority of the people' and exclusion from democracy only of a small minority:

A special apparatus, a special machine for suppression, the 'state', is *still* necessary, but this is now a transitional state; it is no longer a state in the proper sense of the word; for the suppression of the minority of exploiters by the majority of the wage slaves of *yesterday* is comparatively so easy, simple and natural a task that it will entail far less bloodshed than the suppression of the risings of slaves, serfs or wage labourers, and it will cost mankind far less. (Lenin 1965, 107–8; emphasis in original)

Of course, this is Lenin writing a few months *before* the Bolshevik Revolution, before he had to deal with the harsh realities of power, and when he still hoped and believed that revolution in Russia would spread rapidly to the other major capitalist powers. But nevertheless, the idea that the revolutionary state would not only be transitional but *would no longer be a state in the proper sense of the word* must give pause for thought in discussions of the possible forms of Socialism in the twenty-first century.

From a theoretical perspective, then, another crucial error of the Soviets (and most of their Eastern European and East Asian imitators) was to proclaim that they had constructed a stable Socialist system which could continue indefinitely, coexisting with and in competition with, an external capitalist world; and that the construction of a centralised, authoritarian state (and indeed, the *strengthening* of that state) was not incompatible with its eventual 'withering away'. This permitted not only the appalling crimes of Stalinism but also the absurdity, 20 years after 'destalinisation', of Brezhnev's claim that the USSR had reached a 'higher stage' of Socialism, on the road to full Communism. Given the total suffocation of popular initiative and the entrenched power of a centralised bureaucracy, not only was a spontaneous 'withering away' a completely ludicrous notion, but even the possibility of democratic Socialist reforms from above, as attempted by Gorbachev with *glasnost* and *perestroika*, was ruled out. Socialism, or at least an anti-capitalist political and social order, may be able to exist in one country or a group of countries for a significant period of time, but it will always be unstable and in constant tension with both external and internal capitalist pressures, and will require permanent popular initiative from below and a leadership in intimate contact with popular sentiments and initiatives.

The experience of Cuba, but also the partial experience of Nicaragua and especially now that of Venezuela, suggest an alternative analysis.

Social revolutions will continue to occur – at least in the global South – and will produce radical regimes based on popular power and participatory democracy. Such regimes will take measures to promote social justice and independent development – measures which the doctrinaire Trotskyists and Marxist-Leninists will misleadingly criticise as 'reformist' – and will inevitably enter into contradiction with global capital and imperialism, questioning the primacy of the profit motive. The logic of such revolutionary processes and of the popular regimes which lead them will necessarily point in a Socialist direction, although they will never be able to establish a stable Socialist system because this is a contradiction in terms (and more so than ever in today's globalised world). Rather they will exist in permanent tension with imperialism, and their survival will depend on maintaining popular mobilisation and democratic participation at all levels. It will also require a strong state, not in the Stalinist sense of repression but rather in the sense of a state with a solid economic base in key nationalised industries, a solid military base in the form of revolutionary armed forces committed to the defence of the new order, and a solid political base in mass popular organisations supporting and monitoring the actions of the leadership. This could be described as a *revolutionary state of popular power*, which may be what socialism as a transitional stage really amounts to: it cannot operate as a self-contained and distinct mode of production, which was the Stalinist illusion, but through its popular-democratic and military strength it can function with a non-capitalist or anti-capitalist logic, with a combination of nationalised industries, worker cooperatives, other forms of social property, and capitalist enterprises both national and transnational. As a revolutionary state it can negotiate with transnational capital from a position of relative strength, and it can create and protect a society based on a large measure of social justice, participatory democracy and economic sovereignty, but it cannot break completely with the global capitalist system until such time (still remote) as revolution and popular power/ Socialism spreads through most of the world.

It is not so much a question, as in the classic Trotskyist analysis, of the revolution having to spread rapidly in order to survive at all: revolutionary popular power can survive for decades even in a small country like Cuba (although with great difficulty) so long as the leadership remains committed to Socialist goals and closely linked to the mass popular movement. Indeed, *in my view the Trotskyist thesis of the impossibility of 'Socialism in one country' is dangerously misleading*: on the contrary, experience shows that Socialism, or the nearest approximation to it that is viable in an imperialist world, must inevitably be built first in a specific country and maintained there for what may be a considerable period of time until revolutionary conditions mature elsewhere. But until such time as internationalisation of the revolution occurs, neither the people nor the leadership can ever 'rest on their laurels': no social or economic conquest can be assumed to be permanently secure, every advance will always be subject to hostile pressures from within and without in a dynamic tension which will continue indefinitely. This, then, is not Marx's Communist utopia, neither is it the state Socialism of Marxist-Leninist orthodoxy, but it is a real and viable alternative to capitalist globalisation, indeed the only viable strategic option for the Left and the anti-capitalist movement.

As already implied, Cuba can be considered an example of such a revolutionary state, but it can be argued that Venezuela is evolving rapidly in this direction and is in some ways a more relevant example for movements in other countries to learn from. This is because Cuba still has elements of the Soviet state-Socialist model which it is striving to overcome: it is in a sense 'in transition', not to neo-liberal pluralism and capitalism as mainstream scholarship assumes, but to what the Cuban leaders themselves describe as 'the Socialism of the twenty-first century' and which, in an optimistic perspective, will in the end approximate the model of revolutionary popular power described above. The problem for Cuba is that while maintaining an exemplary model of universal public social provision and a leadership dedicated to the popular cause, it has restricted political debate and participation above the municipal level, and this combined with the hardships imposed by the US blockade has produced a dangerous sense of alienation among large sections of Cuban youth.

Venezuela on the other hand is approaching revolutionary popular power from the opposite direction, as a new political process in which popular democracy still has to be consolidated and the anti-capitalist dynamic still has a long way to go. Although its socio-economic system is still predominantly capitalist, the dynamism of the Venezuelan process, its openness and originality are grounds for optimism. But it should also be borne in mind that there cannot be a fixed model and each revolution will produce its own variant of popular power/ Socialism. Once again Aurelio Alonso puts it succinctly:

... neo-liberalism is not going to be overcome on the basis of the socialism established according to the model adapted from Russian twentieth-century experience. We already know that that didn't work. Even the idea of an alternative derived from Cuba faces the double challenge of confronting both the dominant neo-liberal dependent model and the frustrated twentieth-century socialist model. (Alonso 2004, 12)

Alonso then adds, quite correctly, that this does not mean ignoring the important achievements of the Soviet or other models, but it does mean moving on to something new. The alternative cannot be a 'homogenising' system, but one which achieves equity and social justice while recognising difference; and

The legacy of the twentieth century makes it more difficult than before to take up the concept of socialism to designate what we would like to propose as a post-capitalist paradigm, but no other concept has appeared which is better to designate a generic goal .... (Alonso 2004, 11)

Socialism, then, may be the appropriate term for the new concept of revolutionary popular power, but it must be clear that it is significantly different from the Soviet model or any of its variants, and that it cannot in the present era – in other words, within a foreseeable period of time – be regarded as a complete and finished edifice: constant struggle, re-examination and renewal will be required to prevent bureaucratic sclerosis and decay.

This analysis also renders obsolete much of the debate between orthodox Communists, Trotskyists and Maoists over 'stages' of revolution and bourgeois or Socialist 'tasks'. For years Communist parties in Latin America (and elsewhere) argued for supporting bourgeois nationalist governments on the grounds that these countries were still dominated by semi-feudal oligarchies and therefore had to pass through a bourgeois 'stage' before being ripe for Socialism. For this they were rightly castigated by Trotskyists, Maoists and others who maintained that classic bourgeois revolution was no longer possible in the era of imperialism and that any attempt to carry through the 'tasks' of the bourgeoisie (introduction of democratic liberalism, agrarian reform) would inevitably fail if power were not in the hands of a revolutionary proletarian party. But these critics still viewed the first measures to be taken by such a revolutionary regime as 'bourgeois tasks' which the proletariat must complete before it could go on to address its own 'Socialist tasks'. A fine example of this reasoning is to be found in a statement produced by Chilean Socialist Party supporters of President Allende early in 1973:

The Government of Popular Unity, in accordance with its programme of transition to socialism, has as its mission to fulfil the democratic-bourgeois tasks not carried out by the national bourgeoisie and, at the same time, to promote the socialist tasks of the proletariat, under the direction of the parties of the working class .... (Belarmino Elgueta Becker in Casanueva Valencia and Fernández Canque 1973, 13)

But if under conditions of capitalist globalisation – contemporary imperialism – the only viable alternative is a revolutionary state of popular power, which is anti-capitalist and based on popular participatory democracy but is in a state of constant tension and flux, then it is meaningless to talk of bourgeois or Socialist 'tasks'. Any serious measure to promote popular welfare, participatory democracy or national independence is tendentially anti-capitalist and can only be durable to the extent that the popular revolutionary regime consolidates its power and continues to advance.

Here it becomes necessary to engage with the literature on 'dependency' and with 'world systems theory'. Theorists emerging from the Latin American dependency school, such as André Gunder Frank, Theotônio dos Santos, Celso Furtado, Osvaldo Sunkel and Ruy Mauro Marini maintained that colonialism and imperialism created international structures of economic domination (and with them, of political, military and cultural domination as well) which made it impossible for peripheral, 'dependent' countries to follow a similar path of development to that pursued in previous centuries by the central capitalist powers such as Britain, Germany or the USA (Frank 1967, 1969; Dos Santos 1973; Furtado 1970, 1974; Sunkel 1973; Marini 1973). According to the more radical of these theorists (such as Frank and Marini), not only did international structures of dependency make independent capitalist development impossible, but the internal class structures of peripheral countries, where the bourgeoisie was completely 'sold out' or integrated into the international system, meant that no government emerging from the dominant sectors would even attempt an independent policy. The implication was that the only possibility of 'escape', of beating the system, was through anti-imperialist revolution leading to socialism. Other theorists such as Fernando Henrique Cardoso and Enzo Faletto argued for a more nuanced vision based on the concept of 'associated dependent development', by which a combination of the state, national and international capital could bring about a substantial degree of industrialisation and development in certain Third World countries such as Brazil within the limits of the international capitalist system (Cardoso and Faletto 1969), and 'reformist' dependency theorists like Sunkel and Furtado maintained that nationalist and interventionist measures by progressive governments could challenge the structures of dependency; but the radical view counterposing 'dependency and underdevelopment' to 'independence and Socialism' continued to predominate among Latin American revolutionaries (Kay 1989).

At this point the argument was taken a step further by some theorists who moved on from the concept of dependency to 'world systems theory', analysing the emergence from at least the fifteenth century onwards of what they saw as an integrated and self-perpetuating world system. This was Frank's position in his later years, and its best-known exponent is Immanuel Wallerstein (Wallerstein 1980, 1982). One of the more provocative hypotheses of world systems theory is that even the development of the USSR and other Socialist states was ultimately simply an alternative path of development, via a rival world system, enabling these formerly peripheral countries to 'catch up' with the central industrialised countries before being reintegrated into the single world system at a higher level. The implication is that they develop via a form of state capitalism and therefore never really represent a Socialist alternative.

This apparently radical analysis is further developed, with specific reference to Cuba, by the young Puerto Rican scholar Antonio Carmona Báez. Citing the analysis of the Soviet Union as 'state capitalist' by Tony Cliff, Trotskyist founder of the International Marxist Tendency, Carmona Báez goes on to declare that:

> ... production relations and modes of production should not be thought of as very different in countries that claim to be socialist or capitalist ... There were never two separate worlds or systems. Due to the external relations with 'non-socialist' economies and also to its own capitalist mode of production, the Soviet bloc was just another hegemonic realm that took part in the global, competitive capitalist market ... . (Carmona Báez 2004, 26)

Now we have already seen that the complete absence of democratic participation or of genuine workers' or popular power in the Soviet bloc seriously undermined its long-term viability and the possibility that it would pave the way for a transition to the stateless Communist society envisioned by Marx. But Cliff's analysis of it as simply 'capitalist', as just another competitor in the capitalist world market (albeit one run by the state), poses serious conceptual and analytical problems. Although the Soviet Union and its satellites necessarily traded with the rest of the world, it enjoyed a considerable degree of autonomy, even autarchy, and it would be quite misleading to suggest that external economic relations were decisive in its functioning. Moreover, given the high level of centralised economic planning (the 'command economy'), the absence of individual capitalists or of a capital market, and the frequent determination of economic priorities without regard for profitability, it makes little sense to describe it as capitalist. It was precisely these characteristics which made it so unpalatable to real capitalists in the West, who never regarded it as just another rival like Japan or Germany but as a threat to the entire bourgeois order. It may be necessary to invent a new category to describe it – 'bureaucratic state Socialism' is a possibility, as is the 'orthodox' Trotskyist concept of 'degenerate workers' state' – but to describe it as capitalist (even state capitalist) is not very helpful.

To do him credit, Carmona Báez recognises the distinctive features of Cuba, including the much more popular and democratic character of the revolutionary regime. His analysis is also quite original and perceptive in several respects, and it is therefore all the more unfortunate that he insists on this neo-Trotskyist 'state capitalist' analysis. Drawing on other analyses of statist development strategies in the Third World, and various cases in Africa and Asia of one-party regimes with 'Socialist' labels, he asserts that 'In many regards, the Cuban government can be conceived of as having been typical of all states in the periphery of the world system that searched for development' (Carmona Báez 2004, 31). But the difference between Cuba and, say, Nasser's Egypt, Nkrumah's Ghana or the Burmese regime is abysmal, and derives directly from the fact that the Cuban regime has its origins in a popular democratic and anti-imperialist revolution of the most profound kind, whereas nationalist-developmentalist regimes of the type mentioned remain essentially bourgeois and achieve only limited changes in the social and economic structures of their countries.

At another point Carmona Báez almost hits the nail on the head, but once again falls into an excessively schematic structuralist view of the process. Arguing for a relational analysis of the state and of the social forces at work, he refers to the 'party-state apparatus' as the product of a 'social relationship' constituting national power. Social scientists should therefore look for 'state strategies that imply the (im)mobility of social forces that influence policy-making'; in other words, he admits that the Cuban state (the 'party-state apparatus') reflects the pressures and will of the Cuban people, but is loath to admit that this is because it is in fact a popular revolutionary regime, the direct product of one of the most profound revolutions the world has ever seen. He continues with perhaps his most important theoretical statement:

In other words ... there are no 'socialist states', there are only state-led economies run by socialists that might opt for certain market measures, depending on which way the domestic social forces are mobilised and how they are manipulated by global restrictions. Some of these market measures might entail dismantling the entire party/state apparatus, as experienced in Eastern Europe. Though this last experience was seemingly the most popular option during the late 1980s, it was, as demonstrated in other cases, such as Cuba, not the only one. (Carmona Báez 2004, 34–5)

The essential point which Carmona Báez misses here is that these were not simply 'options'; the Soviet and Eastern European regimes, because of their lack of popular roots or legitimacy, had little alternative when faced with the failure of their centralised planning system but to capitulate to capitalist pressures. Cuba, on the other hand, with a state structure and leadership which, although partially weakened by the influence of the Soviet model, still retained its popular foundations and legitimacy, did have the possibility of striving to retain Socialist values. Moreover, once the leadership (represented by the historic prestige of Fidel) indicated its determination to reject *perestroika* and preserve the revolution, the popular response (in terms of the willingness to accept appalling hardship and sacrifice) was extraordinary. It is not mere rhetoric to say that the conditions endured by Cubans from 1990 to around 1996 would have led to the collapse of any other regime in a matter of months: only the strength that comes from a true popular revolution which still retains its essential character can explain such resilience.

Carmona's theoretical argument that 'there are no "socialist states" ... only state-led economies run by socialists' does merit closer examination, however. As we have seen, given Marx's (and Lenin's) definition of Socialism (or 'the lower stage of Communism') as a transitional regime on the road to full Communism, with a minimal state that is on the point of 'withering away', it is questionable whether any regime in a single country or group of countries, and any regime that has hitherto existed or is likely to exist in the near future, can be regarded as socialist under this definition. But, as suggested above, rather than 'state-led economies run by Socialists' I would prefer to call them 'revolutionary states of popular power', because this reflects better the profoundly popular origins and power-base of such regimes; we are not dealing with an abstract state apparatus run by a few Socialist ideologues isolated from the people (as Carmona Báez implies and as bourgeois critics like to suggest), but with the highest political expression yet achieved of the revolutionary Socialist and democratic will of the popular classes. For this reason also, it may be legitimate, as argued by Aurelio Alonso, to call this profoundly radical and popular alternative social order 'Socialism' even though it does not entirely conform to Marx's or Lenin's definition. The Marxist classics remain relevant to today's struggles, but they cannot be treated as sacred writ.

At this point it is necessary to return to the dependency/development debate. If Cuba has had recourse to foreign investment, and if Venezuela is seeking to establish its economic and political autonomy on the basis of a combination of state enterprise, cooperatives and private national and foreign capital, how can their development strategies be reconciled with the implications of dependency and world systems theory? In view of the argument presented above regarding the possibilities and limits of Socialism in today's world and the concept of 'revolutionary states of popular power', it should be clear that in my view it is possible to combat dependency and to achieve a substantial degree of autonomous development if the necessary political conditions are first created. It should also be pointed out that the more extreme versions of dependency and world systems theory have in any case been increasingly challenged; from the beginning there were 'reformist' dependency theorists like Sunkel, Furtado, Cardoso and Faletto who argued that while dependency was a major obstacle to Third World development, it might be overcome by 'structural reforms'. Cardoso, in particular, subsequently betrayed his earlier vision, becoming President of Brazil in the 1990s and implementing essentially neo-liberal measures; but this does not invalidate his earlier insights or those of his colleagues. Of course, what they understood by 'structural reforms' was the polar opposite of what the IMF and the neo-liberals today understand by the same term: for Sunkel and company it meant agrarian reform to distribute land from great estates to peasant cooperatives, nationalisation of key industries, state promotion of national enterprises, and welfare measures to improve the living standards of workers and peasants.

These measures are remarkably similar to those being adopted today by Chávez in Venezuela, but the difference is that what in the 1960s and '70s was regarded as reformist is today a direct challenge to the hegemonic model of capitalism. Sunkel is today quoted by Chávez who regards his concept of *desarrollo desde adentro* – 'development from within' – as a theoretical justification of his strategy of 'endogenous development'. Moreover it is very significant that one of the most highly respected Marxist dependency theorists, the Egyptian Samir Amin, has recently gone on record as questioning the thesis that 'national bourgeoisies' do not exist and that all capitalists in peripheral countries are pawns of globalised finance:

This thesis, presented in a great many writings, is very debatable ... We would be in the presence of mere comprador bourgeoisies, in other words, agents at the service of the transnational capital of the Triad [North America, Europe and Japan] ... But I have to insist: is this a lasting change? ... Would this be acceptable, or accepted in practice, not only by the dominated classes, victims of massive and intensified impoverishment, but also by certain sectors of the ruling classes ... ? (Amin and Herrera 2005, 13)

Amin goes on to insist that the implications of this are so catastrophic for Third World nations, and even to some extent for Europe, that it is possible to conceive of some sectors of the dominant classes in these countries accepting an alliance with the popular sectors to achieve a more balanced type of national development:

Global evolution suggests the creation of great regional associations, above all in peripheral regions, but also in others like Europe, and to give priority in these associations to measures which would permit world-wide modernisation, and which would transform the character of that modernisation, liberating it gradually of capitalist criteria ... In other words, a veritable reconstruction of the international political system which, freed from hegemonic practices, would evolve in a multipolar direction. (Amin and Herrera 2005, 13).

There are signs that such developments are beginning to occur: it is very interesting that Chávez' proposals for a 'Bolivarian Association of the Americas' based on self-sufficiency and equitable exchange have begun to encounter a favourable reception in other Latin American countries, and that his active promotion of a multi-polar international system has been well received in China, Russia, India, the Muslim countries, Spain and France, despite – or perhaps because of – US hostility. It is necessary to insist, however, that the long-term implications of such proposals are Socialist or at least anti-capitalist.

If Cuba, and in a different way Venezuela, are the two main living examples of revolutionary popular power which can inspire current struggles, there is at least one previous Socialist experience which may be very relevant to today's debates, and which deserves more attention than it normally receives: that of Yugoslavia. Although this interesting and original experiment also suffered catastrophic collapse in the 1990s, leading to actual territorial disintegration and ethnic strife, for more than three decades it offered a radically different model of democratic and participatory Socialism based on workers' self-management. In Eastern Europe both Yugoslavia and Albania made their own revolutions without Soviet 'assistance', but where the Albanians adopted their own miniature form of Stalinism, the Yugoslavs reacted to Moscow's hegemonism by rejecting the Soviet model and developing their own participatory system. Although enterprises were state property they were under workers' control and run by elected workers' councils, which took all important decisions regarding the enterprise itself. Initially (in the 1950s) broader planning was imposed by the state which levied substantial taxes on enterprises for this purpose, but in the 1960s pressure from the workers' councils combined with commercial and balance-of-payments problems led to a relaxation of central planning and greater enterprise autonomy, with negative effects on social cohesion (Lebowitz 2005, 4–7).

The relaxation of central planning led to greater competition among enterprises and to greater inequality between enterprises, industrial sectors and regions, and also to a growth in the authority of management technicians at the expense of workers. What is particularly striking is that this led to a reaction in the late 1960s and early 1970s by workers and inhabitants of the poorer regions, attacking the 'techno-bureaucracy' and capitalism, and that this led to a renewed effort at planning and coordination, this time initiated from below with negotiations between different enterprises and social sectors. Tragically this remarkable experiment in democratic Socialist planning was destroyed before it could really prove itself, fundamentally because Yugoslavia had allowed itself to become indebted to international capital, and when high inflation set in during the 1980s the country was forced to accept IMF conditions which led to the end of workers' self-management and subsequently to the break-up of the Yugoslav Federation and civil war (Lebowitz 2005, 7–8). Nevertheless, Lebowitz insists on the positive aspects of the process: in the 1950s and again in the 1970s Yugoslavia enjoyed very high rates of growth, and contrary to the predictions of capitalist and Stalinist sceptics, workers' self-management was very efficient, with high levels of investment and discipline. Workers were both responsible and sophisticated, and the system worked for large enterprises as well as small. Its deficiencies arose above all when central planning was relaxed, leading to disruptive competition between enterprises, uncontrolled borrowing and inflation; but there is no reason to suppose that a similar system combined with democratic Socialist planning could not be both economically and politically viable. At the very least, some elements of the Yugoslav experience may be quite relevant to any new attempt to construct a non-capitalist socio-economic alternative.

There are other fundamental issues to be considered which are relevant both before and after the attainment of power. There is the question of political structure and leadership: given the calamitous failures of 'democratic centralism', what should a revolutionary party or movement look like, and how is its leadership to be chosen or generated? How is 'revolution' to be defined, and what are the paths of revolution in today's world? Since experience has shown that the violent seizure of state power does not necessarily guarantee popular power and Socialism, what is the real difference between reform and revolution? The standard Marxist assumption that anything other than the direct, and usually violent, seizure of state power is no more than reformism needs to be reconsidered. The Venezuelan experience, coupled with the lessons of other experiences such as those of Chile, Nicaragua and Portugal, suggests that it may be possible, and often more feasible, to take power by stages: control of the legislative power and of the formal executive (presidency, central government) must be accompanied by systematic efforts to gain control of the judicial system, the civil service, and above all the armed forces and police. Liberals will denounce this as totalitarian, but it need not be: the crucial issue here is *who* takes control of these state institutions that were hitherto bulwarks of bourgeois power. If it is a bureaucratic centralist party apparatus or revolutionary army, then totalitarianism or at least authoritarian rule is indeed a threat; but if it is a popular democratic movement with a participatory and internally pluralist structure, then the prospects are much more positive. To take power by stages is obviously fraught with difficulties, and it would be foolish to imagine that it can ever be a smooth or entirely peaceful process; revolution will always imply tension and confrontation, and almost certainly a series of ruptures which will be more or less violent depending on the specific correlation of forces and the tactical ability of the popular leadership. But by the steady accumulation of forces and consolidation of existing gains it may be possible to limit the degree of violence, and this also means that specific reforms adopted during what may be a relatively drawn-out process are not necessarily simply 'reformist' but acquire revolutionary significance as part of the broader process.

As for the issue of the political instrument of popular power and revolution, there can be no doubt that a unified movement or party with some kind of effective central leadership is necessary. It must however be internally democratic and above all must have, and must maintain at all times, deep roots in autonomous popular movements, movements which it does not control but which it must strive to represent both in its own structures and in any instances of state power in which it gains influence or power. Its ideology will necessarily be anti-capitalist but must also reflect popular culture and traditions and within those limits, must be open and pluralist. As for the leadership, it must also be as democratic and answerable to the rank-and-file as possible, but at the same time it must actually *lead*; in this respect there can be no concessions to Hollowayesque illusions. Indeed, the crucial point here is that the leadership, whether it be ultimately an individual or a group (and in most cases it will presumably be both, a group with one individual who stands out to a greater or lesser degree), *must demonstrate in practice the capacity to lead*: one of the greatest defects of 'democratic-centralist' parties has been their tendency to impose a bureaucratic leadership which is not only undemocratic but also has very inadequate leadership qualities. In my view this is much more important than the precise institutional structure of the leadership: if the popular movement is to confront the enormous power and resources of the capitalist state, it needs the most sophisticated, determined and responsible leadership possible. But to this we shall return in Chapter 6.

# 4

# Originality and Relevance
# of the Cuban Revolution

The predominant tendency in European intellectual and political circles is to regard the Cuban regime as a kind of fossil, a Stalinist hangover, and even in more traditional leftist circles which see Cuba as an example of social justice and resistance to globalisation, virtually no-one suggests that other countries could learn from the Cuban experience in political terms. The Cuban experience is identified with armed struggle, and since the neutralisation of the Central American guerrilla movements armed revolution has been discredited. Although strong insurgent movements still exist in Colombia – the FARC, ELN and others – their strategy is to combine armed struggle with other methods and to seek a negotiated political solution; their great achievement (which should not be overlooked despite government and media demonisation of them as 'narco-terrorists') has been to maintain popular armed resistance to neo-liberalism. Within the last decade other movements which defend the resort to arms have appeared, notably the Zapatistas in Mexico, but given their limited military capacity and their strategy of 'dissolution' rather than seizure of power, it would be more accurate to describe them as representing 'armed contestation' as opposed to revolutionary armed struggle in the classic sense. Small organisations which advocate armed struggle in theory exist in many countries, and it would be rash to suggest that the question of armed revolution will never again be on the agenda in Latin America; but at present it is clear that political conflicts are resolved through a combination of elections and mass mobilisations which are predominantly peaceful.

For many on the Left, Cuba is to be admired for its achievements in health, education and sport, and to be supported against the injustice and irrationality of the US blockade; but at the same time there is a consensus that it should become more 'democratic'. There is a vague sense that Cuban Socialism is not quite the same as the Soviet variety, that it is more popular and more authentic, but little understanding as to how or why this is the case; and there is widespread scepticism as to the prospects for its long-term survival. Yet if Cuba did not fall in the early 1990s along with the rest of the Soviet bloc, if it survived the extraordinary rigours of the 'Special Period' resulting from Soviet collapse and the intensification of the US blockade, if moreover it has recovered economically with less concessions to capitalism than China or Vietnam, then its prospects for survival cannot be lightly dismissed. 'Democratisation' along liberal lines would undoubtedly undermine Socialism and would open the door to domination by the US and the Miami exile mafia; Cuba has its own system of Socialist democracy, which may have limitations but merits serious examination. This chapter will attempt to explain how and why the Cuban revolution has achieved so much and why, despite its deficiencies, it is still very significant for Latin America and for the entire world.

## ORIGINS: THE CUBAN REVOLUTIONARY TRADITION

The triumph on 1 January 1959 of the guerrillas of the Rebel Army led by Fidel Castro, and especially the dramatic process of radicalisation of the Cuban political scene and the transition to Socialism during the following three to four years, signalled the beginning of a new era in Latin America. Until then a Socialist revolution in that region, and above all in Central America and the Caribbean – the classic 'backyard' of the United States – was unthinkable. In these 'banana republics' comic-opera tyrants alternated with weak and corrupt civilian regimes, and the rare exceptions like the progressive nationalist government of Jacobo Arbenz in Guatemala from 1951 to1954 were swiftly crushed by the Colossus of the North. In 1959–61 the memory of Guatemala was fresh in everyone's mind, and most observers anticipated a similar fate for the revolutionary regime in Havana. The political establishment in Washington has never forgiven Fidel Castro and the Cuban revolutionaries for their successful defiance of US hegemony, and nearly five decades later Cuba continues to be a thorn in the side of the imperial super-power. The Cuban–US confrontation became a central component of the Cold War, and there is no doubt that from 1962 to 1989 Soviet support was a critical element in Cuban survival; but it is necessary to recognise also that the Soviet Union only committed itself fully after the Cubans had demonstrated their own capacity for political and military resistance with the defeat of the Bay of Pigs invasion in April 1961. This independent Cuban will to resist has reappeared since the collapse of the Soviet bloc, surprising the prophets of the

New World Order who confidently predicted 'the demise of Castro' within months of the fall of the Berlin Wall; both Fidel Castro and the Cuban revolution have confounded the sceptics and demonstrated an unsuspected vitality. But those who really understand Cuban history should not be so surprised.

To understand the success of the Cuban revolution and its continued vigour we have to review the island's history from the nineteenth century, when it was Spain's most important remaining colony (after most of Latin America achieved its independence between 1810 and 1826). This delayed independence, together with the crucial issue of slavery and its abolition, gave the Cuban nationalist movement a more radical and democratic character when it finally emerged with full force from 1868 onwards. Also, the expansionist and annexationist ambitions of the USA, manifested from a very early date, contributed to the formation of a precociously anti-imperialist consciousness in Cuba. Already in 1805 Thomas Jefferson had proclaimed his country's interest in the annexation of the largest of the Antilles, and in 1823 Secretary of State John Quincy Adams declared that with the passage of time Cuba would fall 'like a ripe apple' into the lap of the United States; and in the course of the nineteenth century the US tried to purchase the island from Spain on four occasions (Cantón Navarro 1998, 40). It should not therefore come as a surprise that the literary prophet of the independence movement and founder of the Cuban Revolutionary Party, José Martí, declared in his last letter, shortly before his death in combat in 1895: 'Everything I have done unto now and all that I shall do hereafter has as its objective to prevent, through the independence of Cuba, the United States of America from falling with added weight on Our America' – *Nuestra América*, in other words Latin America as opposed to the Anglo-Saxon world (Martí 1975, 3). It was also Martí who insisted, at a time when racial prejudice was solidly entrenched in all Western countries, on racial equality within the independence movement and on its democratic and popular character. Furthermore, another hero of the independence struggle, General of the Liberating Army Antonio Maceo (a free mulatto known as 'the Titan of Bronze'), declared in reply to a young Cuban who asked him what attitude he would take in the event of a US intervention against Spain: 'In that case, young man, I think I would be on the side of the Spaniards' (Thomas 1971, 300) – an extraordinary declaration, and a clear indication that he agreed with Martí, even at the height of the struggle against

Spanish colonialism, in regarding nascent US imperialism as the greater danger.

The relevance of these warnings by the heroes of the independence struggle was confirmed shortly after their deaths with the US intervention of May 1898 and the Spanish–Cuban–American War. Taking advantage of the mysterious destruction of the battleship *Maine* in Havana harbour, the North Americans rapidly defeated the Spanish forces and occupied Cuba, Puerto Rico, the Philippines and the island of Guam in the Pacific, and then negotiated peace terms with the Spanish in Paris without consulting the Cuban liberation forces which had been fighting off and on for 30 years and were close to victory at that time (Cantón Navarro 1998, 61–74; Collazo 1972; Foner 1972). The US military occupation lasted four years, until in 1902 the island became formally independent. But it was no more than formal independence because Washington imposed as a condition of its withdrawal acceptance by the Cubans of the 'Platt Amendment', which gave the imperial power the right to intervene whenever it saw fit 'for the protection of life, liberty and private property', and also the right to establish naval bases on the island (this was the origin of the notorious Guantánamo base) and various commercial privileges. In the following 30 years Washington intervened militarily in Cuba on four occasions; the Platt Amendment was revoked by Cuba in 1933 and the United States in 1934, but US domination remained the central fact of Cuban affairs until 1959 (Roig de Leuchsenring 1973).

In the neo-colonial 'Plattist' republic it seemed for a while as if the values of Martí and the *mambíses* (the Afro-Cuban nickname of the independence fighters) had been completely forgotten, but from 1922 onwards a new radical consciousness began to emerge with the formation of the FEU (Federación Estudiantil Universitaria, University Students Federation) led by the brilliant and restless student activist Julio Antonio Mella, who also founded the Liga Anticlerical and Liga Antimperialista in 1924 and was one of the founders of the Cuban Communist Party in 1925 (Kapcia 2000, 68–9). The labour movement was also beginning to become a force under anarcho-syndicalist leadership, but with a rapidly increasing Communist presence. Then in the next few years the political situation became more polarised as Cuba underwent its first experience of a classic Latin American dictatorship, as President Gerardo Machado, elected in 1925, began to assume arbitrary powers and held on to power by force until 1933, when a frankly revolutionary situation developed.

Out of the FEU, suppressed by Machado, there emerged a more revolutionary student body, the Directorio Estudiantil, which from 1930 onwards adopted a strategy of armed resistance. In this it was soon imitated by other clandestine organisations, the ABC and OCRR (Organización Celular Radical Revolucionaria), both of petty-bourgeois composition and nationalist/corporatist ideology. The world depression beginning in 1929 had a catastrophic impact on Cuba and contributed strongly to popular discontent (the price of sugar, which accounted for 80 per cent of exports, collapsed completely and long-term unemployment reached over 50 per cent). The early months of 1933 saw a political strike by sugar workers, and as political violence increased rumours of a possible US intervention began to circulate. But the recently inaugurated President Franklin D. Roosevelt had just proclaimed his 'Good Neighbour' policy in relation to Latin America, abandoning military intervention and promising support to democratic governments; so although the US Navy was on patrol in international waters only a few kilometres from the Cuban coast, Washington limited itself to sending a Special Envoy, career diplomat Sumner Welles, with the mission of 'mediating' between Machado and the opposition. But this only helped to undermine Machado's authority, and between May and August 1933 a series of strikes, demonstrations, bombings and assassinations culminated in an ultimatum from the military High Command to Machado, which finally convinced him to leave for exile (Cantón Navarro 1998, 110–16; Kapcia 2000, 72–3).

With Sumner Welles' support a liberal government was installed, but it had no real power base and fell in a matter of weeks. On 4 September 1933 the sergeants and NCOs of the army successfully revolted against the officer corps, putting effective power in the hands of Sergeant Fulgencio Batista who thus appeared on the political scene for the first time. But the rebellious sergeants did not assume governmental office, leaving a power vacuum which was occupied by the Directorio Estudiantil. The students nominated a 'Pentarchy' of distinguished intellectuals, one of whom, the respected medical professor Dr Ramón Grau San Martín, soon emerged as President of a Provisional Government in which the students had significant influence. The new government in effect represented the popular, democratic and anti-imperialist movement, but it did not enjoy the organised support of any political party or force and had to confront the pressure of Batista (who soon revealed himself to be an opportunist) and of the US Embassy.

The most interesting and influential member of Grau San Martín's government was the Minister of the Interior, Antonio Guiteras, a postgraduate student of Socialist ideas but not affiliated to any party. It was above all Guiteras who inspired many radical and popular measures decreed by Grau's government: the revocation of the Platt Amendment, the intervention (public administration) of the Cuban Electric Co. (a US subsidiary), the minimum wage and eight-hour day, female suffrage, the beginning of an agrarian reform, and so on. Many of these measures were never implemented since the government had no real power and was in any case overthrown after only four months, in January 1934, in a military coup carried out by Batista and encouraged by the United States. The 'Government of the Hundred Days' had failed, but the heady experience of these months changed Cuban politics for ever (Aguilar 1972; Cabrera 1977; Tabares del Real 1973). There is a notable similarity between the measures decreed in 1933 and those adopted by the revolutionary government in the first six months of 1959; in fact the 1933 revolution was the direct precedent of 1959, and revealed clearly the weakness of the neo-colonial power structure and the growth among large sectors of the Cuban people of an anti-imperialist and revolutionary consciousness.

From 1934 to 1959 all the main political forces in Cuba had their roots in the events of 1933: the Partido Revolucionario Cubano (Auténtico), formed by Grau and his associates and generally known as the Auténticos, the 'Authentic' Party; the Partido del Pueblo Cubano (Ortodoxo), or Orthodox Party, formed in 1947 as a breakaway from the Auténticos and led by Eduardo Chibás, who as a student had been prominent in the anti-Machado resistance; and Fulgencio Batista, whether as de facto strongman behind a series of puppet presidents (1934–40), democratically elected president (1940–44), or dictator (1952–58). Immediately after the 1934 coup Guiteras began to organise clandestine resistance, creating his own movement called Jóven Cuba (Young Cuba), but he was assassinated in 1935. In the next few years Batista revealed considerable political astuteness, decreeing a series of popular reforms, legalising the Communist Party and permitting the adoption of a remarkably progressive constitution in 1940. In 1944 Grau and the Auténticos won the elections, and this victory by the figurehead of the 1933 revolutionary government aroused great popular enthusiasm; but it soon became clear that the Auténticos had abandoned the ideals of the 'Hundred Days', and the new government descended into a morass of corruption and opportunism. Grau's successor, Carlos

Prío Socarrás (1948–52) was another Auténtico and heir to 1933, but continued on the same corrupt path, thus contributing to the failure of parliamentary liberalism in Cuba and paving the way for Batista's second coup d'état on 10 March 1952 (Ameringer 2000).

Batista's coup provoked almost unanimous repudiation, but the established political parties were unable to channel this sentiment into an effective strategy. Repression hindered open expression of the popular movement against Batista, but soon there was a series of attempts to launch armed struggle, showing the extent and intensity of opposition. The first efforts came from radical intellectuals and students: a philosophy professor at the University of Havana, Dr Rafael García Bárcena, organised the Movimiento Nacional Revolucionario (MNR, National Revolutionary Movement) which began to prepare a civilian-military uprising for early 1953, but he was arrested and his movement disintegrated over the next few months (Hart Dávalos 1997, 37–40). In Santiago, the country's second city and capital of the Province of Oriente, a group of students and young intellectuals led by Frank País created another clandestine armed movement, Acción Revolucionaria Oriental (Revolutionary Action of Oriente). But the first effective armed action was carried out by another clandestine group, as yet unnamed, organised in Havana by the young lawyer Fidel Castro Ruz: it was this group which travelled secretly to Oriente to lead the assault on the military barracks of Moncada (in Santiago) and Bayamo on 26 July 1953, which although unsuccessful would mark the beginning of Castro's emergence as revolutionary leader and would give the movement a name (Movimiento Revolucionario 26 de Julio, the 26 July Revolutionary Movement or M-26–7). Castro's famous 'History Will Absolve Me' speech – delivered at the in camera trial organised by the regime, but clandestinely printed and distributed by his supporters – became the manifesto of the new movement and helped to mobilise a broad civic movement in favour of an amnesty for the imprisoned Moncada survivors, an amnesty which was finally granted by Batista in May 1955 (Mencía 1993; Hart Dávalos 1997).

Fidel Castro had already become a household name in Cuba, and after his release it soon became clear that he was not safe there; so he and his brother Raúl chose exile in Mexico – but with the stated intention of returning to continue the struggle. It was of course in Mexico that they met the young Argentine doctor – already a revolutionary internationalist – Ernesto Guevara, nicknamed 'Che' by the Cubans because of his use of this interjection which means 'mate' in Argentine Spanish; Che Guevara would come to play a role second only to that of Fidel in the Cuban revolution. There followed 17 months of training and preparation for the expedition in the leaky yacht *Granma* across the Gulf of Mexico to land on the coast of Oriente with the aim of linking up with an insurrection in Santiago organised by Frank País and the urban underground of the M-26-7 on 30 November 1956. Once again the plan failed disastrously due to a combination of errors of judgement and sheer bad luck, with most of the expeditionary force dispersed or killed, and only a dozen or so men, including Fidel and Raúl Castro and Che Guevara, surviving to seek refuge in the mountains of the Sierra Maestra. But once again, as with the Moncada assault, this disaster contributed to the heroic aura surrounding Fidel, and his extraordinary knack for snatching victory from the jaws of defeat with the subsequent success of the guerrilla campaign completed his transformation into an iconic figure for the Cuban resistance against Batista. Che Guevara, Raúl and others like Camilo Cienfuegos and Juan Almeida shared, and rightly so, in this aura of revolutionary heroism, but there can be no doubt that the central figure, standing head and shoulders above the rest, was Fidel – popularly referred to from then on by his first name. No-one could dispute the fact that the decisive blows in the triumph over Batista were struck by the Rebel Army emerging from the Sierra Maestra, and that the strategic vision which had made this possible was above all that of Fidel (Hart Dávalos 1997, Ch. 16).

This however should not obscure the fact that the Cuban revolution was a popular mass movement in which tens of thousands of people participated in different ways. Although the rural guerrillas were militarily decisive and the M-26-7 leadership in the Sierra under Fidel was politically decisive, the movement also had many thousands of urban militants and sympathisers in Havana and throughout the island, functioning clandestinely in the urban armed resistance, in the trade unions and many other organisations such as the Resistencia Cívica, the 'Civic Resistance' which brought together thousands of members of the liberal professions – lawyers, doctors, engineers, lecturers – in opposition to Batista (Cuesta Braniella 1997). The scale and importance of urban armed resistance has been reaffirmed in several recent studies, especially Gladys Marel García-Pérez' *Insurrection and Revolution* (García-Pérez 1998) and Julia Sweig's *Inside the Cuban Revolution* (Sweig 2002). When one takes into account also the thousands of militants of the Directorio Revolucionario and further thousands of Partido Socialista Popular activists who collaborated with the revolutionaries despite their party's pacifist line, it becomes apparent that the entire country was in revolutionary turmoil from 1955 to the fall of Batista in January 1959.

In this respect a complex historical and political polemic developed in the 1960s, and has recently been revived, regarding the relative contributions of the *Sierra* and the *Llano* (the Mountains and the Plains) to the revolutionary victory. The *Sierra*, the guerrilla force under Fidel and Che, has traditionally been seen as decisive, with the *Llano*, the urban underground, being regarded as secondary. This interpretation was given semi-official status with the publication of Che Guevara's *Pasajes de la Guerra Revolucionaria* (later translated as *Episodes of the Cuban Revolutionary War*) in 1963, followed in 1967 by Régis Debray's *Revolution in the Revolution*. Debray's thesis, largely based on his interviews with Guevara in Havana and later in Bolivia, was that in Cuba the *Llano* had been reformist and ineffective and that victory had only been possible when the truly revolutionary position of the *Sierra* had its way; and that this strategy could be extrapolated to Latin America as a whole, where the traditional Left, based in the cities and dominated by the conventional pro-Soviet Communist parties, was pacifist and reformist and based its strategy on an illusory alliance with the national bourgeoisie. As against this the Cuban experience had demonstrated that revolutionary conditions existed, or were latent, in the countryside, where the peasantry was ready to take up arms if only the revolutionaries, organised in a guerrilla nucleus (*foco*) would show the way; the guerrilla *foco*, in an inversion of the normal Marxist interpretation, would *create* the conditions for revolution.

This polemic, and the *foquista* strategy derived from Debray's position, contributed significantly to the rash of poorly organised and politically isolated guerrilla expeditions which failed disastrously in many Latin American countries in the 1960s and '70s. The strategy was also based on a misreading of the Cuban experience. Although there is no doubt that the military success of the Sierra Maestra guerrillas was ultimately decisive in the revolutionary victory, this does not mean that urban underground struggle was irrelevant. On the contrary, the urban resistance, both armed and unarmed, had contributed enormously to undermining Batista's regime, and had also played a vital role at certain moments in channelling supplies, arms and recruits to the *Sierra*. The *Sierra/Llano* polemic originally came to a head in relation to the strategy of a revolutionary general strike, which the urban leadership saw as the road to victory and which was reluctantly accepted by Fidel and the *Sierra* in late 1957. The result was the general strike of 9 April 1958, a heroic but disastrous failure in which many militants lost their lives and the urban underground was severely disrupted by repression. In response a crucial meeting was held on 3 May at Altos de Mompié in the Sierra Maestra, attended by all members of the M-26-7 national leadership plus Che Guevara (García-Pérez 1998, 100); after what was by all accounts a difficult discussion, it was decided to unify the guerrilla and *Llano* command structures with Fidel as General Secretary of the Movement and Commander-in-Chief of the Rebel Army. The National Executive was now based in the Sierra and the urban underground, headed by Marcelo Fernández in Santiago, was subordinate to the Executive in the mountains. Those responsible for the general strike were censured for sectarianism in its preparation (marginalising the Partido Socialista Popular which controlled the bulk of the organised working class) and for underestimating the difficulties of armed confrontation with the police and military in an urban environment (Sweig 2002, 148–51).

The Altos de Mompié meeting did therefore conclude that the *Llano* leadership had committed serious errors and that the Cuban struggle had reached a point where rural guerrilla struggle against the regular military was the decisive element; and this proved to be correct. However, this is not the same as saying that the *Llano* leaders were irredeemable reformists or that a rural guerrilla *foco* could bring revolutionary victory in isolation from the urban movement and in any Latin American country, regardless of specific conditions. Whether Che Guevara really believed this or whether it was an unwarranted extrapolation of his views by Régis Debray is debatable, although it is undeniable that Che made tragic errors of judgement, apparently inspired by the *foco* theory, in the Bolivian campaign which would lead to his death.

Another element of the Cuban revolutionary struggle which cannot be overlooked is the contribution of the FEU (the Student Federation) and the Directorio Revolucionario Estudiantil (Student Revolutionary Directorate) which emerged from it. The Directorio leader José Antonio Echevarría had signed a crucial alliance with Fidel and the M-26-7 in Mexico in August 1956, and on 13 March 1957 the Directorio would lead a heroic but unsuccessful armed assault on the presidential palace in Havana with the aim of assassinating Batista. Despite the Mexico agreement, this reflected the Directorio's independent strategy of trying to defeat the dictatorship by 'decapitation'; they were not far from succeeding but were driven off with over 40 dead, including Echevarría (Sweig 2002, 18–19). The Directorio would subsequently rebuild and would develop its own rural guerrilla force in the Escambray mountains in central Cuba, but would never again really be in a position to dispute revolutionary leadership with Fidel and the M-26-7.

After the failure of the April strike, the key development in the revolutionary struggle was the summer offensive by Batista's army, with some 10,000 troops with tanks and aviation launching an all-out offensive on a few hundred guerrillas in the Sierra Maestra. By August the offensive was defeated, and as the guerrilla columns began to fan out into the plains and take the initiative it became clear that the dictator's days were numbered. As Raúl Castro consolidated control of the northern part of Oriente province, Fidel moved on Santiago and two columns under Che Guevara and Camilo Cienfuegos undertook a heroic march through the swamps of Camaguey towards the west of the island, repeating the great feat of Antonio Maceo, the 'Titan of Bronze' in the 1895–98 war of independence. Batista's forces disintegrated and it became clear that the M-26-7 and above all the Rebel Army were victorious.

## 1959: VICTORY AND EUPHORIA

With Batista's hurried departure in the early hours of New Year's Day 1959 and the triumphant entry of the *barbudos* (the bearded guerrilla fighters) into Havana and Santiago, the country was swept by scenes of extraordinary euphoria. In the following weeks and months, with the consolidation of the new regime and the avalanche of decrees by the revolutionary government imposing change in all aspects of public life, it began to become clear that this was a situation without precedent in the history of Cuba or Latin America, and that the new authorities in Havana enjoyed unparalleled freedom of action. At local level a multiplicity of popular initiatives sprang up, the people began to seize control in neighbourhoods and workplaces, and provisional revolutionary town councils replaced the representatives of the dictatorship. With the collapse of Batista's army and police and the purging of *batistianos* from the civil service, the state apparatus was already being transformed. Within three weeks the most notorious of the dictator's agents, responsible for thousands of deaths and other abuses, were being put on trial and in many cases condemned to death; when US Congressmen protested about the trial procedures, it was pointed out that at least the Rebel Army had maintained order and saved them from lynching:

The 12th of August 1933 had been marked in historical memory as the start of disorder, looting and social upheaval. To the amazement of our contemporaries the much-feared spectre of the excesses of 1933 was not repeated, giving the new revolutionary order a different character. (Díaz Castañón 2001, 105–6)

There was of course disorder in other respects, as the new government issued a raft of decrees which often could not be implemented, or in other cases ratified de facto situations which had been created by spontaneous actions.

It quickly became apparent that the only organisation with popular legitimacy and credibility was the M-26–7: for the vast majority of Cubans the Auténticos, the Ortodoxos, and even more so the Liberals and other traditional parties only represented the past – and one of the most remarkable aspects of the revolutionary situation was how these parties virtually disappeared from the political scene. They were not suppressed, they simply faded away over the next 18 months. The only party with a significant presence was the old Communist Party, known since 1944 as the Partido Socialista Popular (PSP), which had won the support of some sectors of the working class since the 1930s but had been somewhat compromised through its collaboration with Batista in his reformist phase (1938–44), and had become further discredited by its opposition to armed struggle against the dictatorship until the last moment: at the time of the Moncada attack it condemned Fidel and the insurgents as 'petty-bourgeois adventurers', and only officially changed its line in mid-1958. In 1959 therefore the PSP could support the revolutionary process and accept the leadership of Fidel and the M-26–7 – and this it did almost immediately – but it could not claim to be the vanguard of the revolution. In Cuban domestic politics the central issue of the next four years would be the relationship between the PSP and the M-26–7, which was at times friendly and collaborative and at times tense and conflictive. Other than these two organisations, the only other movement of any importance was the Directorio Revolucionario, which had emerged from the student movement and had played an important role in the clandestine struggle in Havana, as well as having its own rural guerrilla force in the Sierra del Escambray in central Cuba; its ideology was similar to that of the M-26–7, and after a few moments of tension in the early months of 1959 it also accepted the leadership of Fidel and the larger movement. In mid-1961 these three organisations (M-26–7, PSP and Directorio) united to form the Organizaciones Revolucionarias Integradas (Integrated Revolutionary Organisations, ORI); in 1962 this was transformed into the Partido Único de la Revolución Socialista (PURS, Single Party of the Socialist Revolution), and finally in 1965 into the new Cuban Communist Party. The leading role, however, was that of the M-26–7, and it was fundamentally this movement with Fidel at its head which directed the agrarian reform, the nationalisations, the breach with the US and the transition to Socialism.

It is important to bear in mind these original characteristics of the situation in order to understand the headlong rush of events in the first three to four years. In the first nine months of 1959 some 1,500 decrees and laws were issued. The government decreed the purging of *batistianos*, the compulsory reduction of urban rents, the reduction of telephone rates and – when the US-owned company refused this – the legal intervention of the company, the reduction of electricity rates, wage increases for low-paid workers, and the first agrarian reform law (May 1959) (Pérez 1988, 319–20). The State Department condemned the measures, but the Cuban response was to reject any interference in the country's internal affairs and to press ahead with more reforms. From August 1959 onwards, armed attacks on Cuba began to be mounted by Florida-based exiles with the connivance of US officials; on 5 September the US Ambassador was recalled for a fortnight as an expression of Washington's displeasure with the agrarian reform and the measures affecting the telephone and electricity companies; on 21 October a Cuban Air Force deserter, Major Díaz Lanz, flew over Havana dropping leaflets and incendiary bombs, and in Havana itself counter-revolutionary terrorists planted bombs and machine-gunned people in bus queues; and Fidel announced in response the formation of a popular armed militia (Scheer and Zeitlin 1964, 104–7). This tit-for-tat pattern culminated with the Cuban expropriation of the Standard Oil, Texaco and Shell oil refineries in June–July 1960, the US decision to cut the Cuban sugar quota, and the Cuban expropriation of a series of industrial subsidiaries in August, until in October all remaining US properties were nationalised and Washington imposed its trade embargo, soon to become a virtually complete blockade, which has continued ever since.

What was remarkable in all this was the unflinching determination of the Cubans; where previously in Latin America, and especially in the Caribbean area, any nationalist or reformist government which faced the hostility of the United States had backed down or else had been overthrown, this government in Havana reacted by taking more radical decisions in defiance of Washington. Then in April 1961 when the inevitable armed intervention came at the Bay of Pigs – an invasion by 1,600 counter-revolutionaries sponsored by the CIA, with the US Navy just off the coast waiting to land – the Cubans resisted and crushed the invaders, in an act of revolutionary affirmation which won the admiration of all Latin America and which Washington has never forgiven. It was also at this moment that Fidel proclaimed the Socialist character of the revolution, for the first time and after two years and three months in power; and the alliance with the Soviet Union, hitherto partial and limited principally to a trade agreement, developed fast over the next few months and was extended to the political and military fields as well. The final act of this geo-political drama came 18 months later with the Missile Crisis of October 1962, when Cuba stood at the centre of what was probably the most dangerous confrontation ever between the two super-powers. With the peaceful resolution of this crisis Cuban Socialism became a fait accompli, although subject to a systematic US blockade and integrated into the Soviet bloc in ways that were not necessarily always desired by the Cubans.

These are the bare bones of the Cuban revolutionary transition, of an exceptionally radical and rapid transformation occurring in an island of six million inhabitants (eleven million today) only 180 kilometres from Florida. The Cuban revolution has been studied to death, but there are still aspects of it which are misunderstood. First, it is necessary to look more closely at the political and ideological characteristics of the revolutionary movement itself. It is generally recognised that the PSP had little to do with the revolution, which was the work of Fidel Castro and the M-26–7: a broad, nationalist, democratic and anti-imperialist movement. Most observers also recognise that the movement as such was not Socialist or Marxist until some time after victory, at least in terms of programme and systematic doctrine (although a significant number of its militants were familiar with and sympathised with one or another version of Socialist ideology). Before and for some time after 1 January 1959 it included many individuals of liberal, Social Democratic or Christian Democratic ideology. With the exception of some right-wing US writers or Miami Cubans who regard the revolution as a cleverly disguised Communist plot, most scholars consider that the Cuban leaders became radicalised in the course of the struggle against Batista and especially in the confrontation with the US from 1959 to

1962. It is important to realise that US hostility did not begin when the revolution was declared to be Socialist (which was not until April 1961) but from the very beginning. Even on 1 January 1959 when Batista had just fled and the revolutionaries were in control of Santiago and marching on Havana, the US Embassy supported an attempted coup by General Cantillo to prevent Fidel Castro and the M-26–7 from taking power (Ibarra Guitart 2000, 352–3); it failed because Fidel immediately called for a general strike and confirmed his orders to Che Guevara and Camilo Cienfuegos to march on the capital. In the months that followed, despite conciliatory overtures to Washington by the revolutionary leaders, the US remained fundamentally hostile, and it was later revealed that plans for a counter-revolutionary invasion of Cuba (which would eventually materialise in the Bay of Pigs or Playa Girón expedition of 16–20 April 1961) actually began in May 1959:

... the Agrarian Reform Law was signed on May 17, 1959, and just two days later President Eisenhower signed the Pluto Plan, which aimed to destabilize Cuba. Pluto was the CIA's code name for the comprehensive program of subversion that culminated in the Bay of Pigs invasion. (Blanco 1994, 14)

This was almost two years before Fidel declared the revolution to be Socialist (which, not accidentally, he did on the first day of the invasion), and when Cuba had not yet even re-established diplomatic relations with the Soviet Union. Although Communism would later become an additional factor in US hostility, the fundamental reason was Washington's traditional view of Cuba as a US protectorate where its imperial fiat must be obeyed.

The view of North American liberals is that US hostility and political blunders drove the revolutionary leaders into the arms of the Communists: Robert Scheer and Maurice Zeitlin, writing in 1963, declared that:

An examination of the history of the years since the establishment of the Revolutionary Government demonstrates, we believe, that the tragic course of Cuba–United States relations has been encouraged and accelerated, rather than hindered, by the United States Government's foreign policy towards Cuba. That policy acted both to change political attitudes among the Cuban leaders and to increase the probability that men already holding Communist or pro-Soviet beliefs or both, would move into positions of influence and power within the revolutionary movement. Moreover, United States actions often confronted the Revolutionary Government with alternatives which led them to take steps they apparently had neither anticipated nor desired ... . (Scheer and Zeitlin 1964, 64–5)

The authors are undoubtedly correct in arguing that US hostility was counter-productive, but they probably underestimate the determination of the revolutionary leaders to take radical measures which would inevitably affect US interests – not because of a pre-existing Communist or pro-Soviet disposition but because of their own national-revolutionary ideology. This interpretation also overlooks the original characteristics of the revolutionary movement and the unprecedented character of the political situation obtaining in 1959.

As previously mentioned, one of the most remarkable features of the Cuban political scene in 1959 was the almost total lack of political initiative of the political parties and organisations of the bourgeoisie. It could be objected that the Provisional Government established in January included several figures of clearly bourgeois origin and orientation, beginning with President Manuel Urrutia and Prime Minister José Miró Cardona. But what is striking here is their complete inability to control the course of events, and the almost universal attitude that real authority was in the hands of Fidel Castro and the other *comandantes* of the M-26-7. It only took six weeks to bring about the inglorious resignation of Miró Cardona and Fidel's appointment as Prime Minister, a change widely regarded as natural and inevitable (Buch Rodríguez 1999, 69–75). Five months later (in July) came the crisis provoked by the differences between Castro and Urrutia, which produced first Fidel's resignation as Prime Minister and then Urrutia's resignation from the presidency (to be replaced by Osvaldo Dorticós) and, after several days of overwhelming and almost unanimous demonstrations of support for Fidel, his return to the premiership. In this conflict there can be little doubt that Urrutia's position represented bourgeois interests, but what is remarkable is the weakness of the support he received from traditional political forces.

Apart from questions of personal ethics – for example, the fact that unlike other ministers, Urrutia had not agreed to a 50 per cent reduction of his salary – the fundamental political issue was that in the preceding weeks the President had repeatedly denounced the threat of Communism, just at the time when one of the first revolutionary renegades, former Air Force Major Pedro Díaz Lanz, was doing the same in hearings at the US Senate (Buch Rodríguez

1999, 129–31). Moreover, this was at a time when the revolutionary government was far from being Communist-dominated; in fact there was public friction between the PSP and the M-26–7, and on 22 July the Communists demonstrated in protest outside the offices of the pro-26 July newspaper *Revolución* (Scheer and Zeitlin 1964, 100). By doing this Urrutia was in practice encouraging US interventionism, which was aimed more at the agrarian reform and its possible impact on US interests than at the as yet very marginal Communist influence on the revolutionary government. It would later emerge that Urrutia was a close personal and political associate of another anti-Communist dissident, Major Hubert Matos, whose desertion occurred in October 1959 (Scheer and Zeitlin 1964, 107–11; Buch Rodríguez 1999: 126–7).

The crucial weakness of Urrutia (and also of Hubert Matos and others like them) was the political impossibility of attacking Fidel. Their allegations of Communist influence in the government were known to be directed principally at Raúl Castro, who had previously been a member of the Youth Wing of the PSP, and Che Guevara, who made no secret of his Marxist (but not PSP) views. When Urrutia first learned of Fidel's decision to resign (which he did by reading the report in the morning edition of *Revolución* on 17 July – a circumstance which in itself shows how bad the relationship between the two men had become), his first reaction was to see it as a Communist coup against the *Comandante-en-Jefe*! (Buch Rodríguez 1999, 133). As it quickly became clear that this was not the case and that Fidel had indeed resigned because of disagreements with him, Urrutia had no alternative, given Fidel's overwhelming popularity, but to present his own resignation which would swiftly be followed by Fidel's return as premier. What he had failed to appreciate was that Fidel was determined to carry through the profound and radical revolution that the Cuban people were demanding, and to do so regardless of US hostility and with the support of whatever allies were necessary. Since no politician or party had the prestige to confront the *Comandante-en-Jefe* Urrutia saw that there was, from his point of view, nothing to be done.

With regard to the political parties, it is necessary to examine with some care the circumstances of the collapse of the Auténticos and Ortodoxos, particularly the latter. Supposed heirs of the revolutionary values of 1933 (and therefore of Martí and the mambíses), these parties should theoretically have been the backbone of the resistance against Batista's dictatorship. The Auténticos were profoundly discredited by the corruption and ineptitude of the Grau and Prío administrations (1944–52), although it might have been anticipated that they would be capable of reorganising and recovering to defend their rights as representing the legitimately elected government overthrown by the upstart military tyrant. But it would have been even more logical to expect the Partido Ortodoxo, founded in 1947 as a split from the Auténticos and in opposition to their corruption, to channel resistance against the dictatorship. Indeed it was from the Ortodoxos, and especially from the party's Youth Wing, that many militants of the M-26–7 emerged, among them Fidel Castro himself. But the Ortodoxo Party as such proved to be incapable of offering effective leadership in the anti-Batista struggle; not long after the coup it split into a revolutionary sector and a *pactista* sector, named after the Pact of Montreal which they signed in June 1953 with the Auténticos and other traditional parties. This sector came to accept the classic ineffective strategy of a legal or tolerated opposition to a dictatorship, of searching in vain for a peaceful and constitutional means of forcing the dictator to abandon power (Mencía 1993, 55 [Note 29], 205) – the same dilemma faced for many years by the Portuguese opposition to Salazar. Nevertheless, until the early months of 1957 Fidel insisted on the close links between his movement and *ortodoxia*, and it was in fact this party which contributed more than any other to the formation of the M-26–7. In March 1956 in Mexico Fidel made a categorical statement to this effect:

The 26th of July Revolutionary Movement does not constitute a tendency within the [Ortodoxo] Party: it is the revolutionary instrument of *chibasismo*, firmly rooted in its rank-and-file whence it sprang to struggle against the dictatorship when *ortodoxia* lay impotent, divided in a thousand pieces. (quoted in Harnecker 1986, 24–5)

– in other words, the rank-and-file of the Ortodoxo Party had revolutionary sympathies and remained faithful to Chibás' ideals even when the leadership had betrayed them. This being so, the new movement had to emerge from *ortodoxia* and had to base its legitimacy on the memory of *chibasismo*:

For the *chibasista* masses the 26 July Movement is not something different from *ortodoxia*; it is *ortodoxia* without the leadership of landlords like Fico Fernández Casas, without sugar barons like Gerardo Vázquez, without stock-market speculators, without industrial and commercial magnates, without lawyers working for powerful interests, without provincial *caciques*, without political fixers of any kind. It is the organisation of the common people, by the common people and for the common people. (quoted in Harnecker 1986, 26–7)

This obviously implied the exclusion from the Ortodoxo Party of all bourgeois or oligarchic groups, and it could be objected that any party subjected to a decapitation of this kind would be transformed into a proletarian organisation. But it is noteworthy that Fidel did not make any similar declaration in relation to the Auténtico masses or those of any other party, which tends to suggest that he regarded *ortodoxia* – or perhaps it would be better to say *chibasismo* in the broadest sense – as the principal source of recruitment for the revolutionary movement.

In order to understand this affinity of Fidel Castro for *chibasismo* it is necessary to say a few words about Eduardo Chibás. The founder of *ortodoxia* has more than a few critics among Cuban historians and revolutionaries: they describe him as being excessively emotional, demagogic, as making unfounded accusations against his opponents, and as lacking a clear revolutionary vision or ideology. There is no doubt that in 1951 his accusation against Aureliano Sánchez Arango (Minister of Education in the Auténtico Government), of having stolen public funds for his private investments in Guatemala, lacked documentary proof, and it was the scandal created by this which led Chibás to his final crisis (when he shot himself while on the air in his weekly radio broadcast, dying ten days later) (Alavéz 1994, 64–5). It is also undeniable that Chibás' ideology was contradictory and lacking in coherence. But his emotional speeches conveyed to the people his passion and his conviction of the need for a new politics free from Auténtico corruption; his slogan of 'Honour before Money' (*Vergüenza contra Dinero*) was a reassertion of the profoundly ethical roots of Cuban radicalism since the time of Martí, and his criticism of the telephone and electricity companies and of the US loan reflected a nationalist and anti-imperialist position which was fundamental to the Cuban revolutionary tradition. Moreover, even if he was inconsistent, Chibás did at times take a clearly revolutionary stand: on the eve of the foundation of the Ortodoxo Party in May 1947 he proposed this succinct ideological formula: 'New ideas and procedures, nationalism, anti-imperialism and socialism, economic independence, political freedom and social justice … ' (Alavéz 1994, 53). Even if his conception of Socialism was not Marxist, what we have here is a more explicitly advanced position than that of 'History Will Absolve Me' six years later (which did not mention Socialism).

It is also instructive to read the *Bases* (Principles) of the Ortodoxo Party, approved on 15 May 1947 with a decisive contribution from Chibás: they imply a frankly revolutionary orientation, which however would not be practised by the new party because of the influence of more conservative and/or opportunist leaders. Thus the second article declared that the party should be 'thoroughly revolutionary in its functional structure, which will incorporate the social groups interested in national liberation: productive sectors, workers, peasants, middle classes, youth and women'; the fourth article insisted on the need to avoid a purely electoral structure, because 'it is necessary to adopt forms of organisation and leadership which ensure the discipline and militancy which are indispensable in a modern Revolutionary Party'; and the fifth proposed a method of popular participation which would be 'the result of popular assemblies, and not an empty formula existing on paper only' (Alavéz 1994, 53–4) – in other words, a party of militants and direct popular participation, which would have a revolutionary character.

In the light of these statements by Chibás it is easier to understand why Fidel Castro rendered such explicit homage to the *Adalid de Cuba* (Champion of Cuba) at a public rally on 16 January 1959:

If it had not been for those young people, if it had not been for those teachings, if that seed had not been sown, the 26 July would not have been possible, for it was the continuation of Chibás's work, the flowering of the seed which he sowed among our people. Without Chibás the Cuban revolution would not have been possible. (*Revolución* 17 January 1959)

This does not mean that Fidel was simply a disciple of Chibás or that the M-26-7 was a direct linear successor of the Ortodoxo Party. If Chibás had lived he would not have had Fidel's capacity to develop the political and military strategy to overthrow Batista, or to direct the revolutionary transition after 1 January 1959. The success of the M-26-7 lay in its capacity – which was essentially Fidel's capacity – to bring together all the strands of what Tony Kapcia calls *cubanía revolucionaria*, with its roots in Martí and the *mambíses*, in Mella, in the 1933 revolution and in Guiteras (Kapcia 2000, 46–7, 85–97, 263–8).

An important tendency in the new movement drew its inspiration not from Chibás but from Guiteras, the most coherent protagonist of 1933 who had a clearly Socialist ideology and who subsequently organised a clandestine armed movement, Jóven Cuba (Young Cuba). The memory of Julio Antonio Mella was another source of inspiration, and not only for the Communists: the work of that young student leader of the 1920s went beyond the limits of the Communist Party of which he was a founder, and inspired many who never accepted the Party's line. Figures like Mella and Guiteras formed part of what could be called the Latin American independent Marxist tradition, a school of thought derived from Marx and Lenin but adapted to the realities of the colonised Afro-Indian-Latin-American world and formulated by such thinkers as the Peruvian José Carlos Mariátegui. In view of this the participation in the M-26-7 of the young Che Guevara was not such a chance event, even if it did result from a fortuitous meeting in Mexico; the greatest influence on Guevara's political and intellectual development was precisely this independent Latin American Marxism, and no doubt he identified with the Cuban revolutionaries because he recognised in some of them the same philosophical outlook (Mariátegui 1969; Kohan 1997).

The presence of the Communist Party/PSP cannot be ignored; although it did not participate directly in the revolution until mid-1958, it had organised a large sector of the proletariat along class lines and had disseminated Marxist and Leninist ideas among Cuban intellectuals since the 1920s. As in other Latin American and European countries, many progressive intellectuals and activists had been members of the Communist Party at one time or another and had left or been expelled for differences with the official line. In the 1950s many of those who joined the M-26-7 were also in touch with the PSP but were alienated by its condemnation of Fidel and the *moncadistas* for 'putschism' and 'petty-bourgeois adventurism'. Thus Enrique Oltuski, later head of the M-26-7 in Las Villas Province and holder of various ministerial posts after the revolutionary victory, relates how in 1955 he had a talk with a PSP lawyer who defended the party's 'mass line' of agitation in the unions and among intellectuals to pressure Batista into granting free elections, a notion which Oltuski found completely illusory (Oltuski 2000, 64-8).

In practice, many rank-and-file Communists identified instinctively with the armed struggle and collaborated actively with the M-26-7, disobeying the party line. As the guerrilla struggle advanced, the party leadership came under greater and greater pressure to change its position and began to make contact with the M-26-7, until finally in July 1958 one of the top PSP leaders, Carlos Rafael Rodríguez, went to the Sierra Maestra to hold formal discussions with Fidel and the rebel leadership, and the party officially decided to support the insurrection (Scheer and Zeitlin 1964, 127-9). On 6 January 1959 the

Secretary-General, Blas Roca, publicly declared the PSP's support for Fidel Castro and the victorious revolution, implicitly accepting Fidel's leadership (Matthews 1975, 99–100); but they had little alternative if they wanted to avoid the complete marginalisation of the party. It was only to be expected therefore that the victorious revolutionaries, while accepting the PSP's collaboration, expected it to remain in a subordinate position.

## THE TRANSITION TO SOCIALISM

Does this mean that the subsequent Socialist option was due only to a defensive reaction in the face of US hostility, and to an alliance with the Soviet Union based on geo-political considerations? Not necessarily: it was possible to make a political and military alliance with the USSR without adopting Soviet-style Socialism, as for example in the case of Egypt under Nasser. Moreover this interpretation fails to give sufficient importance to the internal dynamics of the revolution, in which the Cuban bourgeoisie was excluded from the political process (or excluded itself) in little more than a year without any intervention on the part of the Soviets or even of the PSP, whose influence remained minimal until well into 1960. During the transition, leadership was always in the hands of Fidel Castro and the M-26–7 (with the collaboration of some figures from the Directorio Revolucionario), and the social base of support of the revolutionary government consisted from the start overwhelmingly of the popular classes, workers, peasants, blacks, women, middle class; although some representatives of the bourgeoisie and the landlords were involved in the early stages, they had little influence and were quickly marginalised. In a sense the M-26–7 was exactly what Fidel had suggested in 1956, *ortodoxia* without landlords, without industrial magnates, without opportunistic politicians, without lawyers in the service of vested interests, etc. It was therefore tendentially inclined towards Socialism, and the *cubanía revolucionaria* of its leaders, their unflinching commitment to achieving economic independence, political freedom and social justice, evolved necessarily in that direction. In another international context this would not have led to the specifically Soviet model of Socialism, and in this sense the geo-political factor was decisive; but the endogenous revolutionary impulse was leading the country towards some kind of Socialism anyway, a Socialism of original characteristics – and even with the imposition of the Soviet model, elements of Cuban originality remained in what some observers in the 1960s called the 'Cuban heresy'.

From the very beginning the Cuban leaders had to respond to accusations of Communism from right-wing circles in the US and at home; in a press conference on 22 January 1959 Fidel declared, no doubt sincerely, 'I want to make it clear now that I am not Communist.' But at the same time he indicated that the revolutionaries would not allow themselves to be blackmailed by the 'red scare' into abandoning their goals: 'We will act according to circumstances and if they try to exterminate us, we will have to defend ourselves' (*Revolución* 23 January 1959). The leadership had to perform a balancing act in order to preserve unity while maintaining their revolutionary commitment and yet avoiding provocations. Internally there were problems with PSP sectarianism but also with blind anti-Communism from some members of the M-26–7 and Directorio. In May 1959 there was a vigorous polemic because some Communists tried to promote unity 'from below' between local branches of the different organisations in some districts, but on their terms, in a way which would guarantee PSP domination; they were condemned by Fidel in person in a press conference in which he insisted that the philosophy of the revolution was 'humanism and *cubanismo*' (Tamargo 1959, 65; *Revolución* 22 May 1959). Again in November 1959, at the X Congress of the CTC (Confederación de Trabajadores de Cuba, Cuban Confederation of Labour), there were lively arguments between Communist and M-26–7 delegates; in the elections victory went to the M-26–7 list headed by David Salvador, and the PSP delegates withdrew in protest (*Revolución* 20 November 1959; *Hoy* 25 November 1959). But the revolutionary leadership rejected the notion of anti-Communism as a general line: only a few weeks before Fidel had declared in response to right-wing critics that 'the accusations they make that we are Communist show only that they haven't got the courage to say that they are against the revolutionary laws' (*Revolución* 27 October 1959). It is interesting to note also that a year later, David Salvador was arrested as he tried to leave the country in a small yacht (Scheer and Zeitlin 1964, 293); he could not accept the Socialist option which was becoming a reality by then.

A fundamental element in the dramatic transformation of Cuba in this period was mass mobilisation and pressure. Some Trotskyists and other leftist writers, while expressing admiration for the Cuban revolution, lament what they describe as a lack of working-class or popular involvement or initiative, implying that everything was done by fiat of Fidel and a few other *comandantes*. Nothing could be further from the truth: despite the crucial leadership role of Fidel and the M-26–7 commanders, there was enormous mass mobilisation throughout the country. The hundreds of thousands, even millions, who came to listen to Fidel's speeches did so spontaneously, and they came not only to listen but to shout and to answer back and to give their opinions. Workers, peasants, students and people of all backgrounds were active from day one onwards in taking over local governments, reorganising trade unions, demanding the purging of *batistianos* and making demands for wage increases and better conditions. Much of this activity was spontaneous and organised, although in other cases it was led by M-26–7, PSP or Directorio militants emerging from clandestinity. Tens of thousands of people were now joining these organisations, above all the M-26–7, as new recruits. At first the people lacked effective mass social organisations – with the exception of the unions in the CTC – but this soon changed as the process accelerated. The first new organisation was the militia – the Milicias Nacionales Revolucionarias (MNR, National Revolutionary Militia), organised in December 1959 in response to the wave of counter-revolutionary bombings that began in October, and becoming really operational in March 1960:

By bringing together in defence of the homeland everyone from the office worker to the housewife and the combatants of the guerrilla struggle, [the Militia] were the first associative space in which everyone could recognise each other as revolutionaries on the basis of the activity in which they were participating, and not just because of the guerrilla legend. (Díaz Castañón 2001, 119, 126)

The wave of nationalisations and the completion of the rupture with the US between July and October 1960 witnessed intense activity by the militia in their implementation, and they were accompanied by the formation of two major new mass organisations: the Committees for the Defence of the Revolution (Comités de Defensa de la Revolución, CDR) and the Cuban Women's Federation (Federación de Mujeres Cubanas, FMC). The CDRs, committees of militants at street level – one for each city block – were officially founded on 28 September 1960 in response to an appeal by Fidel, with the primary task of rooting out counter-revolutionaries; for this reason they have been condemned by dissidents as instruments for spying on the population, but the fact is that initially they sprang up spontaneously as neighbours rushed to show their enthusiasm to defend the revolution. Within a year they had recruited some 800,000 members, and eventually incorporated 80 per cent of the adult population; they became crucial in mobilising people for all kinds of activities from health to education and recreation. As for the FMC, founded on 23 August 1960, it brought together several previous women's groups to form a national federation which would play a key role in educational and health campaigns and in promoting women's rights (Kapcia 2000, 110–11; Díaz Castañón 2001, 311).

The question of Socialism was resolved in practice between June 1960 and April 1961, with the refusal of the oil companies to refine Soviet oil, the Cuban expropriation of the oil refineries, Eisenhower's decision to cut the Cuban sugar quota on the North American market, Cuba's expropriation of US sugar mills, the imposition of the embargo by Washington and more Cuban expropriations, until the Bay of Pigs/Playa Girón invasion and Fidel's declaration of the Socialist character of the revolution (16 April 1961). Even before this, a key ideological statement was the First Havana Declaration, adopted by a mass assembly of more than a million people in the vast Plaza de la Revolución on 2 September 1960; although not yet explicitly Socialist, it was a militant anti-imperialist proclamation denouncing US interventionism throughout Latin America and defending the revolution in the name of the Cuban people. This declaration, often overlooked in English-language accounts of the revolution, is still relevant to global anti-capitalist politics today:

Close to the monument and the memory of José Martí, in Cuba, free territory of America, the people, in the full exercise of the inalienable powers that proceed from the true exercise of the sovereignty expressed in the direct, universal and public suffrage, has constituted itself in a National General Assembly.

The National General Assembly of the People of Cuba expresses its conviction that democracy cannot consist only in an electoral vote, which is almost always fictitious and handled by big landholders and professional politicians, but in the rights of citizens to decide, as this Assembly of the People is now doing, their own destiny. Moreover, democracy will only exist in Latin America when its people are really free to choose, when the humble people are not reduced – by hunger, social inequality, illiteracy and the judicial systems – to the most degrading impotence. In short, the National General Assembly of the People of Cuba proclaims before America:

The right of peasants to the land; the right of workers to the fruit of their work; the right of children to education; the right of sick people to medical and hospital attention; the right of youth to work; the right of students to free, experimental and scientific education; the right of Negroes and Indians to 'the full dignity of man'; the right of women to civil, social and political equality; the right of the aged to a secure old age; the right of intellectuals, artists and scientists to fight, with their works, for a better world; the right of states to nationalize imperialist monopolies, thus rescuing their wealth and national resources; the right of nations to trade freely with all peoples of the world; the right of nations to their full sovereignty; the right of nations to turn fortresses into schools, and to arm their workers, their peasants, their students, their intellectuals, the Negro, the Indian, the women, the young and the old, the oppressed and exploited people, so that they may defend, by themselves, their rights and their destinies. (quoted in August 1999, 196–7)

This would be followed 17 months later (on 4 February 1962) by a Second Havana Declaration, asserting the right of peoples to self-determination and proclaiming that revolutions cannot be exported (contrary to the view of the US and the Organisation of American States which accused Cuba of doing this), but the Cuban example showed the peoples of Latin America that revolution was possible. In both declarations Cuba was described with the ringing phrase *Primer Territorio Libre de América*, the First Free Territory of the Americas, in itself an enormously symbolic statement which among other things, reclaimed the name 'America' from the imperialist power which had arrogated unto itself exclusive use of what was after all the designation of the entire hemisphere. In the words of the Cuban historian María del Pilar Díaz Castañón, 'the people as a whole is the protagonist of the subversive process', subversive, that is, of the established order (Díaz Castañón 2001, 126); the dramatic cry of '*¡Patria o Muerte!*', 'Fatherland or Death!', first proclaimed after the tragic explosion of the French munitions ship *La Coubre* in Havana harbour in March 1960, marked the identity of the concepts Homeland-Nation-Revolution, a unity which was given formal expression in the two Havana Declarations (Díaz Castañón 2001, 124–6).

The First Havana Declaration was followed after little more than six months by the long-awaited invasion, which would be defeated by the revolutionary armed forces, the militia and the entire people: 'The triumph of Girón consolidated the Homeland-Nation-Revolution identity which lent prestige to the epithet "socialist" in the name of which people fought and won', and gave the collective protagonist, the people as revolutionary subject, a heroic dimension (Díaz Castañón 2001, 133). The people of Cuba – the militia, the CDRs, the FMC, the CTC, workers, peasants, housewives, students – the vast majority contributed to this epic first defeat of US imperialism in Latin America, which gave the Cuban revolution its unique place in history. The adoption of Marxism-Leninism would then become official with Fidel's speech of 2 December 1961 in which he declared 'I am a Marxist-Leninist and will remain so until the end of my days'; this was in part a response to the geo-political situation following the complete break with Washington, but it also reflected the real Socialist option which had developed among the revolutionary leadership and the majority of the Cuban people in the course of the dramatic struggles of the previous three years. Even so, contrary to appearances, it did not indicate total victory for the PSP or for Soviet orthodoxy.

The true orientation of the new regime in Havana began to become clear in March 1962 with the scandal of the 'micro-fraction' or 'Escalante affair'. As explained earlier, in June 1961 agreement had been reached to merge the M-26-7, PSP and Directorio Revolucionario into a single political force, the ORI. The post of Secretary-General of the ORI went to a prominent PSP leader, Aníbal Escalante. After a few months it became clear that Escalante was using his position in classic Stalinist fashion to appoint PSP loyalists to all the key positions in the new structure, often to the exclusion of outstanding guerrilla fighters from the rebel army or the urban underground. In a dramatic speech on 16 March 1962 Fidel publicly denounced this abuse of power; the ORI were completely reorganised, Escalante was sent into 'diplomatic exile' in Eastern Europe and his 'micro-fraction' was dissolved (Kapcia 2000, 130–2). It was made clear that real power in Socialist Cuba was in the hands of veterans of the M-26-7, and that the political, economic and military alliance with the Soviet Union did not imply acceptance of unconditional satellite status (when Escalante returned to Cuba in 1966, he once again tried to organise an ultra-orthodox fraction within the party, but in 1968 he was arrested and sentenced to 30 years in gaol) (Kapcia 2000, 138–9).

The final chapter of the rupture with the United States, the Missile Crisis of October 1962, also marked the limits of Cuban submission to Soviet power. The solution of the crisis by the US and the Soviet Union without consulting the Cubans provoked an indignant reaction in Havana, which refused on-site United Nations inspection to verify removal of the missiles. The end result was a US undertaking not to invade the island (a promise of somewhat dubious reliability), and the consolidation of the Cuban–Soviet alliance on a more realistic basis. Cuba needed, and could rely on, Soviet support, and became a solid bastion of the Soviet bloc right under the nose of Washington, but subject to a systematic blockade by its super-power neighbour. For the next three decades Cuba always defended Soviet interests, but nevertheless insisted on retaining the right to take initiatives of its own, especially with regard to support for revolutionary movements in Latin America and Africa.

Internally the transition to Socialism was confirmed with the Second Agrarian Reform of 1963 (more radical than the first) and the 'Great Revolutionary Offensive' of 1968, which nationalised all small businesses. It was also during these years that the originality of Cuban Socialism was reaffirmed with the primacy of 'moral incentives' and voluntary labour, and the 'Great Debate' between Che Guevara and the defenders of Soviet orthodoxy in economic policy (see Silverman 1973). Similarly in international affairs, Havana's support for guerrilla movements elsewhere aroused Moscow's distrust; but to the Cubans this was an integral part of their revolutionary vision with its pan-Latin-American roots in Martí and Bolívar, naturally extended to Africa because of the history of slavery. Cuban idealism in the 1960s (and later) was the logical expression of the revolutionary populist bond forged between Fidel and the people through the years of armed struggle, the victorious confrontation with imperialism and the Socialist transition: the Cuban people had emerged as a collective subject with an indomitable will and self-confidence, and would not be content with bureaucratic half-measures.

This forging of the identity of the Cuban people as collective revolutionary protagonist through its intimate bond with Fidel as both architect and expression of their unity in the epic struggle of these years was reinforced by the special role of Che Guevara as advocate of Socialist purity and role model of the 'New Man'. The Cuban nation was not only the vanguard of revolution in Latin America and the Third World, it was venturing where no revolution had gone before, to realise the ideal of true Communist equality without waiting for the long transition of 'really existing Socialism' to run its tedious course. Che was also a model of internationalism, and as an Argentinian his acceptance in Cuba – not only at official level but in the popular mind – as second only to Fidel, was truly remarkable. Such acceptance could only occur in a revolutionary process, and is yet further evidence of the depth and authenticity of the Cuban revolution. Che's secret mission to the Congo in 1965, and then a year later his departure for Bolivia in fulfilment of the vision of 'turning the Cordillera of the Andes into the Sierra Maestra of Latin America' were the maximum expression of his, and Cuba's, revolutionary internationalism. Although the circumstances of Che's departure and of his tragic death in Bolivia on 10 October 1967 have given rise to an enormous polemical literature with many critics claiming that Fidel, and Cuba, were in some way responsible, most Cubans and many others who were close to the two leaders regard this as inconceivable:

I knew from the time of Che's disappearance in 1965, that there could have been no ill-feeling or quarrel between the two men ... The cruel libel that Che Guevara and Fidel Castro quarreled and the Cuban leader punished his friend, both in Cuba and by sending him off unaided to his death in Bolivia, will, like so many malicious or ignorant lies, live in books and uninformed minds, either as belief or as doubt. (Matthews 1975, 266)

There are strong grounds for arguing that the Bolivian guerrilla strategy was ill-conceived, and indeed the entire Cuban strategy of supporting armed insurgency throughout Latin America from the 1960s to the 1980s was based on a revolutionary optimism which did not correspond to actual conditions in most countries. But it was entirely consistent with the ideological roots of the revolution, with Martí and Bolívar, which moreover undoubtedly found echoes throughout the continent even in countries where conditions were not ripe for insurrection; and its relevance in some countries was later vindicated by the Central American insurgencies, and arguably by the ongoing struggle in Colombia. In the 1960s Cuba played a central role in the Non-Aligned Movement along with Algeria and Vietnam, despite its close alliance with the USSR; in practice this reflected an autonomous Socialist tendency in the world context, a tacit refusal to accept the Moscow line of 'peaceful coexistence' while remaining faithful to the Soviet bloc in the Cold War confrontation. For many years afterwards the Departamento América (best translated as 'Department of the Americas') of the Cuban Communist Party under Comandante Manuel Piñeiro was the fundamental point of reference for Latin American revolutionaries, indeed down to the present it continues to express Cuban internationalism in a radically different context.

## CHANGING DEVELOPMENT STRATEGIES

In terms of political economy Cuban policy also retained original features, although with very strong Soviet influence. The initial project of accelerated Socialist industrialisation had to be revised in 1963–64 due to the inadequacy of capital accumulation and the bottlenecks caused by the rapidity of the transition; it was at this point that the decision was taken to maximise sugar production as a source of capital, while pursuing a long-term strategy of economic diversification. At the same time Che Guevara as Minister of Industry championed a centralised planning structure known as the Budgetary Finance System, which in contrast to the Soviet system relied on collective moral incentives to achieve labour discipline and growth. But this idealism was not confined to Che: after his departure in 1965 an anti-bureaucratic campaign inspired by Fidel and other ex-guerrilla *comandantes* led to the weakening of the planning and accounting systems in the name of direct Socialist initiative. In 1968 in the 'Great Revolutionary Offensive' all small businesses were nationalised: ' ... private enterprise was banned by fiat, and not as a result of education or a developing socialist "consciousness" ... The result was socialist evangelism, exhorting people to act in the "social" interest' (Cole 1998, 30–1).

This strategy reached its limit with the famous '10 million ton zafra' (sugar harvest) of 1970, an objective which proved impossible and which led to a political and economic crisis only resolved by Fidel's personal assumption of responsibility and the adoption of a more realistic and orthodox economic project. In 1972 Cuba joined COMECON, the Soviet bloc's integrated economic structure, and in 1973 it adopted a Soviet-style planning system known as the Sistema de Dirección y Planificación de la Economía (SDPE, Economic Management and Planning System). This certainly produced results, with a GDP growth rate estimated at 7.8 per cent per annum from 1972 to 1981 and continued growth through most of the 1980s when the rest of Latin America was suffering actual per capita decline during the 'lost decade'. But it was based on the exchange of Cuban sugar and nickel and a few other primary products for Soviet oil and COMECON manufactured goods, essentially perpetuating Cuban underdevelopment although on more favourable terms than under capitalism. Moreover, in line with post-1965 Soviet policy, the SDPE combined centralised bureaucratic planning with enterprise profitability and individual material incentives, undermining collective Socialist consciousness. Although trade unions expanded in the 1970s and were in theory given much greater opportunities to participate in enterprise management, in practice their scope for decision-making was severely limited by the requirements of the central plan and the international division of labour imposed by COMECON (Cole 1998, 32–6).

These deficiencies of the SDPE led to more and more outspoken criticisms until the system was abandoned in the mid-1980s. One of the most interesting critical Cuban writers, Juan Antonio Blanco, declares that in economics it led to a 'primitive and incompetent' style of authoritarian planning, and politically to the bureaucratisation of organisations that had been full of creativity and initiative:

In fact, I would say that the worst error we committed, the one with the most dramatic and lasting effects, was the decision to follow the Soviet model of socialism. Those 15 years of 'Russification' of our socialism left us with problems in almost every realm of society. (Blanco 1994, 24)

The defects of the SDPE were not limited to lack of popular participation. In the long run, just as in the Soviet Union, it also proved to be seriously inefficient. Enterprise autonomy was a fiction as ministries imposed central decisions, profitability was artificially maintained through arbitrary price increases, goods were hoarded to conceal overproduction, and workers slacked so as not to surpass norms. 'The bureaucratic centralism of the SDPE was reflected in the bureaucratic habits and elitist pretensions of planners, with ministries keeping close control of their respective areas of concern, competing with other ministries for resources, which went as far as ministries ordering enterprises not to declare their excess and unused resources as "superfluous"' (Cole 1998, 35). The result was a lack of real coordination, unfinished projects, inefficiency and cynicism. Also, Cuba had never ceased to trade with the capitalist world, and when world market conditions were favourable in the 1970s with high prices for sugar and re-exported Soviet oil, it made the mistake of contracting hard-currency debt. In the 1980s, just like other Latin American countries, it was unable to meet the debt payments; the difference was that it was sheltered by COMECON and thus was able to avoid IMF restrictions and continue to expand its economy, but the long-term result was to cut it off from Western sources of credit when the Soviet bloc collapsed.

As the negative effects, both political and economic, of this Soviet-style planning system became apparent, pressure grew from the more politically conscious revolutionaries for a radical reassessment. Once again the *Comandante-en-Jefe* took the lead in 1985 in denouncing the negative tendencies which threatened to undermine the revolution, promoting instead the policy of 'rectification' which was adopted at the Third Party Congress in 1986. Centralised bureaucratic planning was replaced in 1988 by what was called 'continuous planning', allowing greater flexibility and autonomy in drawing up plans and greater worker participation. Work norms were made more realistic, there were general wage increases for the lowest paid (first in agriculture, later for nurses and teachers), and voluntary labour schemes were reintroduced. Private farmers' markets, authorised in 1980, were closed down because they had led to greater inequality (although this measure would have to be reversed a few years later in the 'Special Period') (Cole 1998, 45–50).

It was also in these years that the international situation began to take a much less favourable turn, with the intensified hostility of the United States under Reagan and the reformism of Gorbachev in the Soviet Union. Fidel surprised many observers by taking a strong stand against *glasnost* and *perestroika*, a stand which was widely criticised as 'Stalinist' or 'conservative' but which was in reality a reaffirmation of Cuban originality, of the more popular and participatory character of Cuban Socialism which did not therefore need a liberal 'opening' – an option which in any case, and in this Fidel once again showed remarkable foresight, would lead almost inevitably to capitalist restoration in the Soviet Union.

In fact 'rectification' began a process of debate and of return to the autochthonous roots of the revolution which contributed significantly to Cuban survival in the unprecedented crisis provoked by the fall of the Berlin Wall in 1989 and the collapse of the Soviet Union in 1992. In that period almost all observers were predicting the imminent collapse of the Cuban revolution, and the Miami mafia was eagerly preparing to celebrate the fall of Castro. The impact on Cuba of the disappearance of the Soviet bloc was indeed catastrophic: in three years the country lost 85 per cent of its foreign trade and its GNP fell by 35 per cent. The lack of Soviet oil was particularly serious: many factories closed for lack of fuel, there was scarcely any public transport, mechanised agriculture could not function because there was no fuel for tractors, harvesters or pumps, crops rotted in the fields because they could not be transported to market, there were blackouts 16 hours a day and for the first time since the revolution there was real hunger and malnutrition. The government announced the inauguration of the 'Special Period', defined as a war economy in peacetime, in order to administer a situation of extreme scarcity. It has been said, quite rightly, that in any other country such a critical situation would have provoked the overthrow of the government in a matter of months, and the regime's survival in these circumstances is the most convincing demonstration of the continued vitality of the revolution. Furthermore the crisis was aggravated by the intensification of the US blockade: the Torricelli and Helms-Burton Laws (of 1992 and 1996 respectively) tried to tighten the noose around Cuba by forcing third countries to apply the same restrictions.

To understand Cuban survival in these circumstances it is necessary to take into account several factors: first, that even faced with such a grave economic crisis Cuba, unlike any other Latin American country (even Sandinista Nicaragua) did not adopt IMF-type deflationary measures; secondly, that it maintained universal free health care and education, the distribution of cheap rations (when the products were available), the control of rents which could not exceed 20 per cent of wages, and highly subsidised prices of gas, electricity and other basic services; and thirdly, that the reforms which were introduced in 1993–94 – free circulation of the dollar, individual self-employment for those that wanted it, joint ventures with foreign capital and a new tax system – were only adopted after an extensive process of consultation with the population. Another indication of the popular character of Cuban Socialism is the country's defence doctrine, which was revised in the mid-1980s following the US invasion of revolutionary Grenada: rather than just relying on the regular army, it was at this time that the Cubans devised the strategy of 'War of the Whole People', reviving the popular militia which had been neglected since the 1960s:

... some three million people were organized and trained in martial arts or tasks related to defense ... We distributed weapons in factories, farms, universities, different neighborhoods in cities and small towns throughout the island to make sure that the population would have access to them in case of a U.S. invasion ... . (Blanco 1994, 25–6)

As Blanco points out, to arm the population in this manner was to show great confidence in popular support for the revolution. Finally, and without any doubt, the leadership of Fidel was once again crucial in the survival of the revolution, with his insistence that Cuba would not capitulate to US blackmail and neither would it follow the self-destructive path of *perestroika*; that it would remain Socialist and forge its own model in the new and hostile world which was emerging. What also became apparent as the country struggled through the hardships of the Special Period was that in some ways it was also returning to its original Cuban and Latin roots, as a distinctive variety of Socialism with strong participatory characteristics.

From 1995 onwards there was a steady recovery of the economy, with a cumulative growth of about 25 per cent by 2002, and significant diversification of production also (the most promising sector being pharmaceuticals and biotechnology). Many state farms, particularly in the sugar sector, have been converted into cooperatives known as UBPCs (Unidades Básicas de Producción Cooperativa, Basic Units of Cooperative Production) in which the state still owns the land but planning and management is in the hands of the workers; the UBPCs have also diversified to produce other crops. Industrial management has been reformed to reflect market conditions within planning priorities set by the state, under the SPE (Sistema de Perfeccionamiento Empresarial, Management Optimisation System) which has been criticised as creating a new capitalist-minded management class (Carmona Báez 2004, 166–80). But Carlos Lage, Executive Secretary of the Cuban Cabinet (Council of Ministers), who is highly respected in Cuba for his Socialist commitment, argues that the SPE combines entrepreneurial efficiency with worker participation in planning and union and party involvement to ensure social justice; and even Carmona Báez recognises that 'what is experienced in the application of the SPE is the maximisation of state influence over the market' (ibid., 182–3). In Cuba there is extensive debate about alternative economic strategies, possibly involving greater enterprise autonomy (Carranza Valdés et al. 1996) or more small and medium-size individually or collectively owned businesses, and greater worker participation in management of state enterprises (Blanco 1994, 48–50).

Politically the most significant development has been the leading role assumed by Cuba in the international opposition to neo-liberal globalisation, and the internal debate on the quest for a new post-Soviet model of Socialism, appropriate to the circumstances of the twenty-first century but also faithful to the revolution's Cuban and Latin American roots. Constant US harassment has probably limited the scope of this debate, since any sign of division or weakness is immediately exploited by Washington to undermine the revolutionary regime as such. But the opening to religious organisations ranging from the Catholic Church to the evangelicals, the promotion of organic agriculture, the increasing acceptance of gay rights, and Fidel's active participation in international gatherings such as the Ibero-American Heads of States meetings and the UN 'Earth Summit' in Rio de Janeiro, are all indications of a Cuban desire to innovate and to engage in discussion on the major issues of the day. Cuban leaders insist on the continued relevance of Socialism and the need to find a non-capitalist solution to the world's problems, but they do not pretend to export the Cuban model and have demonstrated a very open approach to supporting a variety of progressive regimes such as those of Chávez in Venezuela and Lula in Brazil. Cuba is the best example in today's world of a revolutionary regime which still remains a centre of interest and debate decades after coming to power, and this is why it is important to re-examine its origins, development and original characteristics.

## THE TRUE ORIGINALITY OF CUBA

The originality of the Cuban experience, then, lies not so much in the recourse to arms as in its unorthodox origins and course of development. A careful analysis based on a detailed knowledge of Cuban history reveals at least four aspects of the Cuban revolution which were quite original. The first of these was the achievement of a remarkably broad consensus, an overwhelming degree of unity around a popular democratic ideology with deep roots in the national culture; in 1959 and later the political expression of the 'opposition', whether openly reactionary or liberal, was minimal. The second remarkable originality of the Cuban process was the achievement of a surprisingly rapid and complete transition to Socialism without any major rupture in the initial popular consensus: the popular democratic ideology evolved in a Socialist direction without trauma and without losing its original characteristics. The third original feature was the central role in the entire process of one man, Fidel Castro, whose significance cannot be overestimated; although – as has been well analysed by María del Pilar Díaz Castañón – the revolution was the work of the Cuban people as collective subject, Fidel was the personification of this collective subject, its intuitive mouthpiece. This has naturally led to accusations of 'populism' in the negative sense, of *caudillismo* and even dictatorship; accusations which are fundamentally misguided and incorrect, but which cannot be refuted without a clear analysis of the origins and characteristics of Fidel's protagonism. However, such accusations are also discredited by an understanding of the fourth and final original feature of the process, namely its essentially democratic character: despite limitations which will be discussed below, the revolution has striven constantly to forge a genuine participatory socialist democracy, and its achievements in this respect should not be dismissed. The first two of these original characteristics – the broad revolutionary consensus and the swift transition to Socialism – have been analysed above, but the personal protagonism of Fidel and the issue of democracy need to be discussed further.

## FIDEL: POPULIST *CAUDILLO* OR MARXIST REVOLUTIONARY?

On the basis of these original features of the revolution it should immediately be clear that those who describe the regime in Havana as 'Stalinist' have no understanding of Cuban history; despite strong Soviet influence from 1961 to 1989 the revolution had different roots and characteristics which never disappeared, and the theory and practice of Fidel, Che and the M-26-7 were anything but Stalinist. Almost all observers recognise its deep roots in Cuban popular traditions; in Fidel's words, 'The Revolution is as Cuban as the palm trees' (*Bohemia* 22 March 1959, 75). There is also general recognition of its continuity with earlier popular struggles, beginning with Martí, Maceo and the *mambíses* of the independence wars and continuing with Mella, Guiteras, the 1933 revolution and Chibás, a continuity which was constantly referred to by Fidel and the other leaders. Fidel's personal leadership of the popular resistance against Batista was affirmed at the Moncada and confirmed with his active organisational role from exile in Mexico, the *Granma* expedition and the success of the guerrilla struggle in the Sierra Maestra. Although the M-26-7 was a national organisation with a collective leadership, there was never any doubt that the supreme leader was Fidel and that the strategic vision was Fidel's, and as time went on it became clear that the greatest inspiration for thousands of militants throughout the country was the charisma and political genius of Fidel (only rivalled, for a time, by that of Che Guevara).

This makes it easier to understand why in January 1959, after the revolutionary victory, the explosion of popular enthusiasm did not find expression in any political party, not even – or perhaps especially not – in the PSP. The 26 July Movement had become the national liberation movement of the Cuban people, and it was identified in the popular mind less with a political programme than with the figure of Fidel and with the rest of the *barbudos* like Raúl, Che Guevara and Camilo Cienfuegos. This does not mean that policy decisions could be completely arbitrary (Herbert Matthews, who in general had a remarkably perceptive understanding of Cuba, at one point made the absurd suggestion that Fidel would have embraced any ideology from liberal to Fascist if it seemed to produce results!) (Matthews 1975, 228). The movement did have an ideology (although not a dogmatic formula), summed up in what Kapcia calls *cubanía revolucionaria*; and there were essential popular demands like the agrarian reform, popular education and the purging of *batistianos* from the state apparatus which the leadership had to satisfy to retain the trust of the people. But within these broad parameters the leadership had great freedom of action: the people felt that their deepest desires were interpreted by Fidel and the M-26-7, they wanted and expected decisive action from the leaders, and they regarded party politics and elections as irrelevant or even as a betrayal of the revolution. Democracy – the power of the people – meant the absolute power of the movement which had overthrown Batista's tyranny and which expressed popular hopes and dreams after decades of frustration. These hopes and dreams, the popular will forged in struggle against the tyranny, were now expressed openly in Fidel's speeches which became the voice of the collective subject of the revolution, the Cuban people as protagonist of its own destiny.

The Cuban revolution, then, had the classic features of a left-populist movement: charismatic leadership, massive popular mobilisation, relative ideological fluidity (which does not imply lack of ideology), organisational and tactical flexibility, a radical but non-dogmatic discourse, and a remarkable capacity to bypass political parties and established institutions. Fidel Castro's exceptional ability as popular leader, and the particular characteristics of the M-26-7, facilitated during the armed struggle and even more during the radical transformation of 1959–62 the marginalisation of almost all political parties and institutions and the creation of a direct democracy – a structure of popular power – which gravitated automatically towards Socialism. The PSP was dragged along by the process against its initial wishes and in the end came to play an important but secondary role in the revolution. Everyone – Batista, the old Cuban politicians, the USA, the Catholic Church and the international Left – was surprised by the strength and radicalism of the process. Therefore the description of the revolution as populist does not imply that it was in any way reformist, opportunist or demagogic; quite the contrary, it confirms the words of Ernesto Laclau, that a Socialist populism is not the most backward form of working-class consciousness but the most advanced (Laclau 1977, 174; see the discussion below in Chapter 6).

One of the most important, and most misunderstood, features of the revolutionary situation was Fidel Castro's oratory, his interminable speeches to which foreigners could not relate but which held most Cubans spellbound. Often passionate, sometimes calm and methodical, at times didactic, Fidel's speeches ranged in tone from solemn political pronouncements to intimate dialogue in which each listener might feel as if in a private conversation with the *Comandante-en-Jefe*. Moreover, in his constant travels around the country the leader did in fact converse with thousands of workers and peasants and listened to their concerns – and those who know him well say that one of his greatest virtues is his ability to listen. A fundamental aspect of Fidel's leadership of the struggle against Batista, little understood outside Cuba, was his insistence on the unity of the revolutionary movement and on a policy of alliances with all political forces prepared to agree on a minimum revolutionary platform; and in power as well, contrary to the impression of many outsiders who think that every important decision is taken by Fidel, his role has typically been to mediate and build consensus. Although on certain crucial occasions his analytical vigour and rhetorical brilliance have carried the day, at other times he has been in a minority among the leadership and has accepted the majority opinion (Blanco 1994, 30).

To appreciate the significance of Fidel's speeches (and to a lesser extent those of the other revolutionary leaders) it is necessary to bear in mind that there already existed in Cuba, as in other Latin countries, a tradition of grandiloquent and long-winded oratory. What was new and compelling about Fidel's discourse was, first, his direct and down-to-earth language, and second, his passionate sincerity. Where the self-serving politicians of the old regime had been renowned for their pretentious and bombastic rhetoric and hypocritical promises, here was a leader who spoke directly and frankly to the people in their own language and whose actions corresponded to his words. Although he spoke at enormous length his rhetoric was acceptable to the people because it was so frequently the expression of their own deeply held convictions, and they would listen to him for hours in the heat of the day because he was both giving voice to their desires and didactically explaining the reasons for and the implications of revolutionary policies. A distinguished and perceptive observer of this process was Jean-Paul Sartre, who visited Cuba for a fortnight in March 1960 and declared at the end of his visit:

Fidel Castro is very fond of the phrase 'The Revolution of the majority', and it seems to me that that phrase is absolutely correct. It's clear that at the moment he has a relationship with the majority of the people and it is also clear that in that relationship he expresses and fulfils the will of the people ... At this moment there exists between the rulers and the people – and particularly between Fidel Castro and the people – a relationship which we could describe as one of direct democracy, which consists in explaining to the people the implications in terms of work, effort and sacrifice of the desires expressed by the people ...

This is therefore a Revolution which is creating its own ideology and its own instruments through direct contact with the masses. For all these reasons it is the most original Revolution I have seen ... . (*Revolución* 11 March 1960)

When Fidel spoke there was often a sense of dialogue, of mutual interaction, between him and the people, sometimes expressed in shouts, applause or interjections, and sometimes more instinctive ways; 'The dialogue and the incorporation into [public] discourse of anonymous proposals from the people brought about such a level of interaction as to convert the audience from spectators into participants' (Díaz Castañón 2001, 111). Fidel was in effect the mouthpiece of the Cuban nation.

That this was not merely a matter of ideological agreement is apparent from the accounts of various eye-witnesses who testify to the intensity of the experience. Enrique Oltuski, a leader of the M-26–7 in Las Villas who later held various ministerial positions in the revolutionary government, was in Santa Clara on 6 January 1959 when Fidel passed through on his triumphal march to Havana, and he describes the scene as follows:

... Fidel approached the microphone and a sensation of collective hysteria took hold of the crowd. After several attempts Fidel managed to say a few words. It was then that I saw for the first time the emergence of that strange communion between Fidel and the people. The people applauded him because he expressed their feelings, because he said what they were all thinking ... . (Oltuski 2000, 249)

Oltuski saw the same phenomenon the next day in Cienfuegos: 'Despite having passed many hours without rest, Fidel was transformed when he faced the crowd. Then he seemed to forget his tiredness, and the strange communion I had observed in Santa Clara occurred again ...' (Oltuski 2000, 253–4).

This is the essence of the populist phenomenon, and although it has mystical overtones it is not irrational, not just 'collective hysteria'. As we have seen it is based on the deeds, on the actual achievements of the revolutionary *caudillo*, and on his uncanny ability to synthesise and express popular feelings with remarkable force and accuracy. The over-used term 'vox populi' can truly be applied to Castro at his best.

The legitimacy of the system derives precisely from its profoundly popular and revolutionary character. From the very beginning, without recourse to stereotyped formulae, Fidel insisted on the revolutionary character of the new government: 'The revolution cannot be made in a day, but rest assured that we will carry out the revolution. Rest assured that for the first time the Republic will be completely free and the people will have what they deserve ... ' (*Revolución* 4 January 1959). Less than two months later, and once again in Santiago, he proclaimed: 'Many people have not yet realised the scope of the change which has occurred in our country ... ' (*Revolución* 25 February 1959). The same message was delivered by Raúl Castro in a speech on 13 March in Havana: 'On the First of January 1959 we had done no more than conclude the war of independence; the Revolution of Martí begins now' – and he went on: 'This Revolution has a series of characteristics which differentiate it from all other revolutions. The world beholds in astonishment the transformation which is taking place in our country in economic, political, social, moral, cultural and all other aspects ... ' (*Revolución* 14 March 1959). There was no talk of Socialism, much less of Marxism-Leninism, indeed not even of class struggle; but there was repeated insistence on the radical character of the revolution, on the decisive break with the past and the need for a real transformation of the country. Fidel came back to this theme in a speech on 25 March:

> If it had been a question of a mere change of individuals, of a mere change of command and if we had left everything just as it was before and had not got involved in the task of reform, in an effort to overcome all the injustices of our republic ... [then it would not be a revolution]. There was a Revolution because there were injustices to overcome and because, in Maceo's words: 'The Revolution will continue as long as there remains an injustice which has not been remedied' .... (*La Calle* 1 August 1959)

Another constant feature of the revolutionary discourse was continuity with the historic struggles of the Cuban people, with the traditions of Céspedes, Martí, Maceo, Mella, Guiteras, Chibás and others. The revolution was a rupture with the structures of the past, with vested interests, with corruption and dictatorship, but a continuation and fulfilment of national and popular traditions. This reclaiming of historical memory was a fundamental component of the movement's ideology and a central factor in its acceptance by the people as the legitimate expression of their interests. As already mentioned, Fidel said, 'the Revolution is as Cuban as the palm trees', and therefore it needed no lessons from abroad; and 'The *mambíses* began the war for independence which we concluded on 1 January 1959 ... ' (*Revolución* 25 February 1959). The same process of emancipation was now continuing, and this in itself implied the need for radical change. In February Marcelo Fernández, National Secretary of Organisation of the M-26–7, wrote an article with the title 'Permanent Revolution' insisting that the revolutionary transformation was only just beginning: 'The War of '68 ended with the Pact of Zanjón, that of '98 ended with the Platt Amendment, and the 1933 Revolution led to Welles' Mediation. But this Revolution cannot be shipwrecked with Pacts, Amendments or Mediations ... ' (*Revolución* 16 February 1959). In the same way, when faced with criticisms by vested interests and reactionary attacks, the revolutionary government defended itself by appealing to the legitimacy of its continuity with Martí and the *mambíses*; in June 1959, when the attacks on the agrarian reform intensified, Fidel declared that ' ... what we are doing, you gentlemen who defend powerful interests, what we are doing is to fulfil the declarations and the doctrine of our Apostle, who said that the fatherland belonged to all and was for the good of all ... ' (*Revolución* 8 June 1959).

This insistence on Cuban national and popular traditions was logically connected with a defence of the Latin American character of the revolution, its identification with the struggles of the entire continent and with Bolívar's dream of unity. The victorious insurgents felt instinctively that their triumph was part of a larger movement, that they had a duty to support the struggles of fellow Latin Americans: 'Above all we feel the interests of our Fatherland and of our America, which is also a greater Fatherland', declared Fidel at a press conference in the Hotel Riviera on 22 January 1959, just before leaving for Venezuela on his first trip abroad after the victory (*Revolución* 23 January 1959). In the same press conference he suggested that the Cuban example would be imitated, and spoke out explicitly in favour of the Bolivarian vision: ' ... a dream I have in my heart and which I believe is shared by everyone in Latin America, is one day to see Latin America completely united, that it should be a single force, because we are of the same race, the same language, the same feelings'. This is the concept of race as *criollo* ethnicity, as the common heritage of indigenous, black and European citizens of

*Nuestra América*, and it was a constant reference for all representatives of the movement. In a television interview on 5 March 1959 Armando Hart declared that

at this moment this Revolution is making a contribution to the thought of Latin America; *Nuestra América*, to the South of the Río Grande, is in need of a system of thought for a continent which needs to unite and achieve integration as the Cuban people have done, overcoming any sectarianism. (*Revolución* 6 March 1959)

Similarly – and for obvious reasons – this was a frequent topic of Che Guevara's speeches: '... we are carrying the Revolution forward in the midst of forces that want to destroy it even more because of what it represents for all the Americas, as a special beacon for [our] America at this time ... ' (*Revolución* 2 May 1959). Finally in July 1959, in relation to the aggressive plots being hatched against Cuba in the Dominican Republic, Camilo Cienfuegos declared that

Trujillo's provocative plans won't be successful because the peoples of the Americas are watching the development of the Cuban Revolution, because they know that the historic destiny of all the nations of the Hemisphere depends on the process which Cuba is going through at present. (*Revolución* 10 July 1959)

Indeed, not content with preventing plots against the revolution by neighbouring dictators, many young Cubans wanted to go the other way and planned assaults on the Dominican Republic, Nicaragua or Panama (Díaz Castañón 2001, 119).

But it was not only the Cubans who proclaimed the revolution's continental significance. Right from the start this view was shared by representatives of other Latin countries, and the impact of the revolution on Cuba's sister republics was enormous. The reasons for this are not difficult to understand: it was due, first, to the remarkable guerrilla victory over Batista's regular army, and second, to the example of national independence and anti-imperialism – and this from the very beginning, at least implicitly, well before the radicalisation of the breach with the United States. At the end of February 1959 the then Chilean Senator Salvador Allende visited Cuba and declared that 'The Cuban Revolution does not belong only to you ... we are dealing with the most significant movement ever to have occurred in the Americas ... ' (*Revolución* 28 February 1959). In the same vein Gloria Gaitán, daughter of the great Colombian popular (and populist) leader Jorge Eliécer Gaitán, declared in an interview in April 1959 that 'The Cuban revolutionary movements correspond to the entire wave of insurrections which in Latin America are challenging the past', and that the work of the M-26–7 was 'the beginning of the great liberation of *Nuestra América* ... ' (*Revolución* 24 April 1959).

These sentiments of Latin American solidarity were one of the prevailing themes in the huge mass rally of 26 July 1959 in Havana, the first celebration of the founding event of the movement after the revolutionary victory. Among those present on the podium were Salvador Allende, Gloria Gaitán and Lázaro Cárdenas, the former Mexican President who had been responsible for that country's oil nationalisation and agrarian reform in the 1930s. Raúl Castro saluted the great Mexican statesman thus:

Brothers of the Latin American Continent, General Lázaro Cárdenas, this revolution is not the exclusive property of our people, neither is it limited to our frontiers. We believe that the hour of the second independence for the whole continent, foretold by our apostle [José Martí], is arriving ... . (*La Calle* 28 July 1959)

Cárdenas replied that ' ... the Cuban Revolution has aroused a profound sentiment of solidarity in the whole Continent, because the cause of Revolution is indivisible ... ' (*Revolución* 27 July 1959). It was clear to all, long before the Socialist definition of the revolution, that Cuba represented the most vigorous expression of the Latin American anti-imperialist and unitary movement with its roots in Bolívar and Martí, and that it was entering a new phase which pointed towards a popular and participatory democracy with a profound social content. This orientation became clearer still in the final months of 1959, after the desertions of Díaz Lanz and Hubert Matos and the first bomb attacks from Florida; in the words of Che Guevara speaking in front of the presidential palace on 26 October, 'We are not Guatemala. We are Cuba, which rises up today at the head of the Americas, responding to each blow with a new step forward ... ' (*Revolución* 27 October 1959).

What becomes clear from this analysis of the revolutionary discourse is that it is not necessary to postulate any supposed concealed Communist intent to explain the radicalisation of the Cuban revolution; this radicalisation sprang naturally from the popular character of the movement, from the structural contradiction with imperialism and from the leadership's ideology of nationalism and social justice, an ideology which had such profound roots in Cuban and Latin American history that it found spontaneous expression in the course of the struggle. The great virtue of Fidel was his unrivalled capacity to synthesise and personify that ideology and the corresponding revolutionary will in a populist dynamic of dialogue with the Cuban people. This does not mean that Marxism was irrelevant to the Cuban revolution, but simply that the revolution would arrive at its Socialist goal by other means and with a different ideological inspiration.

This failure to conform to Marxist-Leninist stereotypes was also evident in relation to issues of class and class conflict. The revolutionary discourse made frequent reference to the movement's popular and anti-oligarchic character, but the protagonist referred to was not the proletariat or working class as such, rather it was the people, the popular classes, the humble: in other words, the great majority of the Cuban nation. The enemies of the revolution were the oligarchy and imperialism, the rich and the privileged; but the door was left open even for them, since if they abandoned their privileges they were welcome in the new country that was being built. This was very well formulated by Fidel in the phrase: 'The privileged [classes] will not be executed, but privileges will be ... ' (*Revolución* 15 June 1959). But, he insisted, if the rich thought they could prevent revolutionary measures by bribery and corruption, they were badly mistaken:

They helped the Revolution in order to buy us out. So, as I could see that in that phase [of the armed struggle] everyone helped the Revolution, I ask them to make a sacrifice, to continue making a sacrifice for the Country, not just during the insurrection but in this creative effort, because the Revolution doesn't preach hatred, the Revolution preaches justice ... I know everyone helped, yes, but the Revolution was not made in order to maintain privilege, the Revolution was made to establish justice, the Revolution wasn't made to enrich those who were already rich, but to give to those in need, to give to those who had nothing, to give food to those that work ... . (*Revolución* 12 March 1959)

Similarly, on several occasions Fidel insisted that those who wanted to provoke class confrontation were the counter-revolutionaries; speaking on Lawyers' Day (8 June) to the members of the Havana Bar Association, he declared: 'What do they want? To provoke class war? To incite class hatred when it is our purpose that the revolution should be seen as the work of the whole nation?' – because, he pointed out, here there were more than a thousand lawyers, who were far from being poor or underprivileged, but who supported the revolution as they showed by their applause (*Revolución* 9 June 1959). In the same sense Raúl Castro also insisted that they were not closing the door on anyone, 'And that to those who in minuscule numbers are against the Revolution, we tell them in good faith – because in principle we don't wish evil for anyone – we make a patriotic appeal to them to adapt to the new situation, to adapt to the brilliant process which began on the First of January ... ' (*Revolución* 14 March 1959).

The discourse of the revolution, especially in the first euphoric 18 months in power, was profoundly anti-oligarchic and anti-imperialist, but also generous and open-minded, with a powerful ethical commitment and an emphasis on social justice. It was therefore not a class discourse but a populist one: the protagonist of the revolution was the Cuban people, all of those who worked with the sweat of their brow, but also the intellectuals and even businessmen and industrialists if they were honest and supported the process. As the revolution radicalised and became more egalitarian, the discourse became explicitly Socialist and finally Marxist-Leninist, but the stereotyped formulae of the international Communist movement never became totally dominant in Cuba, and in the post-Soviet world Cuban representatives – Fidel, of course, but not only Fidel – have been able to engage in constructive dialogue with the new anti-globalisation and anti-capitalist movements and the new political and social movements in Latin America. It remains to be seen how Cuba will adapt in the long run to the new world situation, but perhaps the most striking development in Cuban policy is the intimate relationship with, and total support for, Hugo Chávez and the Bolivarian revolution in Venezuela. Despite obvious differences, the two revolutions share the same left-populist roots and the same popular-democratic and anti-imperialist characteristics, and Fidel has clearly recognised that Venezuela is showing the way ahead for the Latin American revolution in the twenty-first century.

## THE ISSUE OF DEMOCRACY

Fidel's extraordinary dialectical relationship with the people is what Sartre described as direct democracy, and it was fundamental to the Cuban process. Liberals have always praised the social achievements of the Cuban revolution but labelled it as undemocratic because of the lack of Western-style elections, but it is necessary to understand that from the beginning the Cubans rejected the liberal-pluralist model as irrelevant, and this attitude was shared by a majority of the population. Early in 1959, as in any country just emerging from dictatorship, the question of elections was raised, and the typical response of the revolutionary leaders was that they would be held in 18 months to two years, when the revolutionary process was consolidated. Pressed repeatedly on the question by Cuban and North American journalists, Fidel responded in a television interview on 25 March:

> Which of us here has said anything against elections? No-one ... However, such is the weariness that people feel, such is their repugnance at the memory of that verbiage, at the memory of those rallies with hypocrites parading from one platform to the next ... We are favourable to elections, but elections that will really respect the people's will, by means of procedures which put an end to political machinations ... . (*Revolución* 26 March 1959)

Similarly in another interview in June – with a large audience – when a journalist quoted the opinion that anyone who spoke against elections was 'Communist, Fascist or Nazi', Fidel replied in a more polemical tone:

> Do you want to have elections right away, tomorrow? Shall we call on the people to vote tomorrow? [The audience shouted 'No!'] Supposedly elections mean consulting the people's will, so you people must be Fascists or Communists because you've shouted against elections. What a poor sense of judgement! Instead of blaming those who are responsible for the people's distrust of elections, those who converted politics into a quest for spoils ... What is really odd is that those who have no popular support talk about elections ... . (*Revolución* 15 June 1959)

Rather than elections, he explained, what was needed was genuine democracy: 'There is democracy in the Government. The Government is at the service of the people, not of political cliques or oligarchies ... We have democracy today, for the first time in our history ... ' – because real democracy, government of the people, he explained, only existed once before in Cuba, and that was with Guiteras in 1933; and that was destroyed by reaction (*Revolución* 15 June 1959).

Indeed, everything suggested that the people did not want elections, at least not at that time and not in the conventional form. An opinion poll conducted by *Bohemia* magazine in June showed that almost 60 per cent were against elections, at least for the next three to four years, whereas 90 per cent were in favour of the revolutionary government and the agrarian reform (*Bohemia* 28 June 1959, 70–3, 96). This poll also revealed the interesting fact that opposition to elections was stronger among workers and peasants, while those who did want elections were proprietors, executives and professionals. The reasons given by those opposed to elections were that they would interrupt the work of the revolution, that they would encourage petty politicking and that they would mislead the people. On the other hand, the same social classes that opposed conventional elections also declared themselves in favour of a different type of elections, of a system (yet to be developed) of revolutionary democracy. This is why they responded so favourably to Fidel's repeated statements in favour of such a system, as when he referred to the agrarian reform:

And by redeeming the peasant, the Revolution is taking the first step towards building a true democracy; a democracy without slaves, a democracy without helots; which is also the strange phenomenon of a non-representative democracy, but one which is yet more pure: a democracy which lives through the direct participation of the people in political problems ... . (*Revolución* 28 July 1959)

This was one of the most sensitive and crucial issues of the revolution, and indeed of any revolution. As Raúl Castro also pointed out, if those who wanted to redirect the process towards 'those false democracies, those democracies of privilege', then true peace would never exist and in another 15 or 20 years at the most, 'as well as still facing all the problems we are fighting against today, another Machado or Batista would arise' (*Revolución* 7 September 1959). In other words, liberal democracy would not resolve the country's major social and economic problems, and this would lead to further political turmoil and eventually another dictatorship.

For some 15 years the revolutionary notion of direct popular democracy functioned in Cuba on an informal basis, and mass organisations like the CDRs, the CTC, the FMC and the UJC (Unión de Jóvenes Comunistas, Union of Young Communists) were the only institutional channels for popular participation. The spontaneous interaction with Fidel and other leaders was genuine and important, but it could not substitute for organised structures where popular concerns could be expressed. It was to overcome this deficiency that the system of 'People's Power' was created in the mid-1970s and given permanent status in the 1976 Constitution. The 'Organs of People's Power' (Órganos de Poder Popular, OPP) are elected governing bodies at municipal, provincial and national level, with delegates elected by universal suffrage and secret ballot. Municipal delegates represent small wards of 1,000 to 1,500 voters and candidates are nominated in public mass meetings; by law at this level there must be between two and eight candidates for every seat. Both the Communist Party and the mass organisations like the CTC and FMC are forbidden by law from intervening in the nomination process, so that people nominate whomever they consider to be best for the job based on local personal reputation. Peter Roman, author of a detailed study of Poder Popular, points to three crucial differences between the Cuban system and that obtaining in the former Soviet Union: that in Cuba municipal delegates must reside in their electoral district; that the municipal elections are competitive by law; and that the Communist Party does not choose the candidates (Roman 2003, 103).

Attendance at nomination meetings averages from 70 to 90 per cent of eligible voters, and most delegates say that when they were first nominated they had no idea they were going to be proposed (Roman 2003, 107). The only campaigning allowed is the distribution of candidates' photographs and biographies. Once elected, municipal delegates are responsible for all local affairs including supervision of schools, hospitals, factories and other productive facilities within the municipality, obviously within the parameters laid down at national level. They serve for two and a half years and may be re-elected, but they also have to report back to their electors in public meetings every six months and may be recalled if there is widespread dissatisfaction with their performance. This is not an idle threat: in 1989, for example, 114 delegates were recalled, and only 45 per cent of delegates were re-elected overall (Cole 1998, 38). I have attended some report-back meetings (*rendición de cuentas*), and some of them at least are vigorous public cross-examinations in which the community asserts its authority in no uncertain terms. Moreover, the six-monthly reporting back is not limited to one public meeting per delegate: the size of each meeting is limited by law to 120 people, so most delegates have to hold between four and ten such meetings depending on the size of their ward.

One of the reasons for the non-re-election of delegates (as distinct from recall) is that the task is extremely demanding. Roman points out that 'The public conceives that their delegates are on call at all hours and for any reason. Many citizens with emergencies or personal problems contact their delegate first' (Roman 2003, 77). Delegates at all levels are non-salaried volunteers and continue to work in their regular jobs in addition to their representative duties, and with the pressure of popular demands and reporting back they are often under considerable stress; in many cases therefore they themselves refuse to serve more than one term. The reason for the insistence on nonpayment of delegates is to prevent the emergence of a professional political class, to ensure that as in Rousseau's ideal or in the Paris Commune, delegates should be just like the working people they are mandated to serve.

It seems clear that there is a close, even intimate relationship between municipal delegates and the electors they serve. In 1990 a survey conducted by *Bohemia* magazine found that 75.2 per cent knew the name of their municipal delegate, and asked whether they trusted their delegate, 59.1 per cent said Yes, 23.3 per cent said Somewhat, and only 17.6 per cent said No (Roman 2003, 78): a level of confidence which compares very favourably with that found in most liberal systems. One aspect of Poder Popular which cannot be emphasised too much is the small size of municipal wards and the sense of direct responsibility of delegates to their constituents, who are after all their immediate neighbours: with only 1,500 or so voters in most cases, the typical ward consists of half a dozen city blocks or a small village in the countryside (August 1999, 256–7). This creates a sense of direct involvement in the political process lacking in most countries, where even local councillors typically represent 10,000 people or more. If Cuban municipal delegates are tied up with what is sometimes disparagingly referred to as 'parish pump' politics, this is where involvement in the political process should logically begin; and if in most countries including Britain turnout in local elections is appallingly low (30 per cent or less), one reason for this is undoubtedly the remoteness of local councillors.

The other reason commonly cited for lack of participation in local elections in 'advanced' Western countries is the sense that local councils lack real power (a situation which in Britain has been accentuated as a matter of deliberate central government policy since Thatcher). In Cuba a similar problem emerged during the worst years of the 'Special Period' when very frequently delegates simply could not resolve concrete problems raised by their constituents because of the extreme scarcity of many goods: if a delegate were asked to improve the street lighting or paving, for example, they could not do it even with the best will in the world because light bulbs, asphalt and cement were not available. According to some reports this did lead to frustration and some loss of confidence in the system, but with improved conditions in recent years this is not such an important problem.

It should also be emphasised that Cuban local delegates do hold significant authority over social and economic affairs going well beyond the 'parish pump'; through the municipal assembly they are responsible for all aspects of local administration. They do not legislate, but they do supervise the running of everything from schools and hospitals to recreational and productive facilities in their municipality: in Cole's words, 'Poder Popular decentralized the management of productive and service enterprises and institutions to the areas or constituencies which they serve' (Cole 1998, 36). Even large factories, although ultimately controlled by the central government, are supervised on a day-to-day basis by commissions of the municipal assemblies, which may report managers to higher authorities for poor performance, sometimes leading to their dismissal.

In addition to the municipal assemblies there is a further instrument of local democracy which was introduced in 1988, the people's councils. These operate on a smaller scale than the municipalities; each municipality is divided into several units, each with its own people's council consisting of the municipal delegates from that district plus representatives of the mass organisations and state enterprises in the district. The president and vice-president of the people's council are elected by its members and must be popular delegates, not appointees of the mass organisations or enterprises. Unlike the municipal assemblies, these councils do not have administrative responsibilities, but they do have extensive powers to investigate and make complaints about corruption, inefficiency and other problems, and have become an increasingly significant instrument for citizens to gain access to higher authorities and resolve important issues:

On the one hand, people's councils became part of the convergence of civil and political societies, by amplifying constituents' frequent and personal contacts with their elected municipal representatives; and strengthening the application of the *mandat impératif*, that is, the responses and responsibilities of municipal delegates regarding citizens' *planteamientos* [complaints]. On the other hand, people's councils have also supported the development of a more autonomous civil society ... (Roman 2003, 234)

The development and popularity of the people's councils has sometimes led to conflicts of authority with the municipal assemblies, but this can probably be taken as a healthy sign of local democratic vigour.

At higher level Popular Power as an expression of the direct will or interests of the people suffers from greater limitations. Under the 1976 Constitution provincial delegates were chosen by the municipal assembly, and national delegates were likewise chosen by provincial assemblies from among their members. This pyramidal structure obviously severely limited popular influence on the process, and in 1992 it was replaced by direct election at all levels. But it is still the case that there is only one candidate for each position at provincial or national level, and the nomination process is less open than at municipal level, so that the election is more like a popular ratification of a preselected list of candidates. The one significant qualification of this is a requirement introduced in 1992 for delegates to receive the votes of at least 50 per cent of the registered electorate in their districts; if turnout is too low, the process has to be repeated, and this can be a mechanism for voters to reject unpopular candidates. National delegates, like local ones, are unpaid, except for those selected as officers of the Assembly or its commissions.

The Council of State, the country's supreme authority, is elected by the National Assembly whose deputies vote in secret ballot on a list drawn up by a candidacy commission which takes into account deputies' proposals but modifies the list to achieve 'balance'. It clearly does make an effort to include figures representative of different areas of national life and to achieve consensus in the Assembly on this, but the process is more one of negotiation within the governing elite than of democratic election. Decisions of the Council of State have to be ratified by the National Assembly, which has supreme legislative authority. However, the National Assembly meets in plenary session only twice a year for a few days, and its votes are always unanimous because of a convention that favours consensus; controversial proposals are usually withdrawn and redrafted. Most of the work is done by specialised commissions of the Assembly, on which about half the delegates serve and which have much longer sessions including public hearings, often meeting in the provinces (Roman 2003, 85–9). The commissions clearly do allow for a significant degree of debate and public input, but this does not alter the fact that debate in the Assembly as such is limited and many delegates feel pressure to conform. This is in part due to the need for national unity in the face of US hostility, but may also reflect the heritage of Soviet influence.

However, popular input into policy is not limited to the formal structures of Poder Popular; the Constitution provides for processes of popular consultation on major issues, and even if formal national consultation processes are not very frequent, they are remarkably extensive and thorough when they occur. The 1976 Constitution was circulated in draft form to the mass organisations and debated extensively in thousands of local branches, and revised in accordance with these discussions before being put to popular referendum. In the summer of 1990 there were some 89,000 workplace meetings in preparation for the Fourth Party Congress of 1991, plus many meetings in neighbourhoods, schools and universities, generating a multitude of comments which served as input for the delegates in considering the constitutional amendments which would be adopted in 1992 (Cole 1998, 37). Also for the first time many delegates to the Party Congress were nominated directly by the rank-and-file, rather than members just being given a prearranged list to vote on; and in the Congress itself, in contrast to the Soviet-style tradition which had prevailed for the previous 20 years, the General Secretary (Fidel) did not pre-empt discussion by giving guidelines for discussion, but limited his opening remarks to a presentation of the country's problems and then opened the floor for debate (Blanco 1994, 30). In 1993–94 a similar process took place, again with over 80,000 'workers' parliaments' in workplaces discussing the proposed economic reforms (legalisation of the dollar and of foreign investment, self-employment, introduction of income tax and so on). Opinions expressed were synthesised and reported to the National Assembly, and the proposed legislation was modified accordingly. As a result of this consultation process the proposed income tax was limited to incomes from self-employment or private property, and was not applied to wages as originally proposed.

Direct popular involvement in economic policy and management is in fact a crucial element of popular democracy and Socialism: Cuban development policy cannot be understood in purely economic terms, divorced from the politics of Socialist participation. Thus the Rectification Campaign was conceived explicitly in these terms, as explained by Fidel himself:

The most serious error of economic policy put in practice between 1975 and 1985 was undoubtedly its reliance upon economic mechanisms to resolve all the problems faced by a new society, ignoring the role assigned to *political* factors in the construction of socialism. (quoted in Cole 1998, 44)

Ken Cole points out that the Soviet-style SDPE planning system was ended for *political* reasons: 'Economic regulation and control was to be a conscious political process of choosing priorities, and not considered to be the "inevitable" economic result of technical specialization ... or the necessary effect of the anarchy of market forces ... ' (Cole 1998, 45). The directly political implications of the Rectification Campaign, relating to popular socialist consciousness and participation, were constantly emphasised both by the Cuban leadership and by the most critical and creative intellectuals. Thus Haroldo Dilla and others at the Centro de Estudios sobre América (Centre for the Study of the Americas) wrote in 1993: 'It would be wrong to see these changes ... as basically issues of economic administration ... the basic challenge of rectification was the problem of participation, the problems of which have been *less significant than the advances in socialist democracy*' (quoted in Cole 1998, 121; Cole's emphasis). This was further borne out by the measures adopted in the 'Special Period'; although the economic crisis obliged the leadership to reverse some of the policy changes of rectification (for instance, allowing private farmers' markets and self-employment, both of which had existed in the early 1980s and had been banned under rectification), in political terms the emphasis of the 1992 reforms was very much on improving participation and democracy.

The question of Communist Party intervention or influence in Cuban elections is a complex one. The legal prohibition of party intervention was designed to ensure separation of party and state, unlike the situation in the Soviet Union. At local level there is much evidence to suggest that delegate nomination is indeed free and independent, but at national level this is much less clear. Approximately 15 per cent of the Cuban adult population belong to the party, and 70 per cent of both municipal and national delegates are party members. The fact that 30 per cent are not does suggest a degree of independence in delegate selection; national delegates have included members of Catholic and Protestant churches, for example, an indication that the process is partially open to non-party interests. Since recruitment to the party is by popular nomination, in which workers in each enterprise propose for party membership those individuals they consider to be most outstanding, it seems only natural that there should be considerable overlap with the choice of OPP delegates; it should also be borne in mind that outstanding non-party delegates are often invited to join the party, another factor boosting the percentage who belong to the party without implying that it controls the electoral process (Roman 2003, 93). At local level it seems clear that there is a large degree of popular autonomy in both elections and municipal assembly discussions, but at national level there is little doubt that basic policy is decided by the Communist Party leadership and ratified by a National Assembly which it in fact controls. It is possible to justify this as necessary to preserve the basic components of popular power and Socialism in the face of US sabotage, but it cannot convincingly be described as fully democratic.

The role of the Communist Party cannot be separated from the issue of multi-party liberalism versus direct, participatory democracy. The concept of a single party expressing national unity and consensus did not begin in Cuba after 1959, and neither was it borrowed from or imposed by the Soviet Union. Rather, it originated in the late nineteenth century with José Martí and the Partido Revolucionario Cubano, the Cuban Revolutionary Party which united many different political clubs in Cuba and among Cuban émigrés in the US and the Caribbean. Party politics – multi-party politics, that is – was seen as factional and divisive. The single-party system, therefore, is not only a defensive reaction to the US blockade, and once again a very interesting perspective is provided by Juan Antonio Blanco:

... rather than advocating an evolution toward a multi-party system, which is a system that emerged in the world some 200 years ago as a response to a specific historical reality, I would prefer to see us create a new kind of democracy using different tools. I think it is entirely possible to achieve a pluralist one-party system if in that system there were strong sectoral organizations – women's organizations, farmers' groups, neighborhood committees, etc. These sectoral organizations exist in Cuba today, but would have to be stronger at the grassroots level to play the role, when necessary, of challenging government policies. (Blanco 1994, 68–9)

One of the key issues here, as argued in my discussion of democracy, is the role and ideology of the single party. If it is to be truly democratic and an instrument of genuine unity and consensus (unity achieved from the grass roots and not imposed), it cannot be a vehicle of a very specific ideology such as Marxism-Leninism; in other words, it cannot be a Communist party as conventionally understood. Undoubtedly it should express a general commitment to popular power, participatory democracy and socialism, but within those broad parameters it should be open to all currents of thought and ideologies. The Cuban Communist Party has become more open in recent years; this can be seen in its practice of recruiting the best workers as recommended by their colleagues, and by the decision to accept religious believers as members. But it is still the case that members are then indoctrinated with Marxism-Leninism, by all accounts on the basis of very traditional, even dogmatic manuals;

and this cannot be the basis for a free and open Socialist democracy. Of course the ideas of Marx, Engels, Lenin and all the revolutionary classics should be studied, but on a critical basis and along with creative and progressive thought of all kinds – as already occurs in Cuba, but not with the blessing of the party.

The Cuban system of popular participation has been the subject of two interesting recent studies, one by the Canadian author Arnold August and the second by Peter Roman of the City University of New York (August 1999; Roman 2003). August's work suffers from a poor writing style and a number of historical errors, but it does have the virtue of being the first attempt to study the Cuban system seriously on the basis of direct observation; while Roman's study is a thorough and closely argued piece of academic research which sets the Cuban system in the context of the philosophy and practice of direct and/or Socialist democracy from Rousseau and Marx onwards, and constitutes an excellent antidote to the superficiality of most liberal accounts of Cuban 'dictatorship'. These two studies demonstrate that grass-roots participatory democracy is a reality in Cuba, and although the system has limitations in terms of freedom of expression and participation in decision-making at national level (to which US policy has powerfully contributed), it can in no way be dismissed as merely authoritarian. The crucial error of liberals has always been to judge Cuba in terms of formal political institutions, without understanding that Socialist democracy is about popular participation and decision-making in all spheres of the economy and society: municipal delegates of Popular Power appointing the managers and supervising the operations of local facilities from schools to factories or health clinics, trade unionists intervening in the management and planning of their enterprises, mini-brigades building houses for themselves and their communities, or people in local neighbourhoods organising their own *organopónico* allotments. It is this, coupled with the reality of social justice, which gives the Cuban system legitimacy with or without Fidel, and which makes it relevant today in the quest for an alternative to capitalist globalisation. The Cuban revolution is not over and it too will continue to change, but contrary to the prevailing opinion, that change does not have to be in the direction of liberal pluralism and a 'market economy'; rather it may well be towards a deepening of participatory democracy and socialism.

# 5
# Hugo Chávez and the Bolivarian Revolution in Venezuela

Before the 1990s Venezuela was regarded as a 'model democracy' in Latin America, and as a most unlikely place for a radical social revolution. Certainly from the 1960s to the mid-1980s it appeared to meet all the conventional requirements of a liberal-pluralist system, with regular multi-party elections, freedom of speech and organisation, two dominant parties alternating in office, a rudimentary welfare state and a relatively stable economy. There might be corruption and gross inequality, but by comparison with most of its Latin American neighbours it seemed to offer a shining example of liberal success, and social scientists debated 'Venezuelan exceptionalism', the possible causes of the country's freedom from the military dictatorships and civil wars which plagued other countries in the region. Yet in 1992 there were two unsuccessful coups, or to be more accurate, military-civilian uprisings, and in December 1998 the leader of one of them, Lt-Col. Hugo Chávez Frías, was elected President with a large majority. Both the 1992 uprisings and Chávez' election victory were cause for anguished hand-wringing by establishment observers in Venezuela and internationally, who lamented this 'atavistic regression to militarism and populism' in what they had hitherto viewed as a 'consolidated democracy'; but for the mass of poor and marginalised Venezuelans Chávez' arrival represented the hope that social justice and true democracy might finally be theirs. Over the next seven years (and the process is still continuing) Chávez' 'Bolivarian Revolution' would turn the country's politics on its head and would create the most profound social transformation in Latin America since the early years of the Sandinista revolution in Nicaragua, 20 years before. The fact that such a revolution should have occurred not in a despotic dictatorship like Batista's Cuba or Somoza's Nicaragua but in a liberal 'democracy' makes it all the more interesting. It is very instructive to examine just how and why this transformation came about, and why in my view Venezuela now represents the greatest hope for progressive movements throughout the world.

## CAUSES OF THE VENEZUELAN CRISIS

Before Chávez Venezuela was little known internationally except for one thing: oil. The fifth-largest petroleum producer in the world and the third-largest exporter to the US, it exhibited many of the typical features of oil states: corruption, easy money for the elite, gross inequality, cultural Americanisation and an unbalanced economy in which almost any productive activity not closely linked to petroleum was unviable.

But to understand Venezuela it is necessary to go back briefly to the early nineteenth century, when as a peripheral outpost of the Spanish Empire it suddenly acquired remarkable prominence as the birthplace of the most important colonial liberation movement in South America. Motivated by resentment against Spanish taxation, commercial restrictions and discriminatory laws, but also inspired by Enlightenment ideals, a section of the creole elite leapt at the opportunity presented by Napoleon's occupation of the Iberian peninsula to seize power from the Spanish Captain-General in April 1810 and then to declare full independence in 1811. The creole movement, led first by the Anglophile intellectual Francisco de Miranda and then by a truly extraordinary visionary and man of action, Simón Bolívar, suffered through successive triumphs and defeats in a bloody war lasting over a decade, but in the process it became radicalised and incorporated the despised 'lower castes' – slaves, free blacks and *pardos* of mixed race – and carried the struggle to neighbouring provinces of the Spanish Empire which would later become independent as the countries of Colombia, Ecuador, Peru and Bolivia. Bolívar, whose ideal was Spanish-American unity and who tried to liberate the slaves, was defeated by the narrow interests of local landed elites, the Catholic Church and the manipulation of the great powers (above all Britain, France and the US); betrayed and embittered, he died in 1830 on the point of setting sail for European exile. But his name and his ideals lived on throughout Latin America, and above all in his native Venezuela where it is no accident that Chávez decided to call his revolutionary organisation the 'Bolivarian Movement' and the new post-1999 political order the 'Bolivarian Republic of Venezuela'.

The year 1830 witnessed not only the death of the Liberator but also the final collapse of the union of at least three of the new republics (Colombia, Venezuela and Ecuador). For the rest of the nineteenth century and well into the twentieth, Venezuela was dominated by military *caudillos*, strongmen from the landed elite who governed by a combination of force, fraud and demagogy while paying lip-service to liberalism. With a small population, the country had a backward agrarian economy dominated by production of plantation crops (cacao and coffee) in the settled coastal region and cattle-raising in the vast *llanos* (plains) of the interior. This only began to change with the discovery of oil early in the twentieth century and its large-scale exploitation which got going after 1922 when the dictator Juan Vicente Gómez passed a petroleum code on terms acceptable to the international companies.

The oil boom transformed the country beyond recognition, producing a new commercial elite, a middle class and an urban working class in the oilfields around Maracaibo and the coastal cities in general, and a dependency of both the state and the economy on petroleum rent. From the late 1940s onwards it attracted large-scale European immigration, mainly from Italy, Portugal and Spain, which further strengthened the urban middle class. It was these changes which underlay the first, student-led protests for democracy in 1928 and the broader protests in 1935 on the death of Gómez. Military rule continued under Gómez' two successors, Generals Eleazar López Contreras (1936–41) and Isaías Medina Angarita (1941–45), but both were reformist-minded and Medina Angarita in particular was an outstanding progressive leader, legalising political parties including the Communists, introducing an income tax and a more nationalist petroleum law which gave the state a 50 per cent share in profits, and preparing the way for democracy. But as the issue of the succession to Medina Angarita became complicated by the death of his preferred (and generally popular) candidate, the reformist opposition party Acción Democrática (AD) made common cause with dissident military officers to seize power in October 1945 (Ewell 1984, 61–95; Buxton 2001, 9–14). In Venezuela the concept of the civilian-military alliance did not originate with Hugo Chávez.

What followed in the *Trienio* (three-year period) of 1945–48 is conventionally seen as the foundation of Venezuelan democracy, interrupted by a coup in November 1948 leading to more than nine years of military dictatorship. AD was subsequently criticised for being sectarian and monopolising power, and for siding with the US in the Cold War. Certainly the party capitalised on its popularity to consolidate control of unions and peasant leagues at the expense of the Communists (the Partido Comunista Venezolano, PCV) and to ensure partisan control of state agencies like the Social Security Institute, the

Central Bank, the public airline and so on, and its Anti-Communism made it a favourite of Washington. However, it cannot be denied that it held basically free elections for a Constituent Assembly and then for the presidency, Congress and local governments, and AD leaders Rómulo Betancourt (provisional President 1945–47) and Rómulo Gallegos (elected President 1947–48) were extremely popular. AD also implemented an extensive reformist programme including a measure of agrarian reform, promotion of public health and education and social security. The PCV was outmanoeuvred and the other parties, COPEI (Christian Democrat) and URD (radical nationalist) had only limited appeal. The reasons for AD's overthrow were partly its sectarianism and clientelism, but also conservative resistance to its programme from the landlords and the Catholic Church.

The military faction which took over in 1948 was initially led by a relatively progressive General, Carlos Delgado Chalbaud, who was murdered in 1950; from then onwards power was effectively in the hands of General Marcos Pérez Jiménez, who repressed political parties and unions and imposed press censorship. Pérez Jiménez was a nationalist and did promote national industry and infrastructure and maintained welfare measures, which is why he would later be favourably remembered by some sectors of the popular classes in comparison with the corrupt 'democrats' who came later (Derham 2002); but it cannot be denied that his rule was also repressive and corrupt. By 1957 discontent with Pérez Jiménez was widespread and led to the formation of a clandestine Junta Patriótica including AD, COPEI, URD and the PCV, with support from a faction of the military; and a joint military-civilian uprising culminated in popular victory on 23 January 1958.

The revolution of 23 January was unquestionably a popular democratic triumph, and in the following months there was something approaching a revolutionary atmosphere. But on 31 October 1958 three of the major parties, AD, COPEI and URD, formalised an agreement, the Pact of Punto Fijo, to share power and patronage and ensure 'stability', pointedly excluding the fourth party, the PCV. This pact, which gave its name to what came to be known as *puntofijismo*, symbolised the neutralisation of the popular revolutionary impulse and would vitiate the new democracy during its 40-year existence; the closed patronage system led to corruption and the exclusion of the Left caused discontent and conflict. Although the victor of the December 1958 elections, Rómulo Betancourt of AD, fulfilled the Pact by forming a government of national unity with representatives of

COPEI and URD, the exclusive definition of 'national unity' led to unrest. AD was less progressive than it had been in the *Trienio* and Betancourt in particular had come under strong US influence during his years in exile under Pérez Jiménez; in his inaugural address on 13 February 1959 he declared that 'the philosophy of Communism is not compatible with the development of Venezuela' (Gott 1973, 159–60, 165).

Despite the appearance of a democratic mandate and the adoption of popular reforms, the governments of the 1960s repressed popular protests and left-wing dissidence with a heavy hand: already in August 1959 workers' and students' demonstrations were fired on by police, causing several deaths (Gott 1973, 166–7) Such actions provoked serious discontent within AD itself, and between March and July 1960 virtually the entire youth wing withdrew from AD and formed a new party, the Movimiento de la Izquierda Revolucionaria (MIR, Movement of the Revolutionary Left). As protests and repression continued, URD left the government and *puntofijismo* became, as it would remain almost to the end, a two-party system monopolised by AD and COPEI. Betancourt blamed both the MIR and the Communists for the unrest, suspending constitutional guarantees and driving the PCV underground. By late 1961 both the MIR and the PCV were preparing to launch a guerrilla insurgency, and in April 1962 the first rebel detachments went into action (Buxton 2001, 19). Then in May and June there were two armed revolts by naval units at Carúpano and Puerto Cabello, both inspired by sympathy with left-wing ideas, and they were crushed with heavy loss of life (Gott 1973, 187–91).

Although ill-prepared and clearly doomed to failure, these military revolts were of great significance as an indication of the extent of patriotic and socially progressive sentiments among the armed forces, and they are also important for understanding the roots of Chávez' Bolivarian Movement. The Carúpano naval base 250 miles east of Caracas was seized on 4 May 1962 by 450 marines led by Captain Jesús Teodoro Molina; their manifesto denounced 'the excesses of minority groups who are directly benefitting from the heroic efforts of the democratic sectors and the armed forces on the glorious 23 of January' and condemned Betancourt and his government for corruption and repression and for 'attempting to re-open the gap between the people and the armed forces which was a characteristic of former régimes'. The second revolt at the main naval base of Puerto Cabello (west of Caracas) on 2–3 June was more serious and was only put down after heavy fighting, with unofficial estimates of several hundred dead; a number of the defeated rebels would subsequently join the guerrillas. One of them, Captain Elías Manuit Camero, justified his decision as follows in a letter to his comrades: 'It was the time to answer the call which our Liberators have been making to us for so long from beyond the grave. The glorious liberating army was created to defend national sovereignty and to secure the happiness of all its children' (quoted in Gott 1973, 192–3). The appeal to the memory of the liberators, the idea of unity between the people and the armed forces, the notion that the military have a social mission: these would be crucial elements in the ideology of Chávez' movement 30 years later.

Betancourt's hard-line response to the uprisings, banning both the PCV and the MIR, only accelerated the politicisation of the military rebels and the inclination of the leftist parties to take up arms. In February 1963 numerous previously uncoordinated guerrilla fronts came together to form the Fuerzas Armadas de Liberación Nacional (FALN, Armed Forces of National Liberation), with a clandestine political arm, the Frente de Liberación Nacional (FLN, National Liberation Front). The National Commander of the FALN was Captain Manuel Ponte Rodríguez, one of the leaders of the Puerto Cabello uprising, and its manifesto was a broad nationalist, democratic and anti-imperialist document which proclaimed its objectives to be 'To enforce respect for national sovereignty and independence, the freedom and democratic life of the Venezuelan people ... To set up a revolutionary, nationalist and democratic government'; in other words a very progressive platform (Gott 1973, 197–8).

In 1962–3 there was bold and sometimes spectacular guerrilla action in both rural and urban areas. Oil pipelines and other installations of US petroleum companies were blown up, the Sears Roebuck warehouse in Caracas was set on fire and the US military mission was also burnt. A US diplomat and an Argentinian football star were kidnapped and then released. But more seriously, urban combat units attacked the military in popular neighbourhoods of Caracas, sometimes occupying entire areas until driven out by massive and indiscriminate military reprisals (Gott 1973, 206–8; Hellinger 1991, 110–11). In September 1963 the FALN attempted to take over a suburban train, killing five members of the National Guard, and then in November–December they attempted to boycott and sabotage the presidential elections for the succession to Betancourt. But these tactics did not work: popular support was alienated and the elections produced over 90 per cent participation with a victory for the AD candidate Raúl Leoni, demonstrating that liberal reforms and political pluralism (even with the exclusion of the Left) had given the Punto Fijo system legitimacy with a majority of the population (Gott 1973, 209–10; Hellinger 1991, 111).

Although the Communist Party dominated the FLN, from the beginning there were tensions between the urban political leadership and the commanders of the most active rural guerrilla fronts such as Douglas Bravo of the José Manuel Chirinos Front in Falcón State. The PCV leadership and a section of the MIR responded to the failures of 1963 by beginning to question the viability of armed struggle. Already in January 1964 the Secretary-General of MIR, Domingo Alberto Rangel, declared that conditions in Venezuela were not favourable to armed struggle. In May the Communist Party assumed a more cautious position, saying that peaceful methods could be adopted if there were a complete amnesty, legalisation of banned political parties and reintegration into the armed forces of rebel officers. Within three years the Communist position would evolve into one of complete rejection of armed struggle.

But many of the guerrilla commanders took a very different view, in particular Douglas Bravo and Fabricio Ojeda, who both wrote letters to the Central Committee of the PCV in late 1964 and 1965 making the case for continued guerrilla struggle. Their arguments were rejected and in December 1965 they broke away by holding a conference of the commanders of all the insurgent fronts, where they reorganised the FALN/FLN leadership: Douglas Bravo became first *comandante* of the FALN and Fabricio Ojeda President of the FLN, excluding non-combatants from the executive positions. These decisions were rejected by the urban political leadership of both the PCV and the MIR, several of whom had just (March 1966) been released from gaol under Leoni's amnesty programme (Gott 1973, 223–34). The polemic extended to relations with revolutionary Cuba where Fidel Castro publicly defended the positions of Bravo and Ojeda, and became emblematic of the tensions within the entire Latin American Communist movement on the issue of peaceful vs armed struggle. But on 17 June 1966 Fabricio Ojeda was captured by Military Intelligence in La Guaira, the port of Caracas, and four days later he was found hanged in his cell (according to the official version; almost certainly he was murdered). Ojeda, previously of the URD and former head of the Patriotic Junta which had overthrown Pérez Jiménez, 'was one of the few Venezuelans capable of creating a united revolutionary movement' (Gott 1973, 238), and his death was a major blow to the insurgency.

Armed struggle was probably doomed to failure in Venezuela anyway, and its failure had disastrous consequences for the Left which was politically marginalised for years to come. The PCV, which over the period 1959–62 was on the way to becoming a mass party, never again achieved more than about 1 per cent of the vote in elections. But as we have seen the decision to take up arms was in part provoked by the repressive anti-Communism of AD, backed by COPEI. The other element in the situation was of course the Cuban revolution, which rapidly outflanked the Venezuelan *puntofijista* experience on the Left and demonstrated that popular social revolution of the most profound kind was indeed possible in Latin America, even under the nose of the United States. The Venezuelan guerrillas thus represented only one of many attempts throughout the region to imitate the Cuban process, only to discover that (with a few exceptions) conditions in their own countries were not favourable to such an approach. But what did emerge from the Venezuelan attempt at armed insurrection was the existence within the country's military of a significant revolutionary tendency which did not disappear with the abandonment of guerrilla warfare in the 1970s.

The aftermath of the decision to abandon armed struggle soon produced a schism from the PCV. In December 1970 a group led by two of its most prominent leaders, Teodoro Petkoff and Pompeyo Márquez, left to form the Movimiento al Socialismo (MAS, Movement to Socialism) which argued for electoral participation, concentration on urban areas, diversity of forms of struggle and tactical flexibility; they also broke publicly with the Soviet Union. It should be pointed out though that, contrary to most subsequent academic accounts, MAS reaffirmed 'The basic correctness of the non-peaceful road for the Venezuelan revolution, in spite of its recent failure' (quoted in Gott 1973, 264–5); although in practice MAS adopted a completely peaceful and parliamentary strategy, soon becoming the main electoral expression of the Left, in the climate of the early 1970s it was not prepared to issue a blanket condemnation of armed struggle.

Almost immediately after the foundation of MAS it in turn suffered a split, with a tendency led by Alfredo Maneiro breaking away in 1971 to form Venezuela 83 (named in anticipation of the bicentenary of Bolívar's birth) which would be the forerunner of La Causa R (LCR, the Radical Cause). Where MAS made an essentially programmatic critique of the PCV while maintaining a similar centralised party structure, Maneiro and his group argued for a radically different approach to revolutionary politics, defending grass-roots democracy and bottom-up organising based on the autonomy of working-class and popular communities. LCR would develop into an important force both socially and electorally in the late 1980s and 1990s and would be a significant influence on Hugo Chávez and the Bolivarian Movement.

In the meantime the legitimacy of the Punto Fijo system seemed to be dramatically reaffirmed. COPEI won the presidency for the first time in the December 1968 elections, confirming its status as the second party of the system, and its candidate Rafael Caldera gained prestige by continuing a centrist policy of reform and amnesty, not very different from that of AD. For the next decade the continuation of the oil boom created a euphoric atmosphere of easy money among the elite and the growing middle class, with continued European immigration and the spread of a North American consumer culture. It is said that in this period 'Saudi Venezuela' became the largest importer of Scotch whisky in the world, and academics who should have known better fostered the myth of 'Venezuelan exceptionalism', the notion that the country was exceptional in Latin America because of its economic development and liberal politics and was on the point of attaining First-World status. The presidency of Carlos Andrés Pérez (AD, 1974–79) represented the peak of the boom, and it was also the peak of AD reformism, with expanded social programmes, the nationalisation of iron and steel (1975) and oil (1976) and a massive state-sponsored industrialisation plan. As a result Pérez, often known by his initials as CAP, gained a popular reputation which enabled him to return and win the presidency again ten years later, but in very different circumstances which would lead to his downfall. In any case his first presidency was marred by a massive increase in corruption, and within three years of his leaving office the economic bubble burst and Venezuela entered an era of prolonged crisis which would lead to the collapse of *puntofijista* liberalism and the rise of Chávez.

It was the second COPEI President, Luis Herrera Campins, who had to face the music when Venezuela's credit ran out in 1983 with the collapse of the international oil price and the arrival of the Latin American debt crisis. The origins of the crisis were in part structural and in part a reflection of the amazing short-sightedness of the Venezuelan bourgeoisie. The ambitious investments of CAP's presidency had been financed by international credit and the phenomenal oil revenue had been squandered on consumption and corruption, so that Venezuela was no more able to ride out the crisis than its Latin neighbours. The country also faced the classic bottlenecks of import-substitution industrialisation, with massive expansion of new industries requiring large imports of capital goods and failing to increase exports. As the balance of payments began to deteriorate the government made the fatal mistake of contracting large short-term loans to finance it. When the oil price fell in 1982 investment collapsed, inflation rose and the wealthy of Caracas and Maracaibo transferred their money to US banks and Miami real estate. On 'Black Friday' (28 February 1983) the country's currency, the Bolívar – hitherto rock-solid at four to the dollar – was devalued, and soon the government was forced to accept IMF deflationary packages and austerity measures which began to undermine the social consensus of the previous two decades. From this point onwards the economic and social situation deteriorated steadily, and the new President, Jaime Lusinchi of AD (1984–89) could do no more than preside over the decline. Devaluation produced a vicious circle in which production fell, inflation and unemployment rose; Venezuela had virtually no competitive exports except for oil and other minerals for which the market was stagnant. From 1981 to 1989 GDP fell by 3.8 per cent (almost 25 per cent in per capita terms), and in 1989 it fell by more than 8 per cent; inflation reached 81 per cent and unemployment and underemployment were estimated at 50 per cent (Hellinger 1991, 127). Poverty steadily increased among the marginalised masses of the *cerros*, the hillside shanties of Caracas and other cities, and the middle class found its comfortable lifestyle more and more under threat. The only alternative policy would have involved increased taxation of the oligarchy and the transfer of resources to the poor majority, but this was ruled out by the close ties of both AD and COPEI to the oligarchy and by an international climate increasingly dominated by monetarism and neo-liberalism.

It was in this critical situation that CAP returned to the fray in the 1988 election campaign with populist promises to oppose the IMF and to implement reforms to protect popular living standards. Evoking memories of the boom years of his first presidency, CAP easily won the election, but within a fortnight of his inauguration in February 1989 he did a complete volte-face and introduced precisely the kind of IMF deflationary package he had sworn to oppose. The result was an explosion of popular rage which came to be known as the *caracazo* or *sacudón*, in which on 27–28 February tens of thousands of the urban poor descended from the *cerros* in spontaneous riots and looting of supermarkets and stores. The immediate cause of the riots was the rise in bus fares caused by CAP's decision to increase the price of petrol, and the protests began with students hijacking buses and setting up barricades. Workers and the poor soon joined in, and as the unrest spread CAP ordered the military to suppress the disorder by any means necessary. This in effect gave the 'forces of order' carte blanche to use indiscriminate force, and for several days the troops moved in with automatic weapons and machine guns, slaughtering looters and bystanders alike. The unequal contest continued for a week, until 5 March, and the government subsequently recognised a death toll of 276, although some sources estimate figures running into the thousands (Coronil and Skurski 2004, 100). Whatever the number, the impact was catastrophic, and from this point on CAP was totally discredited; indeed the discredit threatened the entire bipartisan political elite of *puntofijismo*, since both main parties were seen as out-of-touch and indifferent to the suffering of the majority. CAP had succeeded in turning a social and economic crisis into a crisis of regime.

It is important to understand that the roots of the problem long preceded the economic downturn. The Venezuelan welfare state was always limited in scope: even in the boom days of the 1960s and '70s, visitors to Caracas would comment on the squalor of the *cerros* juxtaposed to the prosperity of the modern city. The 1960s agrarian reform was also a limited measure, more a reformist response to the Cuban revolution than a serious attempt to end latifundism. Certainly the oil boom masked the underlying problem by providing a limited 'trickle-down' effect, but most of the worthwhile jobs created went to the European immigrants rather than the rural-urban migrants. The poor, especially the blacks, natives and those of mixed race, never ceased to feel like second-class citizens, and with the crisis of the 1980s their exclusion was dramatically intensified.

It was in this situation that Hugo Chávez and the Bolivarian Revolutionary Movement appeared on the scene, with the abortive uprising of 4 February 1992. Chávez' brief televised surrender speech, with the crucial phrase that the rebels' aims had not been achieved 'for now' (implying that they intended to continue the struggle), accounted for his instant popularity. But from then onwards he and many of his comrades were in gaol, and a second military-civilian uprising on 27 November 1992 also failed (its aims and characteristics were in any case less clear than those of the February revolt). Despite their failure, these revolts shook the existing liberal regime to its foundations. The situation of *puntofijismo* was now the chronicle of a death foretold; at best it now had one last chance to salvage itself and avert revolution through genuine and far-reaching reform.

Six months later the political establishment showed some understanding of this when Congress impeached CAP for corruption (May 1993); the corruption charges, although undoubtedly justified, were really a pretext to get rid of a highly unpopular president. But this was not enough to appease popular discontent, and the December 1993 elections revealed the true extent of the political crisis. In a four-way race the presidential vote was split fairly evenly between Claudio Fermín (AD) with 23.6 per cent, Oswaldo Álvarez Paz (COPEI) with 22.7 per cent, Andrés Velázquez of La Causa R (LCR) with 22 per cent and the victor Rafael Caldera with 30 per cent (Gott 2000, 128). It was generally understood that Caldera only won because in a speech in Congress in February 1992 he expressed understanding of Chávez' motives in launching the uprising, and in the interim he had left COPEI and ran as an independent for a new coalition known as Convergencia. Equally significant was the good showing of Andrés Velázquez; in the previous (1988) election he had obtained only 0.37 per cent (Sanoja Hernández 1998, 136), yet now he was virtually level with the AD and COPEI candidates (and it was widely believed that he had really won the election and had been deprived by fraud). Similarly in the congressional elections LCR, which in 1988 had won only three deputies and no senators, in 1993 obtained 40 deputies and nine senators (Buxton 2001, 132); and in 1994 it won several important municipal elections including the mayoralty of Caracas. This spectacular rise of what was essentially an anti-system party, together with a dramatic increase in abstention from 3.4 per cent in 1973 to 18.1 per cent in 1988 and 39.8 per cent in 1993 (Buxton 2001, 59), was the clearest indication possible that the two-party *puntofijista* consensus was dead and that the people wanted fundamental change. Abstention was an indication of popular disillusionment with the political system and also (although this is impossible to quantify) a response to Chávez, who was calling for abstention from his confinement in Yare prison.

Rafael Caldera's victory was probably also a reflection of his election platform which was anti-neo-liberal and reformist, and unlike CAP in 1989, he did make some attempt to implement it during his first year in office. A severe financial crisis led him to nationalise the banks in 1994, but as the economic situation deteriorated further Caldera abandoned any attempt at a heterodox solution and signed up for an IMF stand-by loan in 1996 (Buxton 2001, 105). The government's new stabilisation plan, cosmetically labelled 'Agenda Venezuela', was another nail in the coffin of the *puntofijista* system. Significantly, the minister in charge of implementing this neo-liberal plan was none other than Teodoro Petkoff, the former guerrilla, ex-Communist and leader of the MAS; his participation was symptomatic of the failure of the traditional Left which had now become identified with the system and would become discredited with it.

Caldera did keep one important promise, granting an amnesty for Chávez and his comrades, who were released from gaol in March 1994. With this Caldera was in effect legitimising a revolutionary movement, and although Chávez resigned from the military and proclaimed his adherence to peaceful methods, the implication for many was that the Bolivarian Movement's radical anti-system alternative was gaining in credibility. It was later in 1994 that Chávez visited Cuba for the first time and met Fidel Castro, expressing his admiration for the Cuban revolution while insisting that Venezuela would have to chart its own course. Chávez' initial abstentionist stand in relation to elections only seems to have increased his prestige among the poor and marginalised whose faith in liberal electoral politics was now close to zero. The failure of LCR, which from 1994 onwards allowed itself to be drawn into parliamentary horse-trading with MAS and COPEI, was crucial in opening the way for the rise of Chávez and the Bolivarian Movement; LCR's success had been based precisely on its radically anti-system programme and practice, its roots in grass-roots community organisation and autonomy, and by abandoning this it lost the allegiance of its core constituency (Buxton 2001, 173–7).

The defining issue in the search for a real popular alternative was not electoral participation as such; if armed insurrection was ruled out, with Chávez and virtually all serious political actors committed to peaceful methods, then elections had to be part of the process. But it was LCR's abandonment of its accountability sessions in local communities and its compromising acceptance of traditional elite power-broking arrangements which were seen by the popular classes as betrayal, leaving the Bolivarian Movement as the only credible alternative. The next four years would see the movement recruit and organise throughout the country and then decide to create a mass political party, the Movimiento Quinta República (MVR, Fifth Republic Movement) as an electoral vehicle to contest the 1998 presidential and congressional elections, with Hugo Chávez as presidential candidate; and despite increasingly desperate manoeuvres by the political establishment, in December 1998 the former military rebel won a historic electoral victory which put an end to 40 years of *puntofijista* liberalism and inaugurated the era of the 'Bolivarian Revolution'.

## THE ORIGINS AND DEVELOPMENT OF *CHAVISMO*

Hugo Chávez was born on 28 July 1954 in a provincial lower-middle-class family (his parents were both teachers) in Barinas State, in the tropical plains of the interior. He entered the military as a path to social and professional advancement, being a keen baseball player and seeing the opportunity for further training in the army. But as a cadet he already identified with the poor and oppressed and showed an interest in progressive ideas; entering the Military Academy at the age of 17 in 1970, he benefitted from the Andrés Bello Plan under which for the first time future officers received university courses in social sciences – some of them from Marxist or left-wing lecturers – rather than attending the US-controlled School of the Americas (Harnecker 2002, 19–20). As a student at the Military Academy he also came into contact with a son of Omar Torrijos, the nationalist military President of Panama, and then in 1974 he was sent to Peru to attend the celebrations for the 160th anniversary of the Battle of Ayacucho which ended the Spanish presence in South America. Peru at that time was also governed by a nationalist and progressive military government under General Juan Velasco Alvarado, whom Chávez was lucky enough to meet in person. He recounts how Velasco Alvarado gave him a booklet of speeches, which he kept with him until his arrest following the uprising of 4 February 1992, when it was taken from him (Gott 2000, 37–8; Harnecker 2002, 23–5).

It was with such influences that the young Chávez graduated as a sub-lieutenant in 1975 and within a year was sent to combat a small new guerrilla revolt in eastern Venezuela. Although he saw little action he began to question the repressive role of the military and to sympathise with the guerrillas, even while repudiating their methods (Gott 2000, 38; Harnecker 2002, 26–7). Moreover Chávez was already in contact with the civilian Left; his elder brother Adán was in the MIR in the early 1970s, and soon afterwards joined the Partido de la Revolución Venezolana (Ruptura), PRV (R) or Party of the Venezuelan Revolution (Rupture) which had emerged from the FALN and was led by Douglas Bravo (Elizalde and Báez 2004, 38). At first

Hugo Chávez was unaware of this because his brother was studying in Mérida at the time and they had little contact, but then in the late 1970s they were closer and he thus met Bravo. In the meantime in his home town of Barinas Hugo Chávez knew people who were in La Causa R, and through them he met its founder and theorist Alfredo Maneiro. This was in 1978, and although the two never met again it seems that he was profoundly influenced by Maneiro's ideas; in Chávez' own words:

My meeting with Maneiro and, let's be honest, my certainty that Douglas Bravo's approach was not the solution, led me to get closer to La Causa R, above all because of its work with the popular movement, which was vital for the civil-military vision of the struggle which was taking shape in my mind. At that time I was very clear about the idea of mass work, and that did not exist in Douglas' group; on the other hand in La Causa R I could smell the presence of the masses. (quoted in Harnecker 2002, 29)

Another difference with Douglas Bravo was that the ex-guerrilla leader wanted revolutionary military activists like Chávez to be the armed wing of a civilian political movement and to be controlled by it, something which Chávez could not accept. It seems that as long ago as this Chávez had clear in his mind the basic strategic concept which was to guide his revolutionary action throughout: that of a civil-military vanguard closely linked to the people but independent of political parties.

Another characteristic of Hugo Chávez which was apparent from early in his career was his willingness to take a public stand in defence of his ideas. In 1977 as a sub-lieutenant addressing troops in Barinas at a routine ceremony, he drew their attention to an inscription on the barracks wall which said 'Examples are worth more than words,' and urged them not to let things go on with 'empty words' as was normal in Venezuela, but to 'build the Army of the future, worthy of the free people of the future' (Zago 1998, 60). Chávez was also directly influenced by the long-standing democratic tendencies in the Venezuelan military: he relates how on New Year's Day 1981 he went to see a retired Colonel, Hugo Trejo, who had led an uprising in 1958 and who told him about 'the national project, about Bolívar, and how the Adecos [members of AD] betrayed democracy'; Trejo gave him a copy of his group's political programme, 'The Venezuelan Integral Nationalist Movement', and told the young Chávez not to let himself be corrupted (Elizalde and Báez 2004, 328–9).

It was with such ideas in mind that on 17 December 1982 (by which time he had the rank of captain) Chávez and three other captains, Jesús Urdaneta Hernández, Felipe Acosta Carles and Raúl Baduel, got together symbolically at the Samán de Guere (a tree outside Maracay where Simón Bolívar had sworn to liberate Spanish America) to found the Ejército Bolivariano 200 (EB-200, Bolivarian Army-200) whose name was a reference to the bicentenary of Bolívar's birth the following year (Harnecker 2002, 29–30). The term 'revolutionary' was intended to be part of the name but was excluded for the time being because of the reservations of some of their fellow-officers; a few years later and after intense discussions it was added, so that the organisation became the EBR-200 (Blanco Muñoz 1998, 58–9). Finally, after the *caracazo* uprising and as the organisation came to incorporate more civilians, it changed its name from 'Army' to 'Movement' to reflect this, becoming the Movimiento Bolivariano Revolucionario-200 (MBR-200, Bolivarian Revolutionary Movement-200).

The ideology of Chávez' movement derived explicitly from Venezuelan and Latin American nationalist and revolutionary tradition. From the beginning Chávez talked about the 'Tree of Three Roots', Simón Bolívar, Simón Rodríguez and Ezequiel Zamora, as his ideological inspiration. The reference to Bolívar needs no explanation, and Simón Rodríguez, although little-known in the English-speaking world, was an outstanding Venezuelan intellectual inspired by the Enlightenment who was Bolívar's tutor and mentor. As for Ezequiel Zamora, he was a mid-nineteenth-century liberal *caudillo* who led popular struggles for land and freedom in the 'Federal Wars' of the 1850s and 1860s, a sworn enemy of the landed oligarchy. Just as in Cuba with the memory of Martí and the *mambíses*, so in Venezuela the modern revolutionaries looked for inspiration to the national and popular heroes of the past (although this in no way implied a blanket rejection of Marxism or other international socialist and revolutionary ideologies propagated by the traditional Left). The basic themes of Chávez' ideology were national independence, popular sovereignty, social justice, an end to corruption, and Latin American unity; themes which have remained constant down to the present.

Throughout the 1980s the Bolivarian Movement recruited members in clandestinity, often with great difficulty. One of the leading members, Francisco Arias Cárdenas (who would part company with Chávez in the mid-1990s) joined in 1985 after returning from Colombia where he had completed a postgraduate degree (Blanco

Muñoz 1998, 126); he soon came to be regarded as the intellectual of the movement. Another key figure was Felipe Acosta Chirinos, described by Chávez as the most impetuous and combative member, who joined the day after the founding ceremony at Samán de Guere; he was killed on 1 March 1989 during the *caracazo*, and it was widely suspected that Military Intelligence were responsible (Blanco Muñoz 1998, 124). Evidently the existence of the movement was known or at least suspected by the authorities, and this made recruitment of civilians in particular more hazardous since they were less disciplined and it was more difficult to check their antecedents. Despite this, the movement succeeded in creating several joint civil-military regional commands and in holding five national congresses, demonstrating a considerable organising capacity and a commitment to civilian participation. It was conceived from the beginning as a civilian-military revolutionary alliance, not in any way as a praetorian officers' lodge with corporatist aims, and its development was characterised throughout by dialogue and interaction with the civilian Left.

The spontaneous *caracazo* uprising took the EBR-200 by surprise; all they could do was watch the events unfold and avoid, as far as possible, participating in the indiscriminate repression. Chávez himself was fortunate in being ill in bed during that week, otherwise he might have shared the same fate as Acosta Chirinos. According to some reports a few of the EBR-200 officers actually facilitated 'orderly' looting by the poor; certainly they sympathised with Major Arias Cárdenas, who asked his troops how many of them belonged to the Country Club or came from wealthy neighbourhoods like Altamira; when none of them responded he pointed out that the looters were their brothers and gave orders for no-one to fire unless attacked (Gott 2000, 44–8). The popular revolt and its repression convinced Chávez and his comrades that the time had come for them to act, and during the following year they intensified their contacts with civilians and their discussions of tactics and strategy for the MBR-200, as it was now called.

The authorities continued to have suspicions of Chávez and various other militants of the movement, but their information was partial and often incorrect. On 6 December 1989 they arrested Chávez and several others and accused them of plotting to assassinate CAP, but their information was false and the suspects were released. The authorities tried to break up the conspirators by posting them to different parts of the country, but as often occurs (for example in

Portugal in March 1974 when similar action was taken) the only result was to enable them to spread their subversive ideas more widely.

During the three years between the *caracazo* and Chávez' uprising of 4 February 1992 the MBR-200 had contacts with several civilian political groups. Douglas Bravo held discussions with Chávez again, proposing something like a general strike to be followed by a military revolt; but Chávez was wary of such extensive civilian involvement leading to discovery of the military plans. This led Bravo to say that Chávez 'wanted civil society to applaud but not to participate', whereas Chávez thought Bravo wanted to use the military as a tool of his party, the PRV. Extensive discussions were also held with LCR and its leaders Andrés Velázquez (a steelworkers' leader, elected governor of Bolívar State in December 1989) and Pablo Medina (Alfredo Maneiro had died several years earlier). There was apparently an agreement for LCR militants to go to prearranged points where Chávez' troops would distribute arms to the civilians in the early hours of 4 February, but according to Chávez they failed to appear and the LCR leadership publicly condemned the uprising, betraying their previous commitment (Gott 2000, 63–5; Harnecker 2002, 33–6).Other parties also like the Movimiento Electoral del Pueblo (MEP, Electoral Movement of the People), a left split from AD, supposedly also promised to lend support but failed. What is quite clear is that despite sharing a similar ideology, there was serious distrust between the military and civilian revolutionaries; the 'civil-military alliance' was not yet a functioning reality. Indeed, there were even more serious tensions: according to Chávez an ultra-left tendency called Bandera Roja (Red Flag, of Maoist ideology) infiltrated the MBR-200 and tried to set up their own apparatus inside it, even trying to assassinate Chávez, but they were discovered and expelled (Harnecker 2002, 38; Elizalde and Báez 2004, 362–4).

The actual events of 4 February 1992 have been narrated by Chávez himself and other participants and by journalists and scholars such as Gott and Harnecker. The uprising had already been planned and postponed more than once (the last and most important postponement had been on 16 December 1991), and it had reached the point where the movement's leaders felt that if they did not act within a few weeks all would be lost. Action began on Monday 3 February: within a few hours Arias Cárdenas seized control of Maracaibo and others took over Valencia and Maracay, west of Caracas. But in the capital things did not go according to plan: a captain in the military academy had betrayed the movement a few hours earlier, and when Chávez and his unit arrived in Caracas from Maracay at 1 am on 4 February they met unexpected resistance. Other units also met fierce resistance at various points in the capital, and it soon became clear that the strategic objective of capturing CAP and the high command would not be possible. At 9 am Chávez decided to surrender, but requested and received permission to speak briefly on television in order to communicate his decision to rebel commanders elsewhere and ask them to lay down their arms to avoid further bloodshed (Gott 2000, 66–71; Harnecker 2002, 36–8). This was the speech of about one minute and twenty seconds which made Chávez' name and changed the course of Venezuelan history:

First of all I want to say good morning to all the Venezuelan people and to send this Bolivarian message to the brave soldiers in the Aragua Parachute Regiment and the Valencia Armoured Brigade.

Comrades: unfortunately, for now, the objectives we had set ourselves have not been achieved in the capital. That is to say, we in Caracas did not manage to take power. Where you are you did very well, but now the time has come to avoid further bloodshed. It is time to think things over, new situations will arise and the country must definitively change direction towards a better future.

So listen to what I have to say: listen to Comandante Chávez who is sending you this message, please think and lay down your arms because the fact is that we cannot now achieve the objectives we had set ourselves at national level. Comrades, listen to this message of solidarity. I thank you for your loyalty, for your valour, for your selfless generosity; before the country and before you, I personally take responsibility for this Bolivarian military uprising. Thank you. (Zago 1998, 145–6)

This brief unscripted speech had a totally unanticipated impact and in effect turned defeat into victory. The words 'for now' (*por ahora*) signalled that Chávez had not given up and that there was still hope, a message confirmed by the phrase 'new situations will arise and the country must definitively change direction towards a better future'. Also Chávez' personal acceptance of responsibility for the revolt and its failure won him enormous prestige in a country where public figures never took responsibility for anything.

In the following months it quickly became clear that a sea-change was under way in the country's politics. Chávez and many of his comrades might be in gaol, but their popularity was undeniable and the government's credibility was exhausted. At first Chávez was held in the San Carlos barracks in Caracas, but hundreds of people went to visit him every day and at times they almost broke down the wire fence, so that after a month or so he was moved to Yare prison, about 40 minutes from Caracas by car. His comrades suspected that government agents might try to poison him, and therefore arranged to have trustworthy friends bring him food every day (Elizalde and Báez 2004, 43, 70). It was in this atmosphere that the second military uprising of 1992 occurred, on 27 November. This time it had higher-ranking leadership – Admiral Herman Grüber Odreman of the navy and General Francisco Visconti Osorio of the air force – and involved use of more powerful armaments, including bombing the presidential palace of Miraflores. The casualties were also heavier: over 170 killed, compared to 14 in February. The November rebels were supported from Yare prison by Chávez and members of the MBR-200 took part, as did a number of civilians from LCR; but the evidence suggests that the political orientation of this movement was less progressive and that its leaders were more concerned with narrow professional grievances than with a popular revolutionary programme (Ramírez Rojas 1998, 247–52) . In any case the uprising was badly organised and ended in failure (Gott 2000, 74–9). This second failure put an end to the possibility of military, or military-civilian, revolution: most of the MBR-200 officers were now behind bars, in hiding or in exile. The political establishment would now try to regain its credibility by impeaching CAP six months later and with Caldera's successful presidential candidacy in December 1993. But as we have seen, Caldera had no solution to Venezuela's problems and his election owed much to his speech in defence of Chávez in February 1992.

Hugo Chávez and his comrades were in prison for just two years before being amnestied by Caldera in March 1994. They used this time to good effect, in political reflection and discussions among themselves and with many sympathetic civilian visitors, of different political parties or of none. Some four months after their arrest, on 24 June 1992, they issued a manifesto headed 'From Our Prisons of Dignity' and signed by Hugo Chávez Frías and 36 other officers. Quoting Simón Bolívar's last letter, they spoke of their mission 'to use the sword to defend social guarantees', and condemned CAP's government for having signed an OAS (Organisation of American States) resolution of June 1991, creating a multi-lateral 'democratic' force, 'with the purpose of converting us from a sovereign State into a protectorate of the United States of North America and the Organisation of American States … '. They demanded a national referendum to recall CAP as president and to recall also the entire Congress, the Supreme Court and the National Electoral Council, and the convening of a Constituent Assembly to return sovereignty to the Venezuelan people (Zago 1998, 175, 179, 183). This was strikingly similar to Chávez' agenda of 1998–99.

Among those closest to Chávez at this time were several former members of the PRV, the Venezuelan Revolutionary Party of Douglas Bravo; some of them were now in LCR and some were independent. Among the most important was Kléber Ramírez Rojas, a civil engineer by profession but also a revolutionary intellectual and activist who made a major contribution to the developing ideology of the Bolivarian Movement. Kléber Ramírez argued that the Venezuelan state was fundamentally the same as that constructed by the dictator Juan Vicente Gómez early in the twentieth century; that in 1945 and 1958 Betancourt and AD had 'democratised' it only to the extent of putting the political parties of *puntofijismo* in charge, but with the same military and bureaucratic structures. A revolutionary alternative had emerged with the FALN/FLN but had failed because it was unable to develop a social base of support among the people. The way forward had to be to use the MBR-200 as the nucleus of a new army which would create the Fourth Republic (later they would change this to Fifth Republic by revising the historiography of the independence era), a new type of state based on popular power. The existing political parties – even the most advanced ones – were inadequate for this purpose: 'we must not create political platforms for tendencies which, if they want to be part of this project, must begin by breaking down their own internal structures' (Ramírez Rojas 1998, 276). This was an implicit warning to the PCV, the MAS and other leftist parties, indeed even (it would seem) to LCR. Significantly, Kléber Ramírez referred to the example of Cuba in 1959 and how there the revolutionaries had found it necessary to begin by appointing an inadequate figure, Manuel Urrutia, as president, 'with whom the Cuban Revolution could never have been consolidated'; but crucially, the Cubans possessed the rebel army forged in the Sierra Maestra which made it possible to move forward with popular support to create a new revolutionary state. In Venezuela on the other hand (and this was written by Ramírez in a letter to 'Gabriel' – Arias Cárdenas – on 24 June 1992) the nation's conscience had been stirred by the heroic gesture of the 4F (the 4 February uprising); as a result there was an ongoing crisis of hegemony in which both internal and external social and political forces were striving to impose their interests. The United States, along with the Venezuelan oligarchy, would try to impose their solution, 'which would be to preserve representative or liberal democracy, and this is one of the fundamental objectives which we want to change by means of the broadening of democracy'. In order to achieve this, in his view,

we must be open towards the different social sectors: intellectuals, productive sectors, religious, popular, military, students, etc., but not towards the political factors such as parties or individuals who may call themselves independent but all their action, background and training has come from the political parties which have upheld and developed this system. (Ramírez Rojas 1998, 272–3)

Here we can see the ideal of popular unity independent of parties of any kind, combined with the notion of a revolutionary reconstruction of the state including both its military apparatus and civilian bureaucracy, and the concept of a broader and deeper popular democracy as opposed to the liberal version. These ideas were shared to a large extent by LCR, which did not see itself as a conventional political party but as a grass-roots popular movement; but evidently LCR's compromises and abandonment of its ideals were already suspected or foreseen by Kléber Ramírez in mid-1992. Of course, Chávez' movement would eventually be obliged to create a political party, the MVR, and to negotiate alliances with other parties such as the PCV, a sector of the MAS and a sector of LCR; but it is significant that to this day Chávez has striven to maintain popular unity over and above all of these parties, repeatedly indicating his dissatisfaction even with the MVR. Here we have in essence Marx's vision as presented in the *Manifesto*, that 'the Communists ... have no interests separate and apart from those of the proletariat as a whole' (Marx and Engels 1968, 46), the concept of the revolutionary vanguard as a party unlike any other, indeed ultimately as an 'anti-party', linked directly to the mass popular movement and expressing the popular interest as a whole, the 'general will' in Rousseau's terms. But unlike the Communist parties and most of their Trotskyist or Marxist-Leninist derivatives around the world, Chávez and his comrades have not made the mistake of thinking that by assuming the role of popular vanguard they have gained the right to exclude all others: while rejecting or criticising many self-proclaimed revolutionary or left-wing parties, Chávez has not attempted to ban or suppress any of them. Indeed, even the reactionary parties have been allowed to operate freely (within the confines of the law), and Chávez' Bolivarian Movement, whatever its particular organisational expression at a given moment (EBR-200, MBR-200, MVR), has continued to operate on the principle that its vanguard role has to be constantly renewed and tested by direct interaction with the people at grass-roots level.

The revolutionary idealism of the MBR-200 officers is clearly revealed in their correspondence with Kléber Ramírez and others while imprisoned at Yare in 1992–94. In a letter of 27 August 1992 Arias Cárdenas insisted on the need to become

revolutionaries of a new type ... Those who transform themselves into men so as to be able to speak of love of humanity. Those who practise solidarity among themselves and with themselves, so as to be able to speak of solidarity with some propriety. THOSE WHO STRUGGLE TO BE NEW MEN and show the way to those who dream of new relationships which are less and less false and more in harmony with the simple and constant plan of creation ... . (Ramírez Rojas 1998, 282)

This implied a constant search, 'always with the stubborn determination of our master [Simón] Rodríguez' (Ramírez Rojas 1998, 282). Kléber replied that the 'new man' would really only appear when society began to change, and that above all they had to lay the ideological and social foundations of a '*new political system*' (Ramírez Rojas 1998, 286, emphasis in original).

Kléber's correspondence was above all with 'Gabriel' (Arias Cárdenas) whom he knew best and who, with two postgraduate degrees, was considered the intellectual of the MBR-200. But in relation to 'Héctor' (Chávez) 'everything indicated that he was a brilliant officer, with great charisma and that it was not by chance that he was the star of the 4F', a man of innate intelligence, clarity, capacity for action and determination (Ramírez Rojas 1998, 298). Moreover, Kléber's trust in Arias Cárdenas would soon suffer a severe blow when in June 1993 Arias let it be known that he was considering running for deputy or senator on the LCR list in the parliamentary and regional elections scheduled for December of that year. Kléber's response was categorical: 'Brother ... It seems to me that you are acting in a superficial and naive way. A heroic act like the 4F was not undertaken to win a mere seat in the Senate' (Ramírez Rojas 1998, 311). Kléber's position, like that of Chávez and the rest of the MBR-200, was not against electoral participation in all circumstances, but he considered that at that time Venezuelan society was ready for a total change, a transformation which could not take place only through elections. The transformation required a 'social rebellion' which could be promoted by various means, social, political and military, and which could include electoral participation but only if it were undertaken in a coordinated way by all revolutionary sectors and as part of a broader strategy.

Chávez himself has subsequently confirmed Ramírez Rojas' critique; interviewed by Marta Harnecker in 2002, he declared that in 1992–93 La Causa R tried to use the MBR's prestige after the 4F for its own electoral purposes, suggesting that he and other MBR leaders were members of its leadership, which was false. According to Chávez, LCR lobbied the imprisoned officers to get them to run as candidates, and 'That was when Arias Cárdenas began to show signs of weakness.' The imprisoned officers published a communiqué in which they declared that 'to intervene in an electoral process of that kind, with a framework imposed by the elites, would be to become accomplices of a deliberate fraud against popular aspirations'; that they could only have participated if the purpose had been to elect a Constituent Assembly. In fact Arias could not run in those elections since he was still in gaol, but some time after the rebel officers were amnestied in March 1994 he ran for and won the governorship of Zulia State in 'a strange alliance' with LCR and COPEI (Chávez, quoted in Harnecker 2002, 40–2). According to some of their comrades, the differences between Arias and Chávez had begun as early as 1992 while they were in gaol (Elizalde and Báez 2004, 137–8).

The position of Chávez and the MBR-200 at this time was one of 'active abstention: No to the parties, No to the elections and Yes to the alternative proposal of a Popular Constituent Assembly' (in Harnecker 2002, 42). The notion of a Constituent Assembly as the ultimate expression of popular sovereignty, for the refoundation of the republic on an entirely new basis, had been a key component of the original ideology of Alfredo Maneiro and La Causa R, but LCR had since allowed it to become subordinated to conventional electoral politics. It would be fundamental in Chávez' 1998 election platform, and his first act on inauguration as president in February 1999 would be to announce a referendum requesting popular authorisation to convene elections for such an assembly. This was the legal and electoral expression of the revolutionary aim of a total restructuring of the state, and Chávez has since explained that during their time in gaol and afterwards the movement's leaders studied the theoretical writings on this subject by the Italian radical intellectual Toni Negri and the French proponents of the *pouvoir constituant*, as well as Rousseau on the social contract (Harnecker 2002, 45).

The political situation from 1993 to 1997 was complicated; despite the undoubted prestige of Chávez and the MBR-200, the way forward was far from clear. Their support for the second revolt of 27 November 1992 did not help since it was widely understood that this uprising was not so progressive. It was clear that a further uprising would have neither military feasability nor popular support; the strategy now had to be political. Chávez' calls for abstention seem to have been well received initially among the popular sectors, but as time passed pressure grew for electoral participation as the only viable route to power. After Caldera's first year in office it was clear that the attempt at last-minute reform of the system had failed and that *puntofijismo* was truly moribund; but the question for Chávez and his comrades was how to turn the MBR-200, an essentially clandestine structure of revolutionary cadres, into a mass political movement capable of winning elections, and yet avoid being coopted by the system?

When the amnestied rebels left prison they designed a 'strategic map' identifying political allies, which included LCR and a number of smaller left-wing parties, despite their differences. The 'map' also included certain fundamental projects: the Popular Constituent Assembly, or rather Process (since it was conceived as going beyond an actual assembly to become a continuous process of reorganisation of the state); the organisation of the mass popular movement, in which a key element would be grass-roots 'Bolivarian Committees' (the predecessors of the 'Bolivarian Circles' created in 2001); a programmatic project of specific policies; and a project of international liaison. With this orientation the MBR-200 leaders toured Venezuela systematically in 1994–95, visiting towns, villages and *barrios* all over the country, recruiting a mass following and promoting a local organisational structure (Harnecker 2002, 46–50).

As popular pressure for electoral participation by the MBR-200 increased, in 1996–97 the movement organised its own public opinion poll throughout the country, with thousands of militants and sympathisers consulting over 100,000 people. The result was overwhelmingly in favour of participation and in particular in favour of Chávez running for president, and this led in turn to the MBR-200 holding its first National Conference on 19 April 1997. The decision was taken to field candidates in all the elections scheduled for the following year (for president, Congress, state governors and mayors), and to launch a new mass political party to be known as the MVR (Movimiento Quinta República, Fifth Republic Movement). The MBR-200 was not dissolved and continued unofficially as the hard core or 'motive force' of the broader movement, but public political activity by the *chavistas* (as they were increasingly labelled) was conducted by the MVR.

It was evident from the beginning that the MVR, a new and improvised party, could not afford to run alone but must seek alliances with other progressive parties. But by this time it was also clear that the rise of Chávez and his movement was producing profound divisions in virtually all sectors of the Venezuelan Left: its military origins, its apparently vague and unorthodox ideology, the personal protagonism and charisma of Chávez, all these characteristics provoked doubt, mistrust and resentment among politicians raised on Marxist-Leninist orthodoxy, conventional Social Democracy or theories of collective popular initiative. Despite the fact that virtually everyone in Venezuela recognised the progressive character of the MBR-200, despite Chávez' phenomenal popularity among the poor of the *cerros* and his success in galvanising a united mass movement where previously division and demoralisation had reigned, most of the self-proclaimed revolutionaries and Socialist gurus of the past saw him as a dangerous *caudillo*, a populist who could not be trusted.

The one established left-wing party to accept Chávez and the MVR almost immediately was, surprisingly, the PCV: this party of Communist veterans, now reduced to a token electoral force but still enjoying some prestige for its historical significance, at least had the vision to recognise a potentially revolutionary movement when it saw one. As against this La Causa R split later in 1997, with one faction led by Pablo Medina calling itself Patria Para Todos (PPT, Homeland For All) and supporting Chávez, while the other faction led by Andrés Velázquez retained the LCR name and completed the betrayal of its principles by allying with the Right. The MAS also split into pro- and anti-Chávez parties, with historic figures such as Teodoro Petkoff and Pompeyo Márquez joining the bourgeois parties to defend the status quo. The MVR, PCV, PPT and the *chavista* wing of the MAS were joined by five other small parties in a broad coalition called the Polo Patriótico (the Patriotic Pole).

The 1997–98 election campaign was far from straightforward. Originally all the elections were scheduled to take place simultaneously in December 1998, but the government enacted a measure to bring forward the legislative and local elections to 8 November, separating them from the presidential vote in an effort (partially successful) to prevent the *chavistas* from winning a majority by the 'coat-tail' effect. According to Chávez' followers there were several attempts by government agents to assassinate him, and security was a major concern (Elizalde and Báez 2004, 71). Given the complete discrediting of the traditional parties, most of the establishment united around the populist candidacy of the former beauty queen Irene Sáez, who held a clear lead in the opinion polls in the early months of 1998. But by July 1998 Chávez was rapidly rising in the polls, and Sáez made the mistake of accepting the support of COPEI, which was virtually a death-warrant. As Chávez marched ahead in the polls, the political establishment dumped Sáez and in desperation rallied around their last hope, an 'independent' technocrat named Henrique Salas Römer running for an improvised party called Proyecto Venezuela.

## CHÁVEZ IN POWER

By October 1998 it was obvious that nothing short of a coup could prevent the victory of Hugo Chávez, the candidate of the poor, the excluded, the discontented and all those who wanted fundamental change. When the vote occurred on 6 December, Chávez received 56 per cent to 39 per cent for Salas Römer who had succeeded in uniting virtually all of the conservative forces. In the two months from the elections to Chávez' inauguration on 2 February 1999, rumours of a coup or legal manoeuvre to prevent this former military rebel from becoming president continued, but this did not occur for two reasons: first, because of Chávez' military support, and second, because the oligarchy feared the popular reaction that would follow. The events of the next few years would show that, from their point of view, their fears were justified: Venezuela would never be the same again. The vote of 6 December 1998 was no ordinary election: everyone knew that what was really at stake was the electoral ratification of the popular revolt of 27 February 1989 and the military revolts of 4 February and 27 November 1992. In a delayed reaction, the civilian-military alliance had become a reality and a revolutionary insurgency had come to power. But since it had done so, in the end, by peaceful and electoral means, the power struggle to transform all the institutions of the Venezuelan state would continue for several years afterwards.

The popularity of Hugo Chávez among the poor and excluded, the people of the *cerros*, peasants, blacks and indigenous people was overwhelming: this was a victory for Chávez and the MBR-200, the insurgents of February 1992, and not for the left-wing parties or politicians of the Polo Patriótico coalition. It was Chávez' personal example, his charisma, his ability to communicate with the people in their own language, his identification with them, the fact that he like them was of mixed race, with *negro* and indigenous ancestry: it was these things which created a loyalty going far beyond a mere electoral preference. Many of the common people would without doubt be ready to die for Chávez, just as they felt he was ready to die for them. But by the same token most of the elite, the rich, the oligarchy and the middle class feared and hated the man with irrational fervour. Chávez did not talk the language of class or of Socialism, let alone of Marxism-Leninism, but if class is – as argued by E.P. Thompson – a lived reality, a phenomenon which happens and evolves, in Venezuela in these years it was happening with awesome intensity. Anyone attending a *chavista* rally and then a rally of the opposition could immediately see, feel and even smell the difference, which was succinctly expressed in the language of the two sides: the opposition spoke of the *'chavista* hordes', the mob (*chusma*), the rabble, while the *chavistas* branded their opponents as the oligarchy or the *escuálidos* (squalid ones). There were frequently racial overtones to the hostility: as time went on it was not uncommon to hear *escuálidos* declaring that 'We have to get the *Negro* out of Miraflores [the presidential palace]', and at one point a perceptive newspaper columnist wrote an article analysing the reasons for the opposition's violent rejection of Chávez, entitled *No es por Rambo sino por Zambo* – 'It's not because he's a Rambo [i.e. because of his military origins] but because he's a Zambo [a person of mixed black and native ancestry]'.

This polarisation was somewhat muted during Chávez' first few months in office, in what might be described as a political honeymoon; but as soon as it became clear that he really intended to implement his programme of 'Bolivarian revolution', the gloves came off and the political confrontation became bitter and permanent. This was reflected in the media: the four main private TV channels and the great majority of the press and radio were thoroughly, even viciously anti-Chávez, and against this the Bolivarian forces had only the public TV (Channel 8) and radio and a small number of progressive and community outlets, and above all the impassioned and committed rhetoric of the man himself.

Some sectors of the oligarchy initially hoped that they could manipulate the new president, and that his actual performance would not match his revolutionary rhetoric. The manoeuvre of bringing forward the legislative and local elections had been partially successful for the old guard, and during his first year in office Chávez was hindered by the lack of a majority in Congress.

He also found himself obliged to make concessions by appointing as ministers some politicians from the old system who had jumped on the MVR bandwagon but would later betray him, such as Alfredo Peña and Luis Miquilena. Peña was an influential journalist and former leftist who had helped give Chávez media access during the campaign, but within a year of the election victory he would go into opposition, becoming mayor of Metropolitan Caracas and a visceral opponent of the new president. Miquilena had been a Communist back in the 1940s and early 1950s and had always been on the Left, although now without party affiliation; now over 80, he was a skilled and experienced political fixer, and played a key role in putting together the Polo Patriótico coalition (Harnecker 2002, 70–2). Chávez recognised his contribution by making him Interior Minister in 1999 and then putting him in charge of the election campaign for the Constituent Assembly, of which he became president. It would later become apparent that Miquilena's support for the revolutionary transformation had strict limits, which were reached in late 2001 when he deserted to the opposition; by that time it was also clear that as Interior Minister he had stuffed the Supreme Court with unreliable judges, creating serious problems for the government. But given the correlation of forces in 1998–99, it is doubtful if this could have been avoided.

Despite these constraints, Chávez took bold action on a number of fronts soon after his inauguration in order to confirm his progressive orientation and show his commitment to radical change. In his inaugural speech he condemned the existing Constitution as moribund and announced a referendum to be held two months later asking the nation to authorise him to call elections for a Constituent Assembly. Within weeks he launched 'Plan Bolívar 2000', an ambitious programme of public works and social action using the military in cooperation with local communities, repairing roads, schools and community centres, providing basic health care and other services for poor communities. The plan was financed by the pre-existing Macroeconomic Stabilisation Fund (derived from oil receipts) and the military budget, in order to avoid lengthy debates in Congress where Chávez lacked a clear majority (Gott 2000, 177–8). This was also the case with the Bolivarian schools programme launched a couple of months later, under which the armed forces provided facilities on military bases for schools which offered basic education to children from the shanty-towns to study alongside the children of military personnel; soon this programme was providing access to tens of thousands of young people previously excluded from the system.

These programmes immediately became the focus of vitriolic opposition attacks, with charges of militarisation of society, corruption and 'Cubanisation' – although at this point Cubans were not involved at all. What was really at stake here was to demonstrate the reality of the government's commitment to the poor, while simultaneously raising the political consciousness of the military: both developments which the opposition was determined to stop.

The other field in which Chávez took bold action in his first months in office was petroleum policy. As Minister of Oil and Mines he appointed Alí Rodríguez Araque, a former guerrilla commander and member of LCR and later PPT, who immediately began to tour all the OPEC (Organisation of Petroleum Exporting Countries) nations in order to revive the cartel's effectiveness. Venezuela obtained the cooperation of Mexico (a non-OPEC member) as well, and within two months had achieved agreement to cut back production and thereby raise the oil price from its historic low of $9 a barrel in February 1999. By the end of the year, largely as a result of the Venezuelan initiative, the price had almost tripled to around $25 a barrel, reviving the country's economy and providing much-needed funds for the government's social programmes. At the same time, Alí Rodríguez began a much more difficult task: that of reasserting government control over the public oil company, PDVSA (Petróleos de Venezuela SA) which, although nationalised in 1976, had become a 'state within a state' run as a private fiefdom by a corrupt and Americanised management elite with no regard to the national interest. This would prove to be a major political battle contributing directly to the abortive coup against Chávez in April 2002.

Oil policy was closely linked to foreign policy in general, and here also the new government moved quickly to establish its priorities. Chávez made clear his interest in promoting a multi-polar world, reducing Venezuela's enormous dependence on the US and diversifying its foreign relations. As well as the links with the OPEC countries, he moved quickly to forge new economic and diplomatic ties with China and Russia, and to strengthen relations with some European countries, especially France. The other major axis of foreign policy was Latin America, where Chávez' Bolivarian vision logically implied intensifying relations with Venezuela's Latin neighbours in all respects. Relations with Cuba in particular were given a decisive impulse, and Chávez made it very clear that while he had no intentions of copying the Cuban political and economic model, he regarded the island as a revolutionary example of social justice and dignity in the face of imperialism. He made no bones about his personal friendship with Fidel Castro (begun when he first visited Cuba in late 1994) and refused to take the slightest notice of US hostility to this new alliance.

In November 1999, having won his initial political battles over the Constitution, oil policy, Plan Bolívar 2000 and the Bolivarian schools, Chávez went to Havana with a high-level delegation and signed important agreements which would provide Cuba with Venezuelan oil at favourable prices (a major boost for the Cuban economy) in return for Cuban aid in educational, health and sports programmes; this was only the beginning of what would become a very close alliance of fundamental importance for both countries. Five years later, towards the end of 2004, when Chávez was pushing ahead vigorously with his project of 'endogenous development' – independent national development oriented to use of national resources and emphasising cooperative and public enterprise – and was promoting his scheme of the ALBA, the 'Bolivarian Alternative for the Americas' based on the same concept, as an alternative to the US-sponsored Free Trade Area of the Americas, Cuba and Venezuela formally agreed to initiate the ALBA by signing a comprehensive bilateral economic agreement.

But in 1999 the top priority was the Constituent Assembly, as announced in Chávez' inaugural speech and in accordance with the theory of the *pouvoir constituant* and the original ideals of Alfredo Maneiro and La Causa R. The task of the Constituent Assembly was by definition to draft a new Constitution: an important step but one which had many precedents in other countries, such as neighbouring Colombia a few years earlier (1991). But for Chávez and his movement the importance of the Constituent Assembly went far beyond this: it represented the untrammelled sovereign power of the people, and therefore must not be hindered in any way by other institutions or remnants of the outgoing system (the existing Congress or Supreme Court, for example). Hence the importance of winning the clearest possible mandate for the Assembly, with the initial referendum of 25 April authorising the president to convene constituent elections (won with 82 per cent of the popular vote), then the elections themselves (on 25 July) in which Polo Patriótico supporters won 119 out of 131 seats with 67 per cent of the vote, and finally in December 1999 (after the Assembly had completed its work) the referendum to ratify the new Constitution, which was approved by 71 per cent (Molina V. 2002, 223–5). While the Assembly was deliberating, from 3 August to 12 November 1999, considerable efforts were made to promote popular participation, with regional assemblies and delegations of mass organisations having input into the discussions.

The opposition was well aware of the Assembly's importance and therefore attacked it from the start as being irrelevant to the real problems of the people; they also tried to sabotage its decisions by hostile votes in the existing Congress and by negative decisions in the Supreme Court. Although most legal experts considered that the Constituent Assembly had a clear democratic mandate overriding that of the Congress or any other institution, the President of the Supreme Court resigned in protest and the Congress went into emergency session claiming that 'democracy was in danger', and got delegations from international organisations to back their position. But Chávez and the Assembly went ahead, with popular support, and worked day and night to produce one of the most progressive and democratic constitutions in the world. What was at stake here was the future of the entire Bolivarian project, and it is significant that the battle lines in this first major confrontation were clearly drawn between the two conflicting visions of democracy: the old liberal conception of control by elite parliamentary and judicial institutions, and the revolutionary concept of direct popular sovereignty.

The approval of the Constitution was in itself a major victory, and the government swiftly moved ahead to implement it by holding fresh elections under the new rules for all elective positions in the country. These 'mega-elections' were held on 30 July 2000; Chávez won the presidency again with almost 60 per cent of the vote, and the Polo Patriótico won a clear majority in Congress as well as a majority of the state and local governments. Chávez won despite the first serious defection from the MBR-200: his main opponent in the presidential election was none other than Major Arias Cárdenas, whose previous differences with him over electoral strategy had now culminated in open opposition. Beginning with the November 1998 congressional and local elections, seven elections and referenda had been held in less than two years, with clear and in some cases overwhelming victories (of between 56 and 81 per cent) for Chávez and his supporters, and this despite a ferociously hostile media (Molina V. 2002, 223–5). The old political parties – AD, COPEI, LCR, the opposition fraction of the MAS – and the hastily improvised new bourgeois parties such as Proyecto Venezuela and

Primero Justicia – were incapable of mounting an effective challenge to Chávez. Few governments anywhere have won a clearer mandate for change; the question was, would the opposition and the oligarchy that backed them – the *escuálidos* – allow the implementation of the Bolivarian programme?

The new Constitution renamed the country as the Bolivarian Republic of Venezuela; it created a new unicameral National Assembly, a new Supreme Court, a new National Electoral Council, and a system of 'participatory and protagonistic democracy' which is undoubtedly one of the most advanced in the world in terms of entrenchment of human rights and citizen participation; it established the right of recall of all elected officials, from the president on down. At the same time, with the evident intention of permitting the consolidation of the revolutionary project, the presidential term was extended to six years with the option of one re-election. In addition to the traditional executive, legislative and judicial powers the Constitution created the electoral power (the National Electoral Council) and the 'moral' or 'citizen' power (consisting formally of the Ombudsman, the Attorney-General and the Comptroller-General, but really intended to promote popular supervision of all government activities). Throughout the Constitution there was systematic emphasis on popular participation and on collective, social and economic as well as individual rights. It guaranteed a minimum of three congressional seats to the indigenous population and recognised women's rights, including (an international first) the economic value of women's domestic labour. Although recognising the right to private property, it laid the basis for an agrarian reform and for national ownership of petroleum and mineral resources. This was the legal basis for the 'Bolivarian Revolution', but its implementation would depend on a continuing struggle for power at all levels of the state and of society.

Surprisingly, despite the great triumph of Chávez and the Polo Patriótico in the July 2000 elections, the following year witnessed an accumulation of problems for the Bolivarian process. The opposition used every possible legal device to hinder executive action, and in Congress it soon became apparent that many of the Polo Patriótico deputies were unreliable opportunists, some of whom deserted to the opposition; this was a logical consequence of working through existing institutions, even if only partially. The MVR itself, born as an electoral party in 1997–98, underwent mushroom growth as the Chávez phenomenon swept all before it, and inevitably absorbed many careerists and even saboteurs. In power after the

Constituent Assembly and the new elections of 2000, it began to become bureaucratised and many of its officials became distant, manipulative and arbitrary: they became conventional politicians. Chávez himself recounts how he could feel that there was a 'deadly cold' atmosphere in the popular neighbourhoods as people felt that the party had abandoned them, and his blood froze when he realised this (Harnecker 2002, 193). It was for this reason that on 25 April 2001 he announced the relaunching of the MBR-200, a decision which took almost everyone by surprise.

Many initially took this to mean the end of the MVR, but Chávez later explained that the party – and its coalition allies – were still necessary for electoral purposes, while the MBR-200 was not a party but 'the organised people themselves defending and driving forward the revolution'. It was also at this time that he called for the formation of Bolivarian circles, local groups of from seven to 15 people to discuss the movement's ideology and organise to deal with local problems and defend the revolution: 'Everywhere there should be Bolivarian circles and we should build social networks of Bolivarian circles, and several social networks should create a torrent of Bolivarian circles which become like a river ... the basic nuclei of the MBR-200 are the Bolivarian circles and the Bolivarian forces ... ' (Chávez in Harnecker 2002, 195–6). The 'Bolivarian forces' were social movements like the new trade union movement, the women's, peasants' and youth movements. In all these movements and in the circles there were militants of the MVR, the PPT, the PCV and other parties, but mostly there were people without party allegiance, which was also part of the country's reality because most people had no faith in political parties. The circles and the social movements were manifestations of the popular constituent power in action: once again, we see here Chávez' emphasis on popular power as the basis of the entire revolutionary process, independent of parties and institutions. Institutions were of course necessary, up to and including the central government, but they must always be subordinated as far as possible to the direct expressions of popular power.

In response to Chávez' appeal of April 2001, and even more when he repeated it in December, Bolivarian circles began to spring up all over the country in popular neighbourhoods, towns and villages. Apart from being a response to Chávez, in every other respect their growth seems to have been spontaneous; they were not created by bureaucratic agencies or political parties but by the people themselves at grass-roots level, in that dialectical interaction between Chávez and the popular classes which has been the hallmark of the entire process. The Bolivarian circles were almost immediately demonised by the opposition which claimed that they were armed and violent, and financed and organised by the government; it also compared them to the Cuban CDRs (Committees for the Defence of the Revolution). But there is no evidence that the circles are armed, certainly no more than the various opposition organisations which have been responsible for numerous acts of violence and intimidation; it has to be borne in mind that the Venezuelan population, like that of the United States and many other countries in the Western hemisphere, is in any case heavily armed. The government has repeatedly insisted that it does not and will not finance the circles, which must be self-supporting. It also insists that the circles are a Venezuelan phenomenon and not a carbon-copy of the Cuban CDRs. This is no doubt true in a literal sense, but it should also be recognised that rank-and-file local committees of one kind or another are a feature of most popular revolutions, as with the CDRs and the Sandinista Defence Committees (CDSs) in Nicaragua.

## THE COUP AND THE CIVIC-MILITARY ALLIANCE

As opposition sabotage in Congress and the courts and the factionalism of his own supporters continued to hold up progress on the social and economic aspects of the revolution, Chávez became seriously concerned that this would lead to disillusionment among the mass of poor and marginalised people who constituted the foundation of the movement. It was for this reason that in November 2001 he finally resorted to special powers of presidential decree to issue 49 *Leyes Habilitantes* (Enabling Laws) to implement a large part of his socio-economic agenda: the restructuring of PDVSA, agrarian reform, urban property reform, a new fisheries law, support for cooperatives, and so on. It was this decision which precipitated the opposition's first attempt at a general strike (or, to be more accurate, a bosses' lockout) on 6 December 2001: it was now clear that Chávez was serious about attacking the oligarchy's monopoly of economic power.

Signs of crisis multiplied in the following months. Luis Miquilena, who had played such a vital role in the Constituent Assembly and as Interior Minister, urged the President to desist from the Enabling Laws because in his view revolutions could only be made by force of arms and in Venezuela they could do no more than carry out limited reforms. As it subsequently became apparent that Miquilena was working with the opposition, Chávez dismissed him on 24 January 2002 (Elizalde and Báez 2004, 382). Then on 7 February an air force colonel, Pedro Soto, called publicly for Chávez' resignation, and was backed by Rear-Admiral Carlos Molina Tamayo and a National Guard captain. In March Chávez finally dismissed the disloyal board of the public oil company PDVSA; and the Federation of Chambers of Commerce (Fedecámaras), the CTV (Confederación de Trabajadores de Venezuela, Venezuelan Labour Confederation), the Catholic Church and other organisations signed an anti-Chávez pact. These same organisations called once again for a general strike for 9–10 April, then extended it indefinitely and called for a rally 'to save PDVSA' outside one of the oil company's offices in the wealthy East End of Caracas. The rally, held on Thursday 11 April, was suddenly diverted by its organisers towards the presidential palace of Miraflores in the city centre. As Bolivarian activists gathered outside Miraflores to defend the government, the National Guard moved in peacefully to separate the hostile demonstrations, but then gunfire broke out and within a couple of hours some 20 people were killed. In what was clearly a premeditated action, the opposition media blamed Chávez for the bloodshed and the military high command demanded his resignation. They seized Miraflores and detained Chávez, claiming falsely that he had resigned, and in a farcical ceremony on the morning of 12 April the head of Fedecámaras, Pedro Carmona Estanga, swore himself in as provisional president of the 'Republic of Venezuela' (no longer the 'Bolivarian Republic').

With the coup the opposition finally tore off its 'democratic' mask: Carmona's junta included three generals and a Roman Catholic archbishop, and the usurper immediately proclaimed the dissolution of Congress, the dismissal of all elected officials, the dissolution of the Supreme Court, the National Electoral Tribunal and the Ombudsman's office, suspending civil liberties and starting a witch-hunt against *chavistas*. The circumstantial evidence of US and Spanish involvement in the coup only increased the grotesque parallels with Pinochet in Chile and with the brutal Latin American militarism of earlier decades. But the defeat of the coup within 48 hours by a mass popular uprising supported by the progressive military showed that the Bolivarian Movement was much stronger than the Fascist opposition suspected, and that this was indeed a popular revolution.

Anyone who has seen the extraordinary documentary *The Revolution Will Not Be Televised* filmed by the Irish team of Kim Bartley and Donnacha O'Briain (Bartley and O'Briain 2003) will realise how massive and spontaneous was the popular reaction to the coup and how euphoric was the return of Chávez from what looked like certain death or indefinite exile. It is also clear from this documentary, and even more so from the more recent production of Venezuelan public television, *Puente Llaguno: Imágenes de una Masacre* (Palacios 2004), that the murder of peaceful demonstrators on 11 April was carried out by carefully placed sharpshooters and that the private media were crucial and conscious actors in the coup, manipulating a well-planned *montage* to justify the government's overthrow. But what is not so clear even from these sources is the absolutely crucial role of the revolutionary military in the defeat of the coup. The mass protest by hundreds of thousands, even millions of Venezuelans, demanding the return of Chávez and of democracy, many of them waving their little blue pocket editions of the Bolivarian Constitution: this has rightly gained international recognition as one of the greatest moments of popular power in recent times. But it is essential to analyse clearly the events of 11–14 April: the conventional wisdom on the Left is that it was the people in the streets who defeated the Fascist Carmona and his acolytes, but this is at best a half-truth. Of course the popular reaction was vital and inspiring, but the fact of the matter is that those brave people, despite their passion and unanimity, would almost certainly have been massacred had it not been for the actions of the revolutionary military in rejecting the coup. The testimony of Chávez and others, collected by Marta Harnecker and the Cuban journalists Rosa Miriam Elizalde and Luis Báez, provides essential information for understanding exactly what went on in those dramatic 48 hours.

What saved the revolution was the 'civic-military alliance' to which Chávez frequently refers, a bond between the people in the Bolivarian circles and local committees of all kinds and the officers and troops who constantly worked with them in the Plan Bolívar 2000, the Bolivarian schools and related programmes. On 12–13 April it was not simply that the troops responded to the popular demonstrations outside the barracks (although of course this was a factor); in so many similar situations elsewhere people have appealed to the democratic sentiments of the military, only to be slaughtered or at best ignored. The troops, and many of the officers, were already taking action behind the scenes, and most of them were more than ready to respond to the popular mood because of their Bolivarian ideology and practical experience during the previous three years and before. Neither does this mean – as alleged by some Marxist purists – that the military were paternalistically 'substituting for the masses': on the contrary, on the basis of a long process going back in many cases to the February 1992 uprising or earlier, they were assuming their role as 'the people in uniform', both responding to and leading their fellow-workers in defeating the coup. In this they were of course aided by thousands of civilian activists of the MBR-200 and Polo Patriótico, including leaders like José Vicente Rangel and Aristóbulo Astúriz, who took action to reoccupy government ministries, to get the public TV station Channel 8 back on the air, and so on; but without the actions of the revolutionary military, a Pinochet-style repression (or possibly a civil war of uncertain outcome) would almost certainly have followed.

On 12–13 April the people went to the barracks because they knew, or at least expected, that many of the military – and not just the troops but the officers – would respond. Moreover in some areas such as Maracay, Bolivarian officers themselves went into the popular neighbourhoods where they were known by the local population in order to mobilise people against the coup. In Chávez' own words, 'That whole [popular] reaction would not have occurred without that profound contact between the army and the people. That is Mao. The water and the fish. The people is to the army as the water is to the fish. In Venezuela today we have fish in the water ... ' (Harnecker 2002, 96–7). Of course, Mao was talking about a revolutionary army, but what has happened in Venezuela is – quite remarkably – that the conventional military has been in large part transformed into a revolutionary army.

There were also very specific actions taken on 12–13 April by key officers which contributed decisively to the defeat of the *golpistas* (coup-mongers). General Jorge Luis García Carneiro, then commander of the Caracas military region, got together with a number of other officers in Fuerte Tiuna (the main Caracas military base) on the afternoon of 12 April and prepared a plan to rescue Chávez who was at that moment being held by the military police in another part of the same base; the plan failed because the *golpistas* got wind of it and moved Chávez to Turiamo (on the coast) and then to Orchila island. Then on the morning of 13 April the Presidential Guard recaptured Miraflores palace (an action which was captured on film by the Irish team of *The Revolution Will Not Be Televised*), expelling Carmona and his illicit government; but what is not apparent in the documentary (because the journalists were unaware of it) is that the loyal Presidential Guard were acting on an order from García Carneiro. A few hours later García Carneiro was able to recapture the rest of the installations in Fuerte Tiuna without resistance, including the Ministry of Defence building where he found Carmona and arrested him (Elizalde and Báez 2004, 177–83).

A crucial role was also played by General Raúl Baduel, commander of the parachute regiment in Maracay, 80 km west of Caracas. Baduel was one of the first commanding officers to repudiate the coup, and by 13 April he had gathered 14 generals together with 20,000 troops and heavy armament, and sent a manifesto to the *golpistas* demanding the return of Chávez. Baduel was ready to march on Caracas until he received word that García Carneiro and other loyal officers had already taken control there; and it was also Baduel, in coordination with others, who sent three helicopters with elite troops to rescue Chávez from Orchila island on the night of 13–14 April (Elizalde and Báez 2004, 267–76).

As more details of the events become known, it is becoming clear that the *golpistas* never really had control except in Miraflores palace, a few government offices, a minority of military garrisons and the media. Throughout the entire period they met resistance from both civilians and military personnel loyal to Chávez and the revolution. The contrary impression was created on 12 April and for most of 13 April by the media, whose role cannot be overstated: the Venezuelan private media were active participants in the coup, and one of the most illuminating (and repulsive) scenes in the Irish video is a clip in which several of the leading news commentators from the main private TV channels congratulate each other publicly on how they had prearranged their coverage of the opposition demonstration so as to discredit Chávez and justify his overthrow. With the assistance of most of the international media they strove – with alarming success – to legitimise Carmona during the following 48 hours, and when things began to go badly wrong for the *golpistas* on the afternoon of 13 April, the media did everything possible to suppress the truth, broadcasting old Hollywood films and comic strips in an effort to prevent news of the retaking of Miraflores palace from getting out. The Venezuelan experience is an object lesson in the dangers of private media monopolies and the hypocrisy of their loudly trumpeted appeals for 'freedom of the press'.

After Chávez' triumphant return, many of his supporters and even some opponents were dumbfounded by his failure to take reprisals against the *golpistas*. Chávez has since explained his conciliatory approach and has emphasised that the coup-mongers were not pardoned but merely allowed to retain their constitutional rights while the wheels of justice took their normal leisurely course. In the long run his patient and tolerant attitude seems to have worked, as the reactionaries have become even more discredited: they had the effrontery to argue – supported by the Supreme Court which (thanks in part to Miquilena) still had a right-wing majority – that there was no coup, only a 'power vacuum' which Carmona and his military backers generously agreed to fill! But the immediate effect of Chávez' tolerance was to embolden the *escuálidos*, and in the next few months they became more and more strident in their opposition, repeatedly organising 'strikes' and demonstrations until finally on 2 December 2002 they began an indefinite *paro* or 'general strike', really a bosses' lockout designed to paralyse the economy and bring down the government. They began by closing down large-scale commerce – most shopping malls closed completely – and then tried to close the banks and major industries, and finally after about a week of intensifying disruption and shortages of basic commodities, went on to shut down the oil industry.

As many *chavistas* quickly pointed out, this was simply a coup by other means, and no government could tolerate actions which threatened to produce starvation, economic collapse and civil unrest. In any case the *escuálidos* were quite open about their aims, calling for Chávez' resignation or for a referendum against him (but without following the procedures laid down for this in the Constitution). Carlos Ortega, the head of the CTV (the main labour federation, thoroughly corrupt and controlled by Acción Democrática) even called openly for Chávez' assassination (and had the nerve to claim political persecution when the police came to arrest him several months later on charges of treason and incitement to murder). Once again the opposition had over-reached itself, and the *paro* only served to demonstrate the depth and strength of revolutionary feeling among the people. The shutdown of regular commerce merely created a heyday for tens of thousands of street-traders (most of them *chavistas*), and the people refused to be provoked by the shortages, contrary to the expectations of the *escuálidos* who hoped that they would riot in an anti-Chávez repetition of the *caracazo*. In any case the government responded quickly by organising a programme in which the military purchased basic foodstuffs directly from rural producers and distributed them at favourable prices in special markets in working-class areas. This *mercal* programme was very popular and successful, and has since become permanent. The attempt to close down the banks also failed, in part because it directly affected the interests of those who were promoting it; and it also provoked the government to introduce exchange controls in order to limit financial speculation, another measure which has since become permanent.

But the decisive element in the *paro* was the shutdown of the oil industry, threatening to deprive the country of 90 per cent of its export revenue and produce total economic collapse. It also created the paradoxical situation in which there was a serious shortage of petrol in this oil-producing country. The opposition was able to do this because it controlled the board of PDVSA and most of its management and technicians, and (with the help of a US company) the computer programmes which ran the oilfield machinery. By late December 2002 the situation was critical, but the government sent the military to take over the oil installations and, with the help of loyal workers and technicians, succeeded in gradually reviving production. Despite opposition predictions of disaster, the strategy worked, and the result was that for the first time ever, Venezuelan oil began to benefit the entire nation. Some 18,000 disloyal management and technical personnel were sacked, and PDVSA was in effect renationalised in what was one of the most crucial victories yet of the Bolivarian revolution. Once again, as with the coup, what Trotsky called 'the lash of the counter-revolution' served to consolidate the revolutionary process, provoking a further rupture in the existing power structure as the *escuálidos* lost control of another key asset.

## THE MISSIONS AND THE RENEWED REVOLUTIONARY OFFENSIVE

The opposition formally recognised the failure of the *paro* on 2 February 2003, just two months after it started. The popular movement emerged from this crisis stronger than ever before, and Chávez now moved swiftly to accelerate the economic and social revolution. The Venezuelan state, through the Ministry of Mines and Energy, was now at last in control of its own oil company, PDVSA, whose management was finally subordinated to the priorities of the democratically elected government. The petroleum revenue, 80 per cent of which had previously remained outside the country, was now flowing into the public coffers, and a significant proportion of it could be dedicated to the government's priorities of social investment and economic diversification. It was in the following months (March to November 2003) that several of the 'Missions' were created: the

Robinson Mission for literacy, the Ribas Mission to provide access to secondary education for those previously excluded from it, the Sucre Mission to provide access for the poor to higher education (and with it a new 'Bolivarian University' with campuses across the country), the Barrio Adentro ('Into the Neighbourhoods') Mission to provide basic health care for the poor, the Housing Mission which brought together and strengthened existing programmes of housing for the popular sectors, and so on. The Barrio Adentro Mission was staffed by Cuban doctors and nurses, establishing clinics in the *cerros* and in remote villages where Venezuelan doctors were unwilling to go, and the Robinson Mission was based on Cuban literacy programmes. Tens of thousands of Cuban personnel collaborated in the Missions, and despite opposition claims that they were only there to indoctrinate people with Communist ideology, they were immensely popular with the deprived residents of the *cerros*, many of whom had never seen a doctor and never been to school.

Within a year (by the end of March 2004) the Robinson Mission had taught over 1,200,000 illiterate adults to read and write; the Ribas Mission had incorporated more than a quarter of a million people into secondary education; the Bolivarian University had three campuses functioning and six more in the pipeline; the Barrio Adentro Mission had established over 11,000 health clinics and provided more than 21 million consultations to two and a half million families (Ministry of Science & Technology 2004). Pre-existing programmes had also achieved impressive results: since 1999 the Bolivarian schools had incorporated over 600,000 children from deprived backgrounds into primary education, and the 'Avispa' housing plan had provided tens of thousands of dwellings to people from slum communities. But the most important thing about these and other plans and missions is that, contrary to the hostile propaganda of much of the Venezuelan and international media and organisations like the IMF, they are not simply paternalistic or 'populist' handouts by an oil-rich government (although even if they were, one would have thought that this was preferable to 'squeezing the poor' through welfare cutbacks as advocated by these same apologists of neo-liberalism). On the contrary, the emphasis throughout has been on popular participation in the planning and administration of these programmes, on popular empowerment and organisation.

It was in this context of a renewed popular revolutionary offensive that the opposition, having twice failed in attempts to overthrow Chávez by unconstitutional means, decided to play the constitutional card and go for a recall referendum (an option which only existed because the *chavista* Constitutional Assembly had introduced it). For this there were strict procedures regarding collection of the required number of signatures to authorise a referendum, and there were months of wrangling before the opposition finally consented to play by the rules under the supervision of the National Electoral Council (CNE, Consejo Nacional Electoral, an independent body). The formal collection of signatures to request a referendum took place under CNE supervision from 28 to 30 November 2003, and because of numerous irregularities which had allowed the opposition to collect tens of thousands of false signatures, a confirmation process took place from 28 to 30 April 2004. When the CNE confirmed that the opposition had collected slightly more than the approximately two and a half million signatures required, the referendum was set for 15 August of that year.

Despite suspicions that the opposition had still got away with a fair number of fraudulent signatures, Chávez accepted the CNE verdict and called on the people to welcome this opportunity to put into practice another of the democratic instruments of the Bolivarian Constitution. Venezuela is probably the only country in the world where a president or prime minister elected with a solid popular majority has submitted to a recall referendum well before the end of his term. Once again, Chávez triumphed with over 59 per cent of the vote to 40 per cent. But the referendum was more than just one more electoral victory for Chávez and the revolution. It was another major defeat for the opposition, which had invested enormous legal and illegal capital in the campaign. The attempts to register fraudulent signatures and votes were only part of what really amounted to a third attempted coup; during the prolonged wait for the signature confirmation procedure, from February to April 2004, there were repeated opposition demonstrations which became increasingly violent, the so-called *guarimbas* (a slang term basically meaning disorder), in which streets were blocked, public transport disrupted and *chavistas* or members of the National Guard violently assaulted.

The opposition itself cried fraud when the referendum result was announced, despite the fact that it had participated in the designation of members of the CNE and had obtained the international supervision it demanded (by the Organisation of American States [OAS] and the Carter Center). In a pathetic display of sour grapes, the Coordinadora Democrática (Democratic Coordinator, the umbrella organisation of the opposition) launched bitter attacks on US ex-President Jimmy Carter, OAS Secretary-General César Gaviria and other international figures who had certified the fairness of the vote. The net result of this was at long last to discredit the opposition in the eyes of many of its international backers: establishment newspapers like the *New York Times* and *El País* of Spain published editorials condemning its attitude as undemocratic. Moreover the opposition itself was now in crisis: two months later (on 31 October 2004) there were elections for state governorships and mayors throughout Venezuela, and the opposition suffered heavy losses, with *chavistas* winning 20 out of 22 state governorships and a large majority of the mayoral positions. Soon after this the Coordinadora Democrática broke up in acrimony as the opposition was forced to recognise its complete lack of a viable strategy.

At least as important as the actual election victories was the consolidation of the popular movement; indeed, without this victory would have been impossible. One of the Missions launched in late 2003 was the Misión Identidad, the Identity Mission, designed to provide ID cards (and electoral registration) to millions of poor Venezuelans (and Colombian immigrants) who lacked them and therefore could not vote or benefit from social programmes. The result was a big expansion of the electoral roll, from about 11 to 14 million citizens, and most of these new voters would no doubt be *chavistas*. But it was not enough just to register people and to conduct an election campaign in the normal way; given the opposition's resources and continued control of most of the media, popular organisation and mobilisation was more important than ever. Moreover, as in the crucial elections of December 1998 and July 2000, the people had to understand that this was not just an ordinary vote but a fundamental class confrontation in electoral form, in which everything they had gained in the past five years was at stake.

It was for this reason that early in the referendum campaign, Chávez himself called on the people to form Unidades de Batalla Electoral (UBEs, Units of Electoral Battle) to organise the campaign for the 'No' vote ('No' to recall) in their neighbourhoods. It had become obvious once again that the *chavista* political parties, the MVR and others, had neither the confidence of the people nor the right approach to mobilise support on the scale required. But as on other occasions, the Chávez–people dialectic worked wonders: scarcely had Chávez spoken than UBEs began to spring up like mushrooms in the *cerros*, the towns and villages of the Andes mountains and the *llanos* (the interior plains). Members of each UBE undertook to go out individually to talk to their neighbours and convince them of the importance of turning out and voting 'No'. Chávez also reorganised the central coordinating body of the entire movement: more than a year earlier he had formed the Comando Ayacucho (named after the 1824 battle in Peru which ended Spanish rule in South America), but this was dominated by representatives of the political parties and had become paralysed by factionalism, so he now replaced it by the Comando Maisanta (named after Chávez' great-grandfather, a popular guerrilla fighter) composed of the most dynamic military and civilian activists.

Since the referendum and local election victories of August and October 2004 the Venezuelan process has entered a new phase, characterised by opposition weakness, revolutionary advance and internal contradictions. After repeated defeats the opposition (and its US backers) is divided between those who favour a long-term political strategy, trying to work from within the system, and the hard-liners who incline to violence and terrorism. Although the latter tendency suffered resounding defeats in the coup and the *paro*, it resurfaces whenever the oligarchy feels that its fundamental interests are threatened. Thus after the referendum Chávez announced that one of the areas in which more vigorous action was required was the administration of justice, and one reflection of this was that at long last the judicial investigation of responsibility for the coup two and a half years earlier began to move forward seriously. A team of young lawyers from the Fiscalía (the Attorney-General's office) began to issue summonses for the interrogation of some of the most notorious *golpista* officers and businessmen; in retaliation one of these young lawyers, Danilo Anderson, was assassinated by a car bomb on 18 November 2004. The popular and even international reaction to this crime was so strong that for a while afterwards the terrorist option was downplayed, but it will undoubtedly return; indeed in June 2005 the government announced that it had reliable intelligence reports of the latest plot to assassinate Chávez, and suspended a public ceremony planned for 24 June as a result.

Such signs of opposition desperation are a response not only to political defeat but also to further material advances of the revolution. It was on 5 December 2004, at the closing ceremony of the World Meeting of Intellectuals and Artists in Defence of Humanity held in Caracas (and which I had the privilege to attend) that Chávez surprised everyone by declaring for the first time that 'it is necessary to re-examine the history of Socialism and to reclaim the concept of Socialism ... and to search for the way forward to the Socialism of the twenty-first century.' He would return to this theme at the World Social Forum in Porto Alegre in January 2005 and on a visit to India around the same time, proclaiming that 'only a fool could think that the solution to the world's problems lies in capitalism'.

That this was not mere rhetoric was shown by a number of decisions in December 2004 and early 2005. It was in December that Chávez, on another visit to Havana, signed a major agreement with Cuba under which the two countries formally agreed to inaugurate the Bolivarian Alternative for the Americas (ALBA, Alternativa Bolivariana para las Américas), Venezuela's proposal of an alternative to the US-sponsored Free Trade Area of the Americas (ALCA in Spanish). This agreement creates close economic cooperation between the two countries, including the promotion of direct links between their respective public-sector banks and industries. Then in January the government announced the expropriation of Venepal, a packaging company abandoned by its owners during the *paro* and occupied by its workers ever since; responding to the workers' demands, Chávez announced that the factory would now be run under *co-gestión* (a combination of workers' control and state management). Two months later another plant in a similar situation, the National Valve Company (Compañía Nacional de Válvulas) was expropriated and placed under the same regime, and Chávez announced that while the government wanted to continue to work with private capital, any bankrupt or abandoned enterprise would be subjected to the same scheme.

It was also in these months that the agrarian reform, a highly contentious measure originally decreed in the 49 'Enabling Laws' of November 2001 but subject to repeated legal and violent hindrance by the landlords and the opposition, was given a new impulse. Agrarian reform is fundamental both as a measure of social justice for peasants and rural workers and as a development strategy. Although the percentage of the Venezuelan population working in agriculture is small, agrarian reform has great symbolic significance as a challenge to the oligarchy. But also in practical terms, the small number of rural workers is a symptom of the abandonment of agriculture over the previous decades and the flight of capital to speculative activities such as urban real estate, leading to the absurd situation where a country with abundant fertile land imports 75 per cent of its food. One of the aims of the agrarian reform is therefore to revive agricultural production for the domestic market, with a long-term aim of self-sufficiency. A further aim is to reduce the unhealthy concentration of population in a few coastal cities and induce some of the marginalised population of the *cerros* to return to agriculture, by offering them employment, landed property (on a collective basis) and healthier living conditions.

The Ley de Tierras or Land Law, the basis of the agrarian reform, is based on distribution of both public lands and lands expropriated from private estates. Properties over a certain size (which varies according to the quality of the land) may be affected on the basis of a survey carried out by the National Land Institute (INTI), and it is uncultivated land on these estates that is subject to expropriation (with compensation based on the value declared for tax purposes). The expropriated land is distributed to agrarian cooperatives which receive full technical and marketing assistance from the government and the benefits of the various educational, health and social Missions. That such a moderate law should have met violent opposition (along with the petroleum issue it was a major factor in the coup) is symptomatic of the reactionary character of the landlord class in Venezuela, just as in other Latin American countries. After the coup, later in 2002, implementation of the law did begin, and by 28 December 2003, according to official figures, a total of 2,262,467 hectares of land had been distributed to 116,899 families (INTI 2004, 3). But up to this point it was based entirely on distribution of public lands, and it was only later in 2004 that expropriation of land from private estates began. In November 2004, following victory in the state and municipal elections, several *chavista* state governors issued a joint declaration proclaiming their intention to start expropriations of private estates and began to implement the necessary legal measures. The National Land Institute was reorganised and Chávez reiterated the urgency of implementing the law. In some states such as Zulia and Portuguesa hired thugs in the service of the landlords were murdering peasant activists – 138 were killed between 2001 and July 2005 – and Chávez talked of sending in the military to provide protection. Well before there was any talk of Socialism, the class character of the struggle was crystal clear.

As the revolution radicalised at home, relations with the United States became strained once again. Victory in the recall referendum had provided a temporary respite, but it was obvious that the Bolivarian project went directly counter to US plans for Latin America, and Venezuela's friendship with Cuba, Iran and other members of the 'Axis of Evil' made good relations virtually impossible. However democratic the Venezuelan process was – indeed, perhaps especially because here was a country which had the nerve to question the US claim to a monopoly of democratic virtue – it was unacceptable to Washington because of its direct challenge to US hegemony. Venezuela's only hope, as reflected in Chávez' policies, was and is to strengthen the revolution internally through popular support and organisation and military strength, and externally by cultivating close relations both with Latin American neighbours and with other power centres throughout the world: the OPEC countries, Russia, China, India, and sympathetic European countries such as France and now Spain under Zapatero.

From February to August 2005 the indefatigable Chávez continued his incessant travels, again visiting China, India, Iran and many Latin American countries. Venezuela announced purchases of military helicopters and 100,000 rifles from Russia and tanks from Spain; when this aroused further criticism from Washington, the Venezuelan government pointed out that the rifle purchase was long overdue to re-equip the armed forces and that faithful US allies like Colombia had also bought Russian helicopters. In the same period Chávez signed a series of bilateral economic agreements with Latin American countries; even if no country other than Cuba signed up to the ALBA as such, it was obvious that bilateral deals in the spirit of the ALBA were very attractive to other countries in the region. In August 2005 that prestigious mouthpiece of the world capitalist establishment, the *Financial Times*, lamented that Washington had no constructive Latin American policy and was losing the regional initiative to Chávez.

## VENEZUELA'S ALTERNATIVE DEVELOPMENT MODEL: 'ENDOGENOUS DEVELOPMENT' AND SOCIALISM

When Chávez started talking about Socialism being the only way forward, this did not mean that Venezuela was about to follow the same course as Cuba in 1960–61 (and as some Trotskyists and Marxist-Leninists would like) and nationalise virtually the entire economy. Chávez is only too well aware, and has said so on more than one occasion, that in today's world such a course would be suicidal. But apart from this, the Bolivarian model of 'endogenous development' is intended to be radically different from the centralised and bureaucratically controlled economies of the former Soviet bloc.

When Chávez talks of 'searching for the Socialism of the twenty-first century', it has to be understood that he is serious both about Socialism and about seeking a new model which will be much more politically democratic and economically flexible.

The concept of 'endogenous development' is a proposal for development based on the use of national and local resources, with emphasis on popular cooperatives and other forms of social enterprise in conjunction with public corporations (and in some cases Venezuelan private enterprises). It does not rule out large nationalised industries like PDVSA and the Corporación Venezolana de Guyana (which runs the steel, aluminium and other heavy industries), with the possibility of further nationalisations; but the emphasis is on subverting capitalism 'from the bottom up' as well as from the top. It also emphasises that development should be sustainable, and therefore must be environmentally responsible.

This 'bottom-up', community-based development strategy logically favours cooperatives as one of its principal instruments, and one of the 49 'Enabling Laws' of November 2001 was a new Law of Cooperatives. The Bolivarian activists who drafted the law were well aware that in many countries cooperatives have merely become a form of popular capitalism, and the law provides safeguards to try to prevent this, although it is clear that the ultimate fate of cooperative enterprises will depend on the consolidation of non-capitalist principles in the broader economy. Certainly the growth of cooperatives has been exponential, from 762 in 1998 to over 73,000, with over 800,000 members, in mid-2005 (Sunacoop 2005). Another important component of the Bolivarian development strategy is micro-credit, which was pioneered in India and Bangladesh as a means of providing credit to those who would never normally qualify for bank loans; although not in itself revolutionary, by eliminating the requirement for collateral it calls into question the normal logic of capital, and has been of enormous benefit to many poor peasants (especially women). The Venezuelan Women's Development Bank has taken the concept further: not only does it require no collateral but it only makes loans on a collective basis, to groups of women who present community projects. The Women's Bank has already had a major impact, making thousands of loans which have transformed the lives (and raised the political consciousness) of tens of thousands of women in poor communities. On a similar basis there also exists the Bank of the Sovereign People which makes loans to both women and men in community groups.

The concept of 'endogenous development' is the basis of another of the 'Missions', the Misión Vuelvan Caras. The name of this Mission is quite confusing: literally 'To Turn the Face', it derives from the battle cry of a nineteenth-century revolutionary general, and in this context implies a return to the roots, a recovery of national values. One of its aims is to generate employment, and for this reason many observers describe it simply as the 'Employment Mission'. But its real aim goes far beyond employment and is intended to support alternative development projects of all kinds, 'to change the socio-economic, politico-cultural model' on the basis of education and employment, debureaucratisation of the state and democratic planning (Lanz Rodríguez 2004, 5, 10). The goal is to create 'a new productive structure' in which the profit motive is replaced by 'the satisfaction of collective needs', but within a transitional, mixed economy combining state, mixed and private property (both monopolistic and non-monopolistic) and collective self-managed property; this requires social control and regulation, including price and exchange controls. This inevitably implies confronting the economic power of 'oligarchic groups', and this will require a 'strategic alliance between State enterprises, the associative economy, the non-monopolistic sector of national capital, and small and medium enterprises in both the countryside and the city', and in socio-political terms 'the construction of a Social Revolutionary Bloc' (Lanz Rodríguez 2004, 21–2).

For many Marxists such a vision will seem utopian and unviable in the era of imperialism because of the notion of an alliance with 'national capital', which is regarded as completely sold out or subordinated to transnational interests (Frank 1967; Marini 1973). But the weakness of such strategies in the past – as implemented by some Latin American Communist parties – was that they were based on political subordination to bourgeois parties, as with the Mexican CP's critical support for the PRI from the 1940s to the 1970s. In Venezuela those national capitalists who collaborate with the Bolivarian process, in 'poles of endogenous development' and national infrastructure projects, do so on terms imposed by a popular revolutionary government. This does not mean that such capitalist interests may not at times attempt to distort the projects in which they participate and to undermine the process, which is why there is a constant political battle going on within the institutions of the Bolivarian revolution; this is why the issue of popular democratic control is so crucial and is constantly being reiterated by Chávez.

It also means that the social or associative economy – agrarian, industrial and commercial cooperatives, enterprises under workers' control or comanagement, etc. – must constantly be strengthened and promoted by the state so as not to become subordinated to capitalist interests.

The concrete implementation of this strategy was severely hampered during the power struggle of the coup and the *paro*, and is still a matter of permanent contention. But since early 2003 the process has advanced significantly with the recovery of PDVSA, the creation of a growing number of 'endogenous development' projects, the beginnings of implementation of the agrarian reform and the first cases of workers' control in industry. The endogenous development projects are enormously varied in both size and character: they may be minor local schemes with a couple of dozen participants or massive regional projects incorporating tens of thousands of workers, and may be agricultural, industrial, commercial or a combination of all three. A major scheme which I visited in April 2004 is the Complejo Agro-Industrial Azucarero Ezequiel Zamora (CAAEZ, Ezequiel Zamora Agro-Industrial Sugar Complex) in Chávez' home State of Barinas: a huge new sugar mill is being built with assistance from Cuban technicians and Brazilian machinery (an example of the emphasis on Latin American integration), to process sugar cultivated by agrarian reform cooperatives on land which apparently has some of the highest cane yields in the world. But the project is not intended to be limited to sugar monoculture: the farms will produce subsistence crops as well and some other commercial crops which will also be processed locally. It is estimated that the project will eventually provide some 50,000 jobs.

Other endogenous development projects I visited are very modest, such as a collective of a couple of dozen indigenous Wayúu women designing and sewing children's clothes in Mara, Zulia State, or a group of landless peasants in the same region who are receiving training in organic agriculture on a State experimental farm. In the latter case the success of the project depends on them receiving land of their own through the agrarian reform when they finish the course, which is far from guaranteed given the slow progress of the agrarian reform in Zulia where the landlord class is very powerful and the opposition controls the State government.

In rural areas endogenous development is intimately connected with the agrarian reform. Another project I visited, in Chaguaramal, Miranda State, near the coast east of Caracas, is perhaps more typical:

a medium-size cooperative farm, it consists of some 200 hectares of land cleared from the forest, providing a livelihood for some 130 families (as of April 2004). It is producing a variety of subsistence and commercial crops as well as raising cattle and fish farming, with an emphasis on organic methods, and the produce is commercialised via the Mercal programme. The land was first granted in August 2002, but the coop members complained that initially the project was bureaucratically run by technicians from a public agency inherited from the previous government who took decisions without consultation. A year later, as a result of their complaints, it was transferred to INTI and there was a dramatic change: the INTI officials limited their role to the provision of technical and management services and allowed Chaguaramal to be democratically run as a true cooperative, with the full participation of all its members, especially the women who had previously suffered discrimination. A crèche is now provided to permit full involvement by the women, who control some of the key productive activities such as composting, and new housing has been built by the members with recreational facilities designed according to their needs and priorities.

In mid-2005 there was a marked acceleration of the economic and social revolution, with new endogenous development and cooperative or social enterprises being announced every week. On 17 July 2005, in his regular *Aló Presidente* (Hello, Mr President) TV programme, Chávez announced from Cumaná in the poor eastern State of Sucre that across the country 136 enterprises which had been closed down by their owners were being evaluated with a view to expropriation in order to turn them over to the workers in *co-gestión*. 'It is against the Constitution to have closed enterprises in Venezuela. It's just like having idle lands [in agriculture]', said Chávez. As he inaugurated the United Agro-Industrial Cacao Cooperative, an enterprise which had been abandoned for nine years and had now been bought by the workers with state assistance, he declared it to be an example of the Empresas de Producción Social (EPS, Social Production Enterprises) 'which are at the centre of an economic turning-point towards the socialism of the XXI century' (Aporrea 63341). In total, he said, the government had discovered 1,149 enterprises totally or partially closed down by their owners, a situation which could not be allowed.

As always, Chávez also called on 'really serious entrepreneurs' to invest in the country, but he left his audience in no doubt that this self-managed Socialism was the way forward. 'Revolutionary democracy is the road of the transition to Socialism', he continued, and went on to explain how the EPS were intended to go well beyond simple cooperative production to become communal enterprises providing social services to their communities and integrated into the entire local society. Thus the Cacao Cooperative already had a canteen which provided meals for children of the local community and a Barrio Adentro medical clinic for the local inhabitants, both financed by the enterprise (Aporrea 63345). The idea was that the workers' social life should be integrated with their productive labour, and that production should always have a social function; he suggested creating a labour fund and units of community production, communal services and communal distribution, as well as a micro-bank financed by enterprise profits. Finally he declared, 'Let no-one think that we are improvising, we have had a strategic plan for some time past and we are developing, promoting and consolidating it.'

Cooperatives and small and medium-sized local enterprises are one aspect of 'endogenous development', but active intervention by the state in promoting large-scale industrial and infrastructure projects is another. Chávez and the Bolivarian government are very critical of the neo-liberal concept of decentralisation which tends to weaken the central government in the name of local democracy, while in practice handing power to local elites and transnational capital which thus further undermines national sovereignty and the possibility of independent development. In order to prevent this, and in stark contrast to the prevailing tendency in most Latin American countries or other world regions, the Venezuelan state under Chávez has actively strengthened its role in key economic sectors: not only petroleum and petrochemicals, but also power generation, communications, ports and heavy industry. The Caracas metro is being expanded with three new lines and new metros are being built in Maracaibo, Valencia and Los Teques; an ambitious railway construction programme for both passengers and freight is under way with Chinese and Italian assistance, making Venezuela almost the only Latin American country to be expanding its rail network; and the ports are being modernised under public ownership, not privatised as in most countries. The aim of endogenous development and the social economy is indeed to promote local communal self-government in all aspects of social, economic and political affairs, but it does not imply an absence of the central state; rather, the state – which must itself be fully democratic and accountable – provides a favourable and protective national framework for the local social economy.

This means that the principles of popular democratic participation must also be introduced in official agencies and large-scale nationalised industries, which must also become EPSs, social production enterprises. Now that PDVSA has been effectively renationalised, it is not only being used to finance social programmes and alternative development projects, but efforts are being made to democratise its internal structure and to give the people a real sense of ownership of the industry, with regional public forums being held where popular groups can discuss the future of the national oil company. Similarly in the CVG (Corporación Venezolana de Guayana), a massive industrial complex on the River Orinoco centred around publicly owned steel, aluminium and hydroelectric plants, new managements appointed within the last two years are trying to promote workers' control or at least *co-gestión* in which workers have a substantial degree of influence, and to integrate these enterprises more with local communities. Thus the aluminium company Alcasa (Aluminio del Caroni) is now presided over by Carlos Lanz, the theorist of endogenous development and a former guerrilla commander, and its 2,700 workers are already electing two of its five corporate directors and several of its management personnel (Ellsworth 2005).

Without attempting to impose rigid or unrealistic plans, the Bolivarian government has proclaimed a series of broad goals for national development. These include revitalising agriculture so as to achieve a much greater degree of food self-sufficiency; diversifying industry so as to reduce dependence on petroleum and on manufactured imports; encouraging part of the urban marginal population to move back to the countryside; and settling and developing the vast interior plains (*llanos*) in order to reduce the concentration of population and industry in the coastal cities. The other major aim, in economic but also political and cultural terms, is to promote Latin American integration, the great ideal of the liberator Simón Bolívar. The key proposal here is the ALBA, the Bolivarian Alternative for the Americas, a scheme for economic union based less on free trade than on planned integration and strengthening of Latin American autonomy in relation to the United States. Although so far the ALBA has only been accepted by Cuba, a number of important bilateral agreements inspired by similar principles have also been signed, particularly with Brazil, Argentina, Uruguay and the Caribbean nations. Thus Venezuela has agreed to have most of its merchant marine built in Argentine shipyards in return for purchasing large numbers of pedigree cattle from Argentina in order to improve the quality of Venezuelan cattle. Brazil, Argentina and Uruguay have agreed to participate in Chávez' proposal for a joint South American oil company, Petrosur, based on collaboration by their respective national petroleum enterprises; and they have also accepted the proposal for a joint Latin TV station, Telesur, described by some as 'a Latin Al-Jazeera'. Similarly, Venezuela has agreed to provide Uruguay with 100,000 barrels of oil a month at 75 per cent of world market prices in return for imports of high-quality Uruguayan cement. The direction of all of these schemes is to promote Latin American unity and independence in the face of US hegemony, a concept which strikes a chord in many regional leaders no matter how much they may disagree with Chávez' radical internal policies.

## PARTICIPATORY DEMOCRACY AND POPULAR POWER

One of the most interesting aspects of the Venezuelan revolution is its constant emphasis on democracy, and the insistence that democracy should be 'participatory and protagonistic', in other words with protagonism – active participation and decision-making – by the people. The concept of the popular constituent power as the source of legitimacy of the new 'Fifth Republic' and as the ongoing basis of the revolutionary transformation makes this the most profoundly democratic revolution the world has yet seen, at least in terms of its ideology.

What is particularly striking about the process is that it has taken place in a country which had a liberal-democratic regime for 40 years, not a dictatorship like Batista's Cuba or Somoza's Nicaragua; it is a response to the failure of liberal pluralism to provide any real representation for the poor majority. Although *puntofijismo* had its peculiarities, in essence it was a typical liberal-democratic regime: the exclusion of the Left by the original Punto Fijo pact came to an end after 1970 when the PCV and the MAS adopted electoral politics and began to win seats in Congress, and the 1988 reforms allowed the Left to begin winning State governorships and facilitated the electoral advance of LCR. By that time the Venezuelan political system was in many ways more open than those of Britain and the US, but the fundamental problem for the poor was that none of the political parties – in the end not even LCR – was accountable to them. As we have seen, this defect of liberal systems is also present in the 'advanced' countries, but of course in Venezuela the problem of poverty and social exclusion is much greater.

What Venezuela demonstrates is that it is both possible and necessary to recover the concept of democracy from the elites and restore it to the people. The behaviour of the Coordinadora Democrática, until recently the umbrella organisation of the opposition to Chávez, is fascinating precisely because of its undemocratic character: faced with the repeated demonstration that they do not represent the majority of the Venezuelan people, their response is to cry fraud, to rely on legal obstructionism and filibustering, to resort to violence and indeed to promote a military coup (while pretending that it was not really a coup). Equally fascinating is Chávez' response to these manoeuvres: despite the temptation (which must be enormous) to appeal to revolutionary legitimacy and rule by decree (as in Cuba in 1959–61, where there was also massive popular repudiation of corrupt party politics), he insists on maintaining constitutional procedures.

The 1999 Constitution itself is a thoroughly democratic document in terms of both content and the process by which it was produced and ratified, and popular participation is mentioned time and time again in its 350 articles. But the key to the revolutionary process lies in the implementation of the Constitution and the formation and consolidation of popular grass-roots organisations to take real possession of the rights formulated in this abstract document. The formal structures of political authority – Congress, State, municipal and borough (*parroquia*) governments – although themselves very democratic, are not seen as sufficient to ensure real popular participation and control. The new Bolivarian Republic of Venezuela is intended to be as far as possible the direct expression of the popular movement, of popular power in neighbourhoods, factories, farms, schools, towns and indigenous communities: the movement which brought Chávez to power in the first place. Chávez is less concerned with specific institutions like the MVR party or the Bolivarian circles than with ensuring that both he and all public officials stay in touch with and remain responsive to the people in the *barrios*. This is why he is constantly searching for new political and organisational forms for the Bolivarian Movement: faced with criticisms, often legitimate, of the deficiencies of the MVR, the Comando Ayacucho, or the Bolivarian circles, and anxious to avoid the evils of opportunism, authoritarianism, corruption and bureaucracy, he has repeatedly surprised his own followers with new political initiatives and experiments. This also explains, at least in part, what is often seen as a major weakness of the Venezuelan process, namely the lack of a well-structured mediating organisation between Chávez and the mass popular movement: rather than rush to consolidate a revolutionary party or top-down bureaucratic structure which could all too easily be filled with political opportunists, Chávez is anxious to promote the growth and consolidation of popular organisations from the bottom up and to rely on their dynamism and protagonism to push the process forward.

This emphasis on independent popular organisations necessarily diminishes the role of a political party or parties. It is not that parties are totally condemned by Chávez: rather, they are seen as having a secondary role, organising and mobilising people to vote in elections and proposing ideological options, but not monopolising power. Chávez has also repeatedly expressed the idea that a revolutionary party or parties should work constantly to promote popular power and organisation; he quotes Gramsci as saying that 'a party which aspires to lead society should provide leadership before coming to power ... '. He also talks more and more of the notion of creating a political instrument which goes beyond the parties, 'a unitary movement, a popular Bolivarian bloc' (Harnecker 2002, 204–5). It seems clear that the Venezuelan process needs a more structured and effective political organisation than it has at present; but whatever form that organisation takes, it will be neither as centralised nor as exclusive as the Communist parties which ended up controlling most twentieth-century revolutions.

The reliance on local popular initiative was very clear in the formation and development of the first such grass-roots organisation, the Bolivarian circles. Small local groups of seven to 15 people, they are intended to study the ideology of *Bolivarianismo*, discuss local issues and defend the revolution. Formed in response to Chávez' public appeal of 25 April 2001, they sprang up spontaneously in popular neighbourhoods all over the country in late 2001 and early 2002, and played a crucial role in mobilising people to defeat the coup during the tense hours of 11–14 April. They continued to multiply for over a year after that, coming to incorporate 3 or 4 million people according to most estimates. They are still one of the bulwarks of the revolutionary process, although in more recent times it seems as if they have been partially displaced by other forms of grass-roots organisation such as the urban land committees, water committees and UBEs.

The urban land committees (Comités de Tierras Urbanas) emerged as part of the urban land reform, under which inhabitants of squatter settlements (the shanty-towns of the *cerros*) are given title to the land on which their precarious self-built dwellings are situated. The title is vested in the community, not individuals, and the community forms an urban land committee to administer its new collective property and to undertake and demand support for material improvements such as water, sewerage and electricity services or road paving. This project was initiated by a presidential decree early in 2002, in part in order to forestall a similar initiative by the opposition Primero Justicia (Justice First) party which also proposed to give land to urban squatters, but on the neo-liberal basis of individual titles; as so often, internal contradictions delayed government action until the opposition forced the pace.[1] The urban land committees rapidly became one of the most active forms of popular participation in the revolutionary process; recently the government has tried to supplement them by local public planning committees (also directly elected in the neighbourhoods) with broader powers and responsibilities, but so far these seem to have failed and it is the urban land committees which remain one of the most active sites of popular participation.

Another highly successful area of popular participation is in relation to water supply, where Mesas Técnicas de Água (technical water boards) bring together professional technicians with elected popular representatives, and local water committees consisting entirely of popular delegates arrange the distribution of water between neighbouring communities which share the same water mains. This programme actually began in a few Caracas neighbourhoods such as Antímano before Chávez, under the mayoralty of Aristóbulo Asturiz (then of the LCR party, now PPT and a Chávez supporter) in 1994–96; it was taken up and greatly expanded by Chávez.

It is no accident that these successful instruments of popular participation relate to immediate practical necessities: land and water. The same is true of the Barrio Adentro programme, relating to health care, which is administered at local level by neighbourhood health committees with very active popular participation. This actually began as a proposal of a team led by Rubén Alayón of the Central University of Venezuela in March 2003; accepted by Mayor Freddy Bernal of the Municipio Libertador (the central borough of Caracas) it was then taken up by Chávez and launched at national level a few months later as the Misión Barrio Adentro. Once again, the community dynamic was crucial, although subsequently incorporated

1. I owe this information to Professor Dick Parker of the Universidad Central de Venezuela (UCV).

into a more formal administrative structure with clinics staffed by Cuban health professionals.

Popular participation is an essential aspect of all the Missions and similar government programmes. In the housing programmes like the Plan Avispa, although the resources are provided by the military or by government agencies, local communities are consulted first to determine the type and layout of housing required, and local people are employed and given training during the construction. In the *Mercal* food distribution plan (now called the 'Mercal Mission'), although the big markets are run by the military and civilian professionals, an extension of the programme provides free meals to the poorest people in each neighbourhood, and it is local people with the assistance of social workers of the Barrio Adentro Mission who decide which individuals should benefit. By June 2005 there were over 4,000 *casas de alimentación* (community kitchens) where members of local neighbourhoods are paid to cook meals under these *Mercal* and *Proal* programmes (Mercedes Cobo 2005).

The same dynamic of community activism was apparent in the formation of the electoral units, the UBEs: the concept was formulated by Chávez early in the recall referendum campaign when he realised that the MVR and allied political parties were inadequate to the task of popular mobilisation required, and there was an immediate and dramatic popular response as people in the *cerros* of Caracas and in communities across the country began to form UBEs without waiting for detailed instructions or the arrival of public officials of any kind. Chávez announced general guidelines for these new committees – they should divide responsibility for canvassing specific streets among their members, who should each approach their neighbours to explain the significance of the referendum and the importance of voting – but the actual organisation of the UBEs was entirely spontaneous, another reflection of the enormous enthusiasm for Chávez and the revolutionary process at grass-roots level. As with the Bolivarian circles and the urban land committees, the UBEs were accepted by the people as their own, indeed apart from Chávez' initial public appeal, they were created by the people themselves rather than by any party or state bureaucracy. In the same way, when the referendum was over, many UBEs wanted to carry on, and when Chávez became aware of this he suggested that they should be converted into 'units of endogenous battle' with the same acronym, referring to the concept of 'endogenous development' in economic and social terms. This dialectic between Chávez and the people, or between Chávez and the hard core of the MBR-200 on the one hand and the grass-roots popular organisations on the other, is the key to the Bolivarian revolution; and although this may arouse suspicions of populism or *caudillismo* among many progressive observers, so far it has proved more dynamic, more sensitive to the real feelings of the people and more democratic in the profound sense, than any conventional party or government mechanism. What Chávez is attempting to do is to stimulate and give free rein to the popular movement at all levels, without constraint by state or party bureaucracy; what he and his immediate associates do is to provide the minimum necessary central orientation and ensure that the state bureaucracy performs its essential functions without suppressing popular initiative.

If this kind of massive and spontaneous popular response to suggestions and proposals from Chávez is one characteristic of the process, the converse is also true: Chávez responds positively and unequivocally to pressures or grievances expressed by the popular movements. When students occupied the Central University of Venezuela (UCV) in what was seen by many Polo Patriótico politicians as a reactionary movement, Chávez declared that the students' concerns were legitimate and that the universities also had to be reorganised from the bottom up as part of the revolutionary process. In July 2005, after a demonstration in Caracas by peasants expressing dissatisfaction with the slow progress of the agrarian reform and the inadequate work of INTI, Chávez responded by announcing that from that time onwards the directors of INTI would be directly elected by the peasant organisations. In another context, from the very beginning there was general dissatisfaction with the inadequacy of the government's response to the hostility of the private media and the poor quality of programming on the public Channel 8. But when at a press conference in 2003 one of the questions for the President came from an unknown young journalist, Blanca Eekhout, representing an independent community TV station called Catia TV, Chávez' response was immediate and positive: popular community media of this kind must be encouraged and supported, and shortly afterwards he announced plans for a second national public TV channel, TeleVive, and appointed Blanca Eekhout to run it (and more recently she has been moved to the directorship of Channel 8).

Despite the concern for popular autonomy and dynamism, Chávez and the Bolivarian leadership are well aware that popular power must be given institutional expression and structure to guarantee its permanence and effectiveness. Thus basic rules and a national coordinating body were quickly established for the Bolivarian circles, in order to prevent them falling into the kind of disorderly and violent behaviour of which they were accused by the opposition. Then as government programmes like the urban land reform, the agrarian reform and the Missions began to take shape, legal structures were devised to channel the enthusiastic popular response and enable the people to take effective possession of these programmes. But it is precisely at the level of more formal political structures that popular participation falls off, and this remains one of the weaknesses of the Bolivarian revolution: how to ensure effective popular participation at higher levels of administration. This problem is manifest, for example, in the Consejos Locales de Planificación Pública (CLPP, local public planning councils), intended to provide direct popular input into, and indeed control of, municipal administration.

The prologue to the June 2002 Act of Congress establishing the CLPP proclaims 'our right to take collective decisions about fundamental issues for the development of our communities, seated at the same table with the official representatives of the locality' (FIDES 2003, 9). Article 3 establishes that each CLPP will be presided over by the mayor and will include all the municipal councillors and chairpersons of the borough councils, but also the representatives of neighbourhood committees and 'local civil society' who must equal the total plus one of the formal local government officials. 'Local civil society' is understood to mean educational, health, sporting, cultural, business, labour, environmental and other sectoral or voluntary organisations, and the election of delegates of these groups and of the neighbourhood committees must take place in a general meeting of the respective organisation, supervised and recorded by a representative of the local Ombudsman's office. The CLPP must gather, process and prioritise proposals from the community organisations and generate proposals for the municipal development plan and budget, which must in turn be approved by the CLPP and not just by the formal municipal council. Service on the CLPP is honorary, although there will also be a technical office (with salaried local civil servants) to prepare and process documentation; all information must be available to any citizen of the municipality.

In effect the CLPP are intended to put into practice the principles of the 'participatory budget' pioneered by the Brazilian Workers' Party and extend these principles to all aspects of local government, bringing the formal elected councillors under direct popular supervision. But so far, according to most observers, they have singularly failed to arouse popular interest or participation, probably because people regard them as being dominated by professional politicians. This, however, has not led Chávez and the government to abandon the project; on the contrary, they have redoubled efforts to promote popular involvement in these councils. In October 2005 Freddy Bernal, mayor of the Caracas Libertador borough, announced that 1,200 CLPP would be created in that borough because they are 'the fundamental basis of participation, of protagonistic democracy and of twenty-first-century Socialism'; Bernal's declaration was supported by General García Carneiro, by the mayor of Metropolitan Caracas and the governor of neighbouring Miranda State. He added that as a result of efforts by several working groups they had come to an agreement on how to implement the CLPP, whose 'real essence will be seen when each organised community begins in its own area to debate the diagnosis of its problems, the search for solutions and itself becomes involved in those solutions … ' (Aporrea 67532).

What seems clear, then, is that the 'participatory and protagonistic democracy' proclaimed by Chávez and inscribed in the Constitution is gradually becoming a reality, although with inevitable obstacles and deficiencies. Popular mobilisation in the streets, in mass meetings and in neighbourhood institutions is a vital part of the process, and is complemented and balanced by institutionalised legal procedures. But popular participation has real limits which reflect the internal contradictions of the revolutionary process. The popular classes participate on two levels: first, at neighbourhood level in those institutions which are directly relevant to their daily lives (urban land committees, water and health committees); and secondly, at both local and national levels in those institutions and processes which they see as crucial to maintaining revolutionary political power (Bolivarian circles, UBEs, presidential elections and referenda). But they have much less interest in formal administrative structures, even elective ones like Parliament, municipal councils or CLPP, which they see as dominated by professional politicians. A crucial challenge facing the revolution, therefore, is how to create new instruments which the people will accept as their own in order to guarantee their participation in these formal governmental structures. The government's commitment to this was further demonstrated in mid-2005 with the creation of a new Ministry of Popular Participation, headed by one of Chávez' most trusted associates, General Jorge Luis García Carneiro, and with outstanding advisers such as Marta

Harnecker who has exceptional experience in initiatives of popular democracy and participation throughout Latin America.

There is no doubt that the laws and institutions of the Bolivarian Republic of Venezuela go to great lengths to entrench principles of accountability and of participation by working-class and popular sectors of society. Ultimately no constitution or set of laws can alone guarantee the implementation of such principles, and it is the dynamic of popular struggle and organisation, linked to the national revolutionary leadership, which is decisive. Despite its limitations, Venezuela today has what is probably the most genuinely democratic system existing anywhere in the world. In the long run, however, popular power (which is what true democracy is about) can only be sustained on the basis of an alternative, non-capitalist economic structure: the 'socialism of the twenty-first century' which Chávez now says is the only real solution.

### THE REVOLUTIONARY CHARACTER OF THE VENEZUELAN PROCESS

If the reactionary opposition denounces the Bolivarian revolution for being 'Castro-Communist', many left-wing critics condemn it for *not* being precisely that: for not nationalising the means of production and for not adopting what they consider to be a clear Socialist programme. They also question whether a democratic and electoral process can be anything other than reformist, and make ominous comparisons with Chile under Allende.

Fortunately, Venezuela is not another Chile, even if it came close to being one for 48 hours in April 2002. The crucial difference, as already demonstrated, lies in the armed forces, which are not merely 'constitutionalist' as the Chilean military were claimed to be before 1973, but are active participants in the revolutionary process; and this is more so today than ever before, since the Right lost most of its military support in the wake of the coup and the *paro*, and the active military have deepened their political consciousness since then. But there is another major difference, and that is that in Chile Allende was elected with only 36 per cent of the popular vote and even in subsequent legislative and municipal elections barely reached 50 per cent, whereas Chávez and his movement have now won ten elections and referenda with majorities ranging from 56 to 86 per cent. In order to undertake a radical transformation of state and society, control of the legitimate means of violence is indeed one crucial condition, but it is also essential to have a very clear popular mandate.

To understand the Venezuelan process it is also necessary to appreciate that it does have revolutionary origins: it has not been purely constitutional and peaceful. The MBR-200 began as a clandestine revolutionary movement, and the *caracazo* and the two military-civilian revolts of 1992 represented violent ruptures which shook the *puntofijista* regime to its foundations. Even though Chávez subsequently came to power through elections, the combination of military support and massive popular backing meant that the revolutionary potential of the situation was apparent to all. As Chávez has subsequently declared, 'This is a peaceful revolution, but an armed one': in other words, although change is now being carried out by peaceful and constitutional means, if the *escuálidos* again resort to force the government will respond in kind. Moreover, the failure of the coup and of the *paro* represented further ruptures of the old power structure: in effect, the Bolivarian Movement did not seize power in one fell swoop, but it has conquered important segments of state power by stages. There will no doubt be further confrontations and ruptures as the process continues: the struggle over the agrarian reform looks as if it may well precipitate another confrontation.

With regard to the property structure and the absence of major nationalisations, we have already seen that the strategy of 'endogenous development' implies a different and more subtle anti-capitalist strategy. But this does not mean that nationalisations are excluded: the effective renationalisation of PDVSA and the major state initiatives in infrastructure show that the government is more than prepared to intervene in the economy in a manner radically opposed to current neo-liberal orthodoxy. Pragmatic Venezuelan entrepreneurs and transnational companies have come to realise that they can do business perfectly well under Chávez, especially now that the economy has recovered from the crisis provoked by the coup and the *paro* and has registered the highest growth rates in Latin America for 2004 and 2005. But both national and foreign capitalists recognise that the rules of the game have changed: Venezuela has rejected any kind of free trade agreement with the US, it does not accept IMF conditions, it maintains exchange controls and is using petroleum revenue for both social programmes and large-scale public investment, all of which goes directly against the prevailing rules of the game. Capitalists may still be able to make handsome profits, but they do so under conditions dictated by the Venezuelan state and not just as they please. The economic system as a whole is still capitalist, but it is subject to a degree of *dirigisme* not seen anywhere in the so-called 'Free World' for at least two decades. In the context of unipolar US hegemony and neo-liberal orthodoxy, this is a major achievement, and it is only possible on the basis of massive popular mobilisation, military support and control of a vital resource, a combination which enables the Bolivarian regime to negotiate with international capital from a position of strength.

Although private capital can and will continue to do business in Venezuela, the logic of the process is anti-capitalist: state planning and investment, popular cooperative initiative and the emphasis on social justice are replacing private profit as guiding principles of the society and economy. Although members of the national oligarchy still control most of their economic bastions, they have lost both political and military power and look on with consternation as popular empowerment threatens to undermine their economic and social control at all levels. Despite problems and obstacles, the Vuelvan Caras Mission, incorporated since November 2004 into the new Ministry of Popular Economy, is reinforcing popular grass-roots agency throughout the country. All of the Missions and social programmes are based on the principles of collective ownership and control by popular communities: the agrarian reform cooperatives, the distribution of urban property to the urban land committees, the granting of micro-credit by the Women's Development Bank and similar institutions, even the distribution of piped water supplies to slum communities organised in local water committees. The popular distrust of politicians and bureaucrats, not to mention private capitalists, is an expression of a growing political consciousness within the mass movement which is profoundly revolutionary and tendentially Socialist. Progressive empowerment of local communities is linked to a national leadership personified by Chávez and the revolutionary sectors of the military, above all the original nucleus of the MBR-200 and the junior officers and troops; it is they who understand the dynamics of the process in the *barrios* and who have the confidence of the people. To the extent that popular power in the communities becomes consolidated and is both projected and protected at national level by Chávez and the progressive military, Socialist advance is not only possible but probable. The Venezuelan revolution is very much a work in progress and its final outcome is still unpredictable, but it is surely the most promising and inspiring political process in the world today.

# 6
# Revolutions Aborted:
# Chile, Nicaragua, Portugal

If Cuba and Venezuela represent the clearest examples of successful popular revolutionary processes which in different ways maintain their validity, there are a number of other experiences which, although ultimately unsuccessful, may nevertheless provide important lessons – both positive and negative – for the analysis presented in this book. Most relevant are the experiences of Chile and the Popular Unity of 1970–73, the Sandinista revolution in Nicaragua 1979–90, and the Portuguese revolution of 1974–75. In different ways they confirm the analysis of the Cuban and Venezuelan cases: the importance of broad popular unity, the need to overcome partisan divisions and sectarianism, the essential role of national popular culture and tradition, the need for ideological breadth of vision within the limits dictated by popular interests, and the crucial role of leadership. Without attempting an in-depth analysis of these three processes which would make this volume unmanageable, a brief assessment of their most relevant aspects will help to clarify the arguments already developed on the basis of the Cuban and Venezuelan cases.

## THE POPULAR UNITY IN CHILE: FAILURE OF THE TRADITIONAL LEFT

When in September 1970 Salvador Allende was elected president of Chile as candidate of a left-wing coalition called the Popular Unity (Unidad Popular or UP), it was a cause of enormous hope throughout Latin America, and also in Europe and elsewhere. A Marxist candidate running on an explicitly Socialist platform had won a democratic election and promised to carry out a peaceful revolution, 'The Chilean Road to Socialism'. If Cuba had shown that armed revolution was possible, that in certain circumstances it was possible to defeat the armed forces of the state and imperialism, then Chile appeared to show that in different circumstances, in countries with a more complex social structure and a liberal constitutional tradition, it was possible to reach Socialism by peaceful and constitutional means. This was seen as an inspiration for other countries in the Latin American

'Southern Cone', but also for European countries like France and Italy with strong Socialist and Communist parties and a history of working-class militancy. Allende insisted that Chile was different from many other Latin American countries in having a more vigorous democratic tradition and a military which was 'constitutionalist' in orientation and would respect popular decisions expressed through the ballot-box, a claim which was repeated by many observers at the time.

But from the beginning there were several elements in the situation which gave grounds for concern. Allende had been elected in a three-way race with only 36.2 per cent of the vote, against 34.9 per cent for the right-wing candidate Jorge Alessandri and 27.8 per cent for the Christian Democrat Radomiro Tomic. Under the Chilean Constitution this meant that his election had to be ratified by a vote of Congress, and this vote was only forthcoming after Allende accepted certain 'guarantees' demanded by the Christian Democrats. In October the commander-in-chief of the army, General René Schneider, was assassinated in what appears to have been an extreme-right attempt to provoke a military coup to forestall Allende's inauguration. The US also expressed 'dismay' at Allende's election, which was followed by a run on the banks as domestic and foreign capital showed its displeasure.

After his inauguration in November 1970, Allende moved swiftly to nationalise the copper mines (the country's main export industry), followed by nitrates (another key export), coal, most of the banks and many manufacturing industries. The new government also decreed an agrarian reform, expropriating land from estates over a certain size and giving it to peasants organised in cooperative settlements (*asentamientos*). Many new social programmes to benefit workers and the poor were also introduced. The nationalisation of copper was so popular that it was passed by a unanimous vote of Congress; not even the Right dared vote against it. On 4 April 1971, after only five months in office, the UP polled 50.9 per cent of the popular vote in municipal elections, a big increase on its 36.2 per cent showing in the presidential elections seven months earlier, and a sign that its bold Socialist strategy was paying off and helping to consolidate the popular movement in support of the government. But after this problems rapidly accumulated as right-wing hostility to the UP's programme intensified, and the opposition used its congressional majority to block legislation and question Allende's legitimacy. It would soon become apparent that bourgeois hostility to any more profound transformation would make it impossible for Allende to achieve his Socialist goals within the existing constitutional framework, and a growing political stalemate coupled with economic sabotage by the Chilean Right and the US would lead to a critical situation by early 1972. In congressional elections in March 1973 the UP only polled 43.4 per cent, a clear sign that the government's lack of an effective revolutionary strategy was leading to a loss of confidence among the popular sectors. Unless Allende could quickly turn the situation round he would either have to abandon his Socialist goals or face the reality that his days in power were numbered. To his credit he refused to abandon the struggle, but his inability to cut the Gordian knot led to the inevitable with Pinochet's brutal military coup of 11 September 1973.

The UP was an electoral coalition of the Socialist Party, the Communist Party, the Radical Party (essentially middle-class), the MAPU (Movement for United Popular Action, a left split from the Christian Democrats), and two other small middle-class parties, API and PSD. As such it is often compared to the Popular Fronts which existed as anti-Fascist alliances in several European countries in the late 1930s (and indeed Chile itself had Popular Front governments for several years in the late 1930s and 1940s). UP sympathisers emphasised that its programme was more advanced than that of the Popular Fronts and that the balance of power in the UP was in the hands of the working-class parties, the Socialists and Communists, unlike the Popular Fronts which had been dominated by the Radical Party (Roxborough, O'Brien and Roddick 1977, 64–5). This in theory gave it greater revolutionary potential, but it did not prevent UP from being wracked by internal tensions throughout its existence. The Radicals, API and PSD predictably constituted the right wing of the coalition, but more significant were the tensions between the Socialists, Communists and MAPU. Despite their Marxist-Leninist ideology the Communists tended in practice to be the most cautious of the working-class parties, following the practice inherited from Popular Front times of controlling working-class and peasant militancy and condemning any independent mobilisation as 'provocative'. In this they had allies in the right wing of the Socialist Party, including most of the time (although not always) Allende himself. It was the left wing of the Socialists and the MAPU who were much more inclined to ally with militant groups from the popular classes and to favour strikes, land and factory occupations and other forms of direct action. Frequently this would lead them to ally with the MIR (Movimiento de Izquierda Revolucionaria, Movement of the Revolutionary Left), the most important of the extraparliamentary leftist organisations which defended the principle of independent popular organisation with armed struggle as a strategic option, and refused to join the UP (although often giving it critical support).

The UP's ambiguities reflected the history of the Chilean Left. After the fall of the last Popular Front government in 1947, and despite a period of severe repression in which the Communist Party was declared illegal, the Socialists and Communists allied behind a common programme with Salvador Allende as their presidential candidate in 1952, 1958 and 1964. This Popular Action Front (FRAP, Frente de Acción Popular) was thus the direct precursor of the UP, the main difference being that the latter was broadened to include 'bourgeois' parties. It is debatable whether this broadening of the alliance made much difference, because Allende came within a hair's breadth of winning the 1958 elections (coming second with 28.5 per cent of the vote, only 30,000 votes behind the right-wing winner Jorge Alessandri in a five-way race); and in 1964, when the bourgeoisie and the US, alarmed by this experience, persuaded all the bourgeois forces to unite behind Eduardo Frei and the Christian Democrats as a reformist alternative to stop the Left, Frei did indeed win with 56 per cent of the vote, but Allende nevertheless did quite well and polled more votes than he would do in his 1970 victory (Roxborough, O'Brien and Roddick 1977, 31–7, 69). In essence, Chilean electoral politics since the 1930s had been locked in a three-way split between Right, Left and Centre, which the 1964 alliance of Right and Centre had temporarily interrupted. Despite the popular enthusiasm generated by Allende's victory, it is very doubtful whether the UP had the political dynamism to change this. A revolutionary programme – which the 'Chilean Road to Socialism' ultimately represented – could not be forced through without massive popular mobilisation amounting to well over 50 per cent of the electorate, and this the UP never achieved during its three years in power. The issue of the transformation of the armed forces was also very important, but in my view it was less so than this fundamental political weakness. The military is ultimately subject to political pressures just like any other institution, and when a popular programme for transformation repeatedly wins massive majorities at the polls (as recently in Venezuela), even an elitist and corporatist military structure like the Chilean begins to fracture. But with a president voted in by only 36 per cent of the electorate and a coalition which only briefly achieved a little more than 50 per cent (in April 1971), there was no real mandate for revolutionary change.

It can be argued that this encouraging increase in the UP vote – from 36 to nearly 51 per cent of the vote in seven months – indicated that at that point it was indeed beginning to generate the necessary momentum to carry through its programme. Certainly the decisive measures of Allende's first few months helped to generate a popular euphoria lacking in his original election campaign. But for this to have achieved the strength necessary to overcome entrenched bourgeois opposition he would have had to take much more decisive action in the following months, and above all he and the UP would have had to demonstrate much greater confidence in popular initiative, supporting and encouraging independent popular organisation instead of holding it back. It is possible that this would have provoked a coup a year or 18 months earlier than in fact happened, but it was the only option which might have brought success. It is also quite possible that conditions simply did not exist for revolutionary victory in Chile at that time, in which case all we can do is admire the heroism of Allende and his supporters and draw the necessary political lessons. But what are these lessons? One has just been suggested – the need to achieve a much greater majority at the polls – but there are others which may be more controversial.

On the Left, post-mortem debate about Allende's Chile has tended to divide between the hard-line Marxist-Leninists who saw it as proof of the bankruptcy of the electoral road, and gradualists for whom it confirms the need for a more moderate, reformist programme or at least for more effective measures to win over the middle class. The MIR and a few small Marxist-Leninist groups defended the former perspective, which was also expressed by some foreign Marxists such as Alain Labrousse: Allende's 'reformist' policy 'cannot fail to produce the contradictions characteristic of all "middle roads": to gradually turn towards conservative positions, or to be condemned to be overthrown by the Right' (Labrousse 1972, 384). But experience offers little support for the notion of the viability of armed struggle in a country like Chile, and the heroic efforts of the MIR after 1973 only confirmed that such a strategy was completely unviable (see García Naranjo 1996). On the other hand the hostility of the bourgeoisie to Allende's project was such that the second alternative – that of greater moderation in order to win over the Christian Democrats and the middle class – might well have been seen only as a sign of weakness and a pretext for intensified attacks on the UP government.

Rather than repeating the sterile dispute between partisans of armed revolution and those of peaceful reform, what really needs to be reconsidered is the political dynamic of the UP coalition and the structure and functioning of the traditional left-wing parties which controlled the government.

We have already seen that the policy of the Communist Party was the established one of caution and control. Its practice of opposing popular militancy and suppressing any kind of independent organisation was fatal for the popular movement, and this attitude was shared by the right wing of the Socialist Party. Although the Left of the Socialist Party and the MAPU had a different approach, they were rarely able to direct the practice of the UP as a whole which was dominated not only by the tactical caution but also by the bureaucratic and top-down methodology of the dominant sectors. Allende himself was a decidedly uncharismatic figure, partly because of his personality and also because he was a career politician identified with the moderate Socialist Party establishment. Despite this it appears that with the euphoria of his election victory and the bold measures of his first six months he did begin to develop some charisma, but in order to turn this into a decisive advantage he would have had to break decisively with the dead hand of party bureaucracy and appeal directly to the rank-and-file workers and the marginalised masses of the *callampas* (shanty-towns) whom the Christian Democrats had mobilised under Frei and who were now increasingly influenced by the MIR. This he was unable or unwilling to do, and this was an important factor in the stagnation of UP support, which remained solid at around 40 to 45 per cent but was unable to achieve the dramatic growth necessary to overcome the permanent blockade of the Right and the Christian Democrats in Congress, the courts and the media. Certainly there were elements of popular power developing in the *callampas* and working-class areas around Santiago and the other main cities: the outstanding Chilean historian and activist Luis Vitale points out that the 'industrial belts' (*cordones industriales*) and 'communal commands' (*comandos comunales*) were base-level workers' organisations which

on several occasions went beyond the UP parties because they were built from the bottom up by combative non-party trade unionists or leftist sympathisers. Their resolutions did not conform to the zig-zags and conjunctural tactics of government policy or of the CUT [the union federation], but to the democratic decisions of the grass roots … . (Vitale in Vitale et al. 1999, 204–5)

But neither the UP nor Allende personally chose to encourage this popular revolutionary energy.

To his credit Allende did attempt to move beyond the existing constitutional framework, proposing to replace the existing bicameral Congress with a new unicameral legislature; along with other constitutional changes this would be put to a referendum to obtain a popular mandate for more radical change. This proposal was first put to Congress in November 1971, but rejected, and was then incorporated into the UP's programme for the March 1973 elections, but failed again since the UP did not win an outright majority. In any case the situation was becoming steadily more polarised and there were growing rumours of coups, counter-coups or civil war. After booming during Allende's first year in office the economy was in crisis with growing inflation and balance-of-payments deficits, exacerbated by opposition sabotage; in October 1972 a lorry-owners' strike threatened to cause complete economic breakdown but was overcome as the government took emergency measures and workers resorted to direct action to maintain production and distribution networks.

If limited electoral support and lack of political dynamism or charisma were two decisive factors in the UP's failure, the third crucial element was of course the hostility of the military. I have already suggested that massive popular support and mobilisation might have contributed to changing the attitude of the military, but this is not to deny that the elitist recruitment, Prussian training and traditions of the Chilean armed forces made them a more difficult proposition for a progressive government to deal with than, for example, their Venezuelan counterparts. Nevertheless, it is possible that this problem has been exaggerated in many analyses of Chile; there was after all a progressive military tradition here too. It should not be forgotten that in 1924–25 it was progressive officers who backed the first Alessandri, Arturo, in pushing through democratic reforms despite conservative parliamentary opposition, and a few years later there was the remarkable (if short-lived) episode of the Socialist Republic proclaimed in 1931 by Colonel Marmaduke Grove and other left-wing officers (Mason 1986). The attempt to prevent Allende's accession by the provocation of the Schneider assassination did after all fail, and the UP president was able to rely on a progressive general, Carlos Prats, as chief of staff for most of his term in office. Within the officer corps there were even more progressive figures such as General Bachelet who were known UP sympathisers (Roxborough, O'Brien and Roddick 1977, 211), not to mention the rank-and-file who as in any army were of predominantly popular origin and therefore potentially sympathetic.

Even if the armed forces were bound to be problematic, then, they were not necessarily a lost cause. But the UP made serious errors in its handling of this problem. Allende's approach was to rely on the 'constitutionalist' tradition of the military, which was the position proclaimed by Prats and others to justify their defence of Allende's right to hold office. This was fine up to a point – it prevented the success of reactionary plots like those around the Schneider assassination and others up to and including the unsuccessful coup of 29 June 1973 (the *tancazo*). But 'constitutionalism' was also interpreted in such a way as to prevent the government from 'interfering' in military appointments and promotions even when they favoured officers known to be hostile to the UP, and to refrain from taking action to defend loyal junior officers when they were being purged by right-wing commanders on spurious disciplinary charges, as happened systematically in the months leading up to the coup.

As against this 'constitutionalist' approach, from the beginning the different UP parties and the MIR tried to infiltrate the armed forces and recruit officers and troops to their organisations. The effect of this was disastrous: if there is one thing which offends military esprit de corps it is division in the ranks caused by political activism. This was an entirely different matter from what would occur in Venezuela, where Chávez' movement began *within* the armed forces and systematically avoided partisan political alignment; while Chávez and his colleagues were frequently in touch with a wide variety of left-wing parties, they always refused to align themselves with any specific party and took swift action to suppress attempts by any party (like Bandera Roja) to infiltrate the movement. A further error in Chile (admittedly not one favoured by Allende until the very last moment) was the attempt by the UP parties, along with the MIR, to create independent workers' militias and get sympathetic troops to distribute arms to civilians; again, this is like a red flag to a bull to any military establishment, and while arming the workers is a traditional revolutionary ideal, it is suicidal (given the overwhelming superiority of the established armed forces) unless a large section of the military is already sympathetic. Here also, it is notable that Chávez in power has responded very cautiously to appeals by his more militant supporters to arm the people: his position has been to urge those who want to defend the revolutionary government to join the military reserve.

In addition to creating a specifically military revolutionary movement, what Chávez has done in Venezuela is to foster an anti-imperialist and progressive ideology in the armed forces as a whole which identifies military duty and patriotism with defence of popular democratic rights, but not in any way with party-political interests. This progressive military ideology has provided the basis for active incorporation of the armed forces in the implementation of social programmes, thereby further modifying their worldview and bringing them into close contact with workers and the poor. There is reason to believe that such an approach might have functioned in Chile also; although Allende did not have the advantage of being a military officer, key officers like Prats expressed views which were not so different from those of today's *chavistas*, as in November 1972 after the bosses' strike in Chile:

By and large, it was a strike of professionals and businessmen. In previous governments it was the workers who struck against their employers ... The country's workers have given an example of great social responsibility during the development of the strike movement, and their social conscience, their sense of order, and their desire to maintain production merit the respect of the Armed Forces ... . (Prats, quoted in Roxborough, O'Brien and Roddick 1977, 200)

But for such an attitude to become securely entrenched in the majority of the officer corps it would have been necessary to promote more progressive officers and to prevent the purge of the military Left implemented by reactionary generals. It may be that this was politically impossible, although if it had been undertaken in conjunction with a strong position against partisan infiltration of the military and without questioning the military's monopoly of the legitimate use of force, it might have succeeded.

Some readers will be surprised that in this brief discussion of the Chilean debacle I have only made passing mention of US imperialism. Obviously US hostility was a major factor from the very beginning, but it is questionable whether or not it was decisive. In Chile the US did not have to carry out a counter-revolutionary invasion as it did (unsuccessfully) in Cuba, or foment a reactionary guerrilla insurgency as it did in Nicaragua. For sure, it helped to sabotage the Chilean economy and gave logistical support to the coup, but it could be confident in the ability of the Chilean Right, both military and civilian, to dominate the political process anyway, given the failings of the UP. In a country of Chile's size and resources, a revolutionary government with dynamic popular backing and with an effective military policy might very well have been able to resist US pressures; as it was, domestic reaction was quite capable of liquidating the revolutionary threat with only limited (albeit important) US assistance.

The failure of the UP and Pinochet's brutal coup were catastrophic for the Chilean Left and for the popular movement as a whole for at least a generation. Not only did the coup lead to savage repression on a scale which almost no-one had anticipated, but it inaugurated a 17-year dictatorship which succeeded in completely remodelling the country, imposing the world's first successful neo-liberal experiment which would serve as an inspiration not only for the Right elsewhere in Latin America but also for Thatcher in the UK (Beckett 2002, Ch. 12). Even when Pinochet was finally forced out of office, the return to 'democracy' was severely hampered by constitutional provisions imposed by the dictatorship, and the entire social and political climate is still pervaded by a conservative hegemony which will take many years to fade. As in Franco's Spain, this is the high price of revolutionary failure.

The Chilean experience confirms the importance of winning over the armed forces, but also the crucial need to achieve a solid popular majority for radical change: to win what Marx called 'the battle for democracy', or Gramsci's 'war of position' for social and ideological hegemony. It also confirms the inadequacy of traditional left-wing parties to this task and the need for a new and dynamic politics of non-partisan popular empowerment and mobilisation, transcending party structures and divisions to build a broad and united national movement with an independent revolutionary leadership. Allende and the Unidad Popular, admirable though they were, never succeeded in becoming more than a conventional electoral coalition of political parties playing by the established rules of the game, and this ultimately ensured their failure.

## NICARAGUA: POPULAR DEMOCRACY SUFFOCATED BY IMPERIALISM

Only six years after the Chilean disaster, revolutionary hopes were again raised in Latin America by a new popular triumph, and this time through armed struggle which now appeared to be vindicated again exactly 20 years after the Cuban victory. The overthrow of the corrupt and brutal Somoza regime by the Sandinistas (Frente Sandinista de Liberación Nacional, FSLN) had all the characteristics of a genuine national liberation struggle, given the extreme dependency of Nicaragua which was smaller than Cuba in population and considerably poorer. Just as in Cuba, *sandinismo* had its roots in earlier popular and national struggles, in this case the guerrilla struggle of Augusto César Sandino against US occupation from 1927 to 1933 and the earlier campaign of Benjamín Zeledón in 1912 (and indeed the resistance to the earlier, unofficial US interventions of the filibustering adventurer William Walker from 1855 to 1860) (Black 1981, 5–10, 16–26). Once again, revolution had triumphed in one of the smallest and weakest Latin American countries and one of those most thoroughly colonised by US imperialism.

The hope and enthusiasm aroused by the Nicaraguan revolution was all the greater because of its original characteristics: although similar to Cuba in being the military victory of a popular guerrilla force over a corrupt dictatorship, and in being a broadly based, open and flexible movement, its political and ideological evolution was significantly different. In particular, the FSLN was distinguished by the prominence in its ranks of progressive Christians inspired by liberation theology, and by the outstanding role of women in the movement (including some in leadership positions). Although the Sandinistas were inspired by the Cuban example and implemented some policies which were obviously influenced by Cuban practice, such as the literacy campaign and the creation of Sandinista defence committees (Comités de Defensa Sandinista, CDS), they made it clear from the start that they intended to follow an independent line, with a mixed economy and a pluralist political system. The FSLN was certainly hegemonic as *the* revolutionary movement, but other political parties would share power and bourgeois opposition parties could and did participate in elections. Moreover, the Nicaraguan Communists had virtually no influence on the process: the pro-Soviet Partido Socialista Nicaragüense (PSN) did support the Sandinistas at the last minute, like the PSP in Cuba, but was too small to have any real influence, and the more radical Partido Comunista de Nicaragua opposed the Sandinistas throughout and thus guaranteed its own continued insignificance.

Without categorically committing themselves to Socialism – which at that time was still basically identified with the Soviet, or possibly the Cuban, model – the Sandinistas aimed to build a system in which the state sector would be hegemonic, producing 40 to 50 per cent of GDP and controlling the overall orientation of the economy, although collaborating with private capital which would continue to produce the remaining 50 to 60 per cent. Something like 25 per cent of the economy was nationalised simply by taking over the enormous properties of the Somoza family; banking, insurance and some other industries were nationalised; and the agrarian reform expropriated significant amounts of land from large estates to be distributed to peasants in both cooperative and individual forms of tenure. Trade with the Soviet bloc increased from almost zero to 20 per cent by 1985, but there is no sign that the Sandinistas intended it to go much further than that had it not been for the US blockade imposed at that time (Walker 1991, 78–9).

Most interesting and significant from our point of view was the Sandinista political system and the emphasis in the early years on popular democracy and participation by mass organisations. While supreme authority was vested in the Governing Junta of National Reconstruction (Junta de Gobierno de la Reconstrucción Nacional, JGRN), the function of popular representation was performed by the Council of State, a body consisting of 47 (later increased to 51) members elected by political parties, mass organisations and private-sector associations. The FSLN had six representatives and seven other parties, some allied with and some opposed to the Sandinistas, had one each; the Sandinista defence committees had nine, the unions (Sandinista Workers' Central) had three, the Rural Workers' Association had three, the Women's Association (AMNLAE) had one, and so on (Black 1981, 244–9). Although the apportioning of delegate numbers was somewhat arbitrary it did bear some relationship to the relative size of the different organisations. There was often vigorous debate in the Council of State, which shared legislative authority with the Junta, frequently modified Junta decrees and initiated much legislation; and within the mass organisations, especially at local level, there was intense popular participation and discussion. From a progressive point of view the most disappointing aspect was the allocation of only one delegate to the Women's Association, a sign of attitudes which would lead to future tensions.

The authority of both Junta and Council was provisional and was always intended to be replaced through elections, which were held in November 1984. From the beginning the FSLN had promised pluralist elections, but the actual electoral arrangements were not specified and became the subject of fierce discussion during 1983 and early 1984. Although some FSLN leaders and popular representatives in the Council of State argued for formal representation of the mass organisations to be continued in the new National Assembly, they lost the debate to opposition representatives who, with the help of international pressure, succeeded in imposing the conventional liberal model in which only political parties present candidates. While the FSLN still won a massive majority – 67 per cent of the popular vote and 61 out of 96 seats – the direct input of popular organisations was thus excluded and, as the character of the FSLN itself began to change, the people were increasingly disempowered over the next few years.

There was still an attempt to institutionalise an element of popular direct democracy in the constitution-drafting process from 1985 to 1987. A Special Constitutional Commission was appointed by the National Assembly and prepared a draft Constitution on the basis of advice from many sources, including visits to numerous countries in the Americas and Europe. Televised debates were then held and 73 *cabildos abiertos* – open meetings – were held across the country for citizens to make proposals and observations. This commendably democratic procedure did yield several amendments to the draft Constitution which were adopted when the matter was again debated by the National Assembly, but a demand put forward by several *cabildos* for direct representation of mass organisations was rejected because of strong opposition from the bourgeois parties in the National Assembly (Vanden and Prevost 1993, 83–4). Although the Sandinistas insisted on the inclusion of social and economic rights in the Constitution, they gave way on the issue of participatory democracy, and this may well have contributed to their subsequent abandonment of social and economic rights in practice.

Under the enormous pressures of the US-promoted *contra* war and economic embargo, by 1987 the FSLN found itself in an unsustainable position. Defence was absorbing 62 per cent of the budget, production had declined dramatically, hyperinflation had set in and by 1988 real wages were, according to some estimates, at 10 per cent of their 1980 value (Walker 1991, 84–5). These circumstances

led the Sandinista leadership to adopt in February 1988 – without any popular consultation and contrary to its efforts to change the top-down style of political leadership … – a series of economic measures that went against popular welfare: the currency was devalued and fixed in relation to the dollar, subsidies were reduced and prices and markets were liberalised. (Harnecker 1999, 46)

These IMF-style deflationary measures did reduce inflation and increased exports, but the cost of adjustment was borne overwhelmingly by the poor: 'while the government had adopted Sandino's dictum that "only the workers and peasants will go all the way", it did not seem to have gone all the way with its natural constituency – the very same workers and peasants' (Vanden and Prevost 1993, 144). Meanwhile, the Sandinistas bent over backwards to try to obtain private-sector cooperation, but with little success, lending credence to the argument that a more Socialist policy might have been more effective by making available scarce resources for investment in the public sector.

Bourgeois victory in the February 1990 elections – the triumph of Violeta Chamorro and the UNO (Unión Nacional Opositora, National Opposition Union) coalition, with 54.8 per cent to 40.8 per cent for Daniel Ortega and the FSLN – was clearly due to war-weariness and economic desperation on the part of the poor majority. Indeed, after the criminal sabotage and economic strangulation imposed by the Reagan administration and its blatant electoral interference in favour of the opposition, it is in retrospect remarkable that the Sandinistas did so well. But it is still possible to argue that the FSLN might have retained more popular support if they had attempted to maintain basic popular welfare programmes, and also if they had insisted on inserting constitutional mechanisms for the direct governmental participation of the mass organisations. If the CDS, the unions, the Women's Association and so on had still enjoyed direct parliamentary representation in 1987–89 it would probably have proved impossible to impose the neo-liberal measures which proved so unpopular. As it was, not only were the mass organisations excluded from policy-making, they tended to atrophy as their members realised that they were now powerless.

In this melancholy post-mortem it is also important to re-evaluate the political and ideological characteristics of *sandinismo* as a movement. Interestingly, three of the future founders of the FSLN – Carlos Fonseca Amador, Silvio Mayorga and Tomás Borge – were members of the pro-Soviet PSN in the mid-1950s, but left a few years later because they saw its policies as too conciliatory. Inspired by the Cuban example, they founded the FSLN in 1961, consciously choosing the name in honour of Sandino and committing themselves to armed struggle. Like Fidel and Che they stressed the importance of revolutionary will and leadership, and while considering themselves Marxists looked to Nicaraguan and Latin American popular traditions for ideological guidance; theirs was the Marxism of the Peruvian José Carlos Mariátegui rather than that of Moscow or Beijing. Later, in the 1970s, progressive Christians such as Luis Carrión, Miguel D'Escoto and Ernesto and Fernando Cardenal joined the FSLN, giving the Sandinista Front a more explicitly pluralist character:

What is most significant about the Nicaraguan case and the FSLN is that this historic gulf between Marxist and Christian forces was bridged not simply through a brief tactical alliance but through the integration of progressive Christians into the revolutionary party. The result of this unity was that the political philosophy of the FSLN, and in particular its attitude toward Christianity, was virtually unique among revolutionary parties with Marxist origins. (Vanden and Prevost 1993, 41–2)

It was also during this period of intensified revolutionary struggle that tactical and strategic divisions developed in the FSLN, leading to the emergence of three tendencies: the Prolonged People's War tendency identified with Tomás Borge and Bayardo Arce and emphasising rural guerrilla warfare; the Proletarian Tendency led by Jaime Wheelock and Luis Carrión and emphasising urban struggle; and the Insurrectionalists or Terceristas (Third Way) led by Daniel and Humberto Ortega, which argued for rapid and decisive insurrection based on broad alliances and mass mobilisation in all sectors. In a sense the Terceristas mediated between the other two and forged the united strategy which led to victory in July 1979.

The FSLN's broad strategy of unity, its success in mobilising a truly national mass insurrection, and the extreme unpopularity of the Somoza regime, meant that Sandinista hegemony in 1979–80 was comparable to that of the M-26–7 in Cuba in 1959–60. Their generosity in victory, allowing two representatives of the bourgeois opposition to participate alongside three Sandinistas in the Governing Junta of National Reconstruction, announcing a commitment to pluralist elections, and abolishing the death penalty even for Somoza's henchmen in the National Guard, won them enormous admiration throughout Latin America and elsewhere. At the same time their programme of selective nationalisations, agrarian reform, state-led development based on a mixed economy, popular educational, health and welfare campaigns seemed to promise many of the same benefits of the Cuban revolution within a more open and pluralist framework. Their stress on popular participation implied that the revolution would not be hamstrung by liberal elitism, although respecting pluralism:

Democracy neither begins nor ends with elections ... democracy is mass intervention in every aspect of social life ... Effective democracy, like we intend to practice in Nicaragua, consists of ample popular participation; a permanent dynamic of the people's participation in a variety of political and social tasks .... . (Ortega and Ramírez, quoted in Ruchwarger 1987, 3–4)

In many ways the Sandinista programme and strategy foreshadowed that of the Bolivarian revolution in Venezuela today; this makes its defeat all the more tragic, and further emphasises the importance of the Venezuelan process. Indeed, just as in Venezuela (and in a sense, as in Cuba, but without the distortion imposed by the Soviet model), the Sandinistas did towards the end proclaim that their goal was a new form of Socialism, thus prefiguring Chávez' 'Socialism of the twenty-first century'. But the FSLN's loss of state power was catastrophic for Nicaragua, allowing the various bourgeois governments that have held office since to dismantle what remained of the revolutionary gains, and leaving the country as the second or third poorest in the Western hemisphere (after Haiti and perhaps Bolivia). The Sandinistas have since been plagued by divisions and corruption, and it is very questionable whether they could reinitiate a revolutionary policy if re-elected. This is the problem with accepting a purely liberal-pluralist constitution: if the structures of popular participatory democracy (of popular power) are destroyed, then electoral victory will mean no more than Social Democratic rule in a liberal system. The struggle for popular power has to start again from scratch.

One final issue remains to be addressed: that of revolutionary leadership, populism and charisma in the Nicaraguan case. Given the broad appeal and ideological pluralism of the FSLN and its basis in national popular culture and traditions, it may very well be categorised as a progressive populist movement in the final phase of the insurgency and the first years after victory. It was clearly much more than a conventional political party and transcended all existing parties which were insignificant by comparison, and its nine-man-strong national directorate had an undeniable collective charismatic appeal deriving from leadership of the armed struggle. Because its legitimacy – shared by other leading Sandinistas such as Dora María Téllez – was based on revolutionary leadership and not mere electoral preference or bureaucratic authority, this collective body had a charismatic appeal comparable in some degree to that of Fidel in Cuba or Chávez in Venezuela, and the fact that it was collective was (or should have been) an advantage compared to the personal protagonism of the Cuban and Venezuelan leaders. But perhaps inevitably, Daniel Ortega's position as president of the country tended to transfer much of the collective charisma to him alone, a tendency which was greatly accentuated when in the crisis of the 1989–90 election campaign, the FSLN decided to adopt a bourgeois campaigning style which privileged Ortega's personality much more than ever before. Failure in these elections confirms that individual charisma cannot be improvised, and also that charisma alone cannot overcome fundamental political failure (the inability to preserve popular welfare and participation). As previously stated, this failure was to a large extent a product of overwhelming hostile pressure from the US, but it was nonetheless a failure, with fatal consequences.

## PORTUGAL:
### PARTISAN FACTIONALISM DESTROYS POPULAR POWER IN EUROPE

When on 25 April 1974 the pro-Fascist Salazar/Caetano regime, nearly 50 years old, was overthrown in a coup by junior officers, almost no-one anticipated the revolutionary upheaval that was to follow. For 19 months this small and impoverished nation on the Western fringe of the continent was to experience a genuine revolutionary process such as had not been seen in Western Europe for generations. Lisbon was transformed from a peaceful backwater into the vortex of a nationwide whirlwind of demonstrations, factory occupations, land invasions, takeovers of empty buildings by slum-dwellers, and projects of popular power and socialism. Yet on 25 November 1975 a carefully controlled coup restored state authority and put an end to the revolutionary process, ensuring that Portugal would remain a member of NATO and become a conventional liberal parliamentary regime, joining the European Union a few years later. The prevailing wisdom regards this as the logical conclusion of the revolutionary process, but ignores the fact that this liberal capitalist success story was only made possible by the neutralisation of the independent mass movement of Portuguese workers and peasants who in the 'hot summer' of 1975 aspired to much more than bourgeois normality (see Kayman 1987).

The 'Revolution of the Carnations', so called because of the red carnations which people put in the soldiers' rifle-barrels to celebrate the liberating coup, was the result first and foremost of war-weariness among junior officers sent to fight in colonial wars in Portugal's African colonies of Angola, Mozambique and Guinea-Bissau, wars which had dragged on for 13 years and were absorbing nearly half the national budget. It was this frustration which had led to the formation of a semi-clandestine 'Captains' Movement', subsequently named the Movimento das Forças Armadas (MFA or Armed Forces' Movement). The junior officers involved were also influenced by the revolutionary ideologies of the very liberation movements they were sent to suppress, and by the domestic anti-Fascist resistance in Portugal itself which had a long and valiant history although it had hitherto been unable to unseat the regime (see Raby 1988). The MFA's initial programme promised democracy at home, self-determination for the colonies, an 'anti-monopolist economic strategy' at the service of the 'least favoured strata of the population', and a social policy defending the interests of the working class (Rodrigues, Borga and Cardoso 1976, 301–2).

During the months that followed supreme power was in the hands of a Junta of National Salvation headed by General António de Spínola – one of a handful of high-ranking officers to have sided with the MFA – with a provisional government composed of ministers from four different leftist and centrist parties. But it soon became clear that real power was in the street, with the popular movement, and in the hands of the junior officers of the MFA. Spínola tried in vain to put a brake on the revolutionary process and was defeated in several successive crises, being forced to resign as president after an unsuccessful attempt at an *autogolpe* (a coup to reinforce his own authority) on 28 September 1974, and to flee the country to Franco's Spain after another unsuccessful coup attempt on 11 March 1975. These and other crises led also to governmental reorganisation as six provisional governments succeeded each other; the first five were successively more radical, until the formation of the sixth on 19 September 1975 marked the first clear move back towards the Right. But the dynamic determining these changes was that of the popular struggle in the streets, factories and fields of Portugal, the internal faction struggle within the MFA, and the colonial struggles in Africa.

A decisive blow for revolution appeared to have been struck with the defeat of Spínola's second coup on 11 March 1975. This was immediately followed by the formation of a supreme Council of the Revolution of progressive military officers, and by decrees nationalising the banks and insurance companies (and thereby most heavy industry, controlled by the banks) and implementing agrarian reform in the southern region of the country which was dominated by large estates. In the next three months popular struggle intensified and the different tendencies in the MFA became more clearly separated.

First there was the tendency associated with the Communist Party (PCP) and with Col. Vasco Gonçalves, Prime Minister of the second, third, fourth and fifth provisional governments, which favoured a transition to Socialism based on reinforcing control of different components of state power by the MFA and the left-wing parties (above all the Communists). Second were the so-called 'moderates', close to the Socialist Party and the PPD (Partido Popular Democrático, later to be called Partido Social-Democrata or PSD, in reality a right-of-centre liberal formation), who claimed to believe in Socialism but on the basis of conventional liberal elections and parliamentary politics. Finally there were the radicals around Otelo Saraiva de Carvalho, the young major who had been operational commander of the liberating coup of 25 April 1974 and who was now commander of COPCON, the Operational Command of the Continent, which was a special military structure controlling key MFA units and which had become increasingly identified with the popular movement in the streets and the extraparliamentary Left.

To speak of an 'extraparliamentary Left' is to identify one of the crucial issues in Portugal at that critical conjuncture. Strictly speaking there was no parliament, since the puppet Fascist National Assembly had been dissolved along with other institutions of Salazar's *Estado Novo* (New State) immediately after the April liberation. But one of the key promises in the MFA's programme had been to hold elections for a Constituent Assembly within one year of liberation, and true to this promise the elections were held on 25 April 1975. The problem here was that the elections bore little relationship to the dynamics of the revolutionary process; whereas the people participating in neighbourhood committees (*Comissões de Moradores*), workers' committees in factories, land occupations and street demonstrations were increasingly doing so independent of political parties, the elections were held along party lines. Moreover, whereas the people (at least in Lisbon and the South) identified with the MFA and the idea of popular power and Socialism as the ultimate goal, the MFA as such had no candidates and no electoral movement of its own. The result (with a 92 per cent turnout) was that although a hard core of Communist sympathisers voted for the PCP (12.5 per cent) and a closely allied anti-Fascist front party, the MDP/CDE, got 4 per cent, the great majority of those attracted to the general idea of Socialism voted, logically enough, for the Socialist Party (PS),which emerged as the largest party with 38 per cent. With other small parties the Left total was 58 per cent, against 26 per cent for the PPD and 8 per cent for the right-wing CDS (Kayman 1987, 138). This should have been a resounding endorsement of the revolutionary process, but in practice it was not because the PS leadership, despite uttering Marxist rhetoric in order to gain credibility in the radical atmosphere of the time, actually had a typical pro-capitalist Social Democratic agenda and immediately began to ally with the PPD in the Constituent Assembly and to claim greater legitimacy than the provisional government, the Council of the Revolution or the MFA General Assembly.

Some of the more far-sighted MFA leaders, as well as grass-roots activists of the popular movement, had begun to foresee this problem during the previous two months and had argued for the elections to be postponed, but the promise to hold the vote within twelve months was regarded as a solemn undertaking by large sectors of the population, and international pressures also made postponement almost impossible. The Council of the Revolution and the fourth provisional government did come up with the idea of getting the parties to sign a pact guaranteeing the right of the MFA to intervene in all political issues including the drafting of the Constitution, and on 11 April the main political parties signed this agreement; then in the last days of the campaign some MFA leaders began to appeal for a blank vote as a vote of confidence in the MFA. But neither of these ideas worked; the pact had no legal force and parties would feel free to ignore it as the conjuncture changed, and as far as the 'blank vote' idea was concerned, most people naturally felt overwhelming enthusiasm for the first free elections in 50 years and therefore voted for one or another of the party lists on offer. In retrospect, this was the first serious setback for the revolutionary process; although the Constituent Assembly was not the government, and although the Constitution it eventually produced a year later was actually quite progressive, the conventional political parties (above all the PS and PPD) which dominated it could now claim a legitimacy which competed directly with the revolutionary legitimacy of the MFA, the Council of the Revolution and the mass movement in streets and neighbourhoods.

In spite of this, for a few months it looked as if the dynamic of revolutionary activity would carry all before it, leaving the Constituent Assembly as a sideshow. In the southern provinces of Alentejo and Ribatejo, the area of large absentee-owned estates, the Agrarian Reform decree only accelerated the existing process of land occupations by rural labourers. With the nationalisations workers' councils became more and more active, not only in the nationalised industries but in many private enterprises. Although in most heavy industries and in several leading newspapers (now nationalised as properties of the banks) the PCP dominated through its trade union strength, there were increasing numbers of cases where militant workers rejected both PCP and PS and demanded independent, non-partisan workers' control. This became a burning political issue in May–June 1975 when workers took control of *República* newspaper (owned by leading PS politicians) and Rádio Renascença, the radio station of the Catholic Church. Pressure from the PS, the right-wing parties and the Church, who claimed that these actions were part of a Communist takeover, persuaded Prime Minister Vasco Gonçalves to send troops to restore these media outlets to their 'rightful owners'. But as had already happened in some factories, the troops fraternised with the workers and refused to carry out orders; and in any case the workers in both institutions pointed out indignantly that the majority of them were neither Communists nor Socialist Party members but non-party or members of other leftist groups (Rodrigues, Borga and Cardoso 1976, 203–18). So for the next six months *República* and Rádio Renascença served as vehicles of the non-partisan popular revolutionary movement.

Between March and July also the MFA Assembly, composed of officers representing different military units, began to take very interesting and explicit revolutionary positions. Vigorous debates in the Assembly produced on 19 May a document called the Political Action Plan (PAP) which formalised the goal of Socialism, the concept of the MFA as the 'liberation movement of the Portuguese people' and the principle of political pluralism, but at the same time stressed governmental authority and labour discipline. This was a compromise reflecting the position of the PCP and Vasco Gonçalves, but it would soon be modified by approval of a more radical statement, the 'Guiding Document for the Alliance between the People and the MFA', approved on 8 July. Although the broad political goals remained the same as in the PAP, the 'Guiding Document' (DG from its Portuguese initials) placed more emphasis on grass-roots popular mobilisation, stressing the need to create 'conditions for active participation' which would occur through 'forms of popular organisation, with a democratic, independent and unitary practice' (SIPC 1976, 45–6). More significantly, the DG proposed a political structure of popular power which was profoundly revolutionary and in clear contradiction of the perspectives prevailing in the Constituent Assembly: there should be grass-roots popular assemblies based on workers', peasants and neighbourhood committees in each locality, which would be linked to MFA soldiers' committees in each military unit, with a pyramidal structure culminating in a National Assembly of Popular Power (which in turn would incorporate the MFA's General Assembly).

These developments were too much for the bourgeois elements in Portuguese politics, and it was precisely in this period that the PS leaders resigned from the provisional government (on 12 July, over the *República* affair), followed by the PPD (on 16 July) (Rodrigues, Borga and Cardoso 1976, 223–4). It was also in this period that right-wing forces, dominant in the north where the Catholic Church was hegemonic, began to organise violent assaults against provincial offices of left-wing parties. At the same time there were large workers' demonstrations in Lisbon in support of the DG and of the Rádio Renascença workers. The fourth provisional government had collapsed with the departure of the PS and PPD, leaving only the PCP and its close allies, so the Prime Minister Vasco Gonçalves formed a fifth government composed of independent technocrats; but this government was still seen as being dominated by the PCP and was unable to solve the political impasse.

The political crisis deepened the divisions within the MFA. On 7 August the MFA 'moderates' published a manifesto which came to be known as the 'Group of Nine' document, from the number of officers signing it. They attacked Gonçalves and the PCP as being responsible for pushing the revolution too fast and isolating it from the people of the centre and north, and argued for a parliamentary road to Socialism (although claiming not to accept Social Democracy either) and a foreign policy alignment with the Third World. Their emphasis on 'moderation' and parliamentarism clearly implied rejection not only of the PCP/Gonçalves line but also of the independent popular movements and 'popular power' as defended by Otelo and the revolutionary Left. This provoked a swift response from the revolutionary Left within the MFA in the form of their own manifesto, known as the COPCON document, in which officers close to Otelo and the popular movement made a devastating critique of both the 'Document of the Nine' and the PCP/Gonçalves position, arguing for intensification of the revolution on the basis of popular power and non-partisan unity. The result was continued political stalemate until early September when, in a climate of increasing social and political polarisation and rumours of civil war, the MFA right wing finally forced the dismissal of Vasco Gonçalves and the formation of a sixth provisional government led by a 'moderate', Admiral Pinheiro de Azevedo.

The formation of the sixth government clearly showed that counter-revolution was now advancing within the MFA itself and the state apparatus. But it was not yet the end of the revolution, for it quickly became apparent that the sixth government had little authority and could not govern: it sent troops to occupy worker-controlled radio stations but once again the troops fraternised with the workers who remained in control. A revolutionary organisation of rank-and-file soldiers appeared, the SUV (Soldados Unidos Vencerão, Soldiers United Will Win), participating in demonstrations disguised with balaclavas. The final straw came on 12–13 November when thousands of striking construction workers surrounded the Parliament building and the prime minister's office, and when COPCON military units refused to intervene, Pinheiro de Azevedo declared the government to be on strike and offered the workers the keys to the building. But this theatrical gesture was a provocation, and was accompanied by other provocations which led newly radicalised soldiers of the parachute regiment to occupy several key military bases in an uncoordinated revolutionary advance; this gave the Centre-Right the excuse to act, moving its most loyal units (led by the commando regiment from Amadora, a Lisbon suburb) to seize power in the early hours of 25 November. Although many feared civil war, there was no resistance except briefly by the military police regiment, leading to two deaths (or eight according to some sources: Faye 1976, 87–8).

The 25 November coup effectively brought the Portuguese revolution to an end: in the following weeks the military Left was purged from all key positions and a few hundred civilian and military leftists were arrested, although most were released within a few months. The authority of the sixth provisional government was restored, the Constitutional Assembly completed its work and came up with quite a progressive Constitution in April 1976. Legislative elections then produced a relative majority for the Socialist Party which proceeded to form the first constitutional government of the new regime, and in June presidential elections gave a large majority to Col. Ramalho Eanes, the commando officer who had led the November coup and was backed by all the bourgeois parties (although Otelo came second with 16 per cent of the vote in a kind of swan-song for the revolutionary Left). For a few years after this a climate of sullen discontent prevailed in working-class areas, but everyone knew that the revolution was over and as Portugal's entry process into the European Community advanced, the inflow of European funds contributed to a new bourgeois euphoria in the late 1980s and 1990s. The liberal establishment sees this as the triumph of the revolution, and certainly it is preferable to the repression and backwardness of the Salazar dictatorship; but in the late twentieth century incorporation into the prevailing liberal-capitalist world order was scarcely revolutionary, especially when it came about through the destruction of a genuinely revolutionary mass movement for popular power which inspired workers all over Europe and beyond in 1975.

That the November coup did destroy the real revolutionary movement despite its relative moderation is well demonstrated in a recent study by Diego Palacios Cerezales (2003), who argues that there was clearly a crisis of state power in Portugal from 25 April 1974 to 25 November 1975, and that it was because the people instinctively sensed this that they seized the initiative time and time again in the streets, the factories, the fields and neighbourhoods. But after 25 November they saw immediately that their opportunity was over: there was an immediate and dramatic decline in demonstrations, occupations of factories, land or vacant housing, or other forms of direct action, especially those in which political parties had little involvement. Palacios Cerezales takes the example of shanty-town neighbourhood committees (*Commissões de Moradores*) and the SAAL, a special service supporting housing expropriations and community housing initiatives: in 1976 the government declared that elected local councils were the only legitimate form of representation and therefore the SAAL and the neighbourhood committees were irrelevant:

The poor communities which had been mobilised thus ceased to be the source of legitimacy of political power and their interests were diluted in [formal] democratic representation ... From that moment on, public housing plans returned to their classic competitive method, in which each applicant, instead of being just one participant in a collective action, contributing strength to a joint project, was converted into a rival in the sharing-out of scarce commodities' (Palacios Cerezales 2003, 104)

Although the neighbourhood committees were not the object of repression, they gradually atrophied as their members realised that direct action would no longer be tolerated and that any mobilisation needed support by someone in power to achieve results. In other words, popular power (and therefore real participatory democracy) was dead; Palacios Cerezales' example sums up very well the practical difference between formal liberal and popular participatory democracy.

Why did the Portuguese revolution fail? In terms of the actual conjuncture in November 1975, it has to be understood that the military and civilian Left were in an impossible position. Otelo and the COPCON, with the tacit but heavily conditioned support of the PCP and of military units aligned with Vasco Gonçalves, could certainly have seized power in Lisbon and the South, but northern Portugal and the Atlantic islands (Azores and Madeira) were firmly controlled by the Right. The result would have been civil war in which the Right would have been backed by the US, the European Community and neighbouring Spain (where Franco died on 20 November, but hard-line *franquistas*, alarmed by the revolutionary developments in Portugal, would have been more than willing to intervene). This is why Otelo and the COPCON, and also the forces aligned with the PCP, resisted all provocations until 25 November, and even then when the coup came they refused to take up the gauntlet: despite the growing strength of the popular revolutionary movement in Lisbon and the south, all the other cards were stacked against them.

The official version of these events is contained in a two-volume *Report on 25 November* (Relatório 1976) subsequently produced by the government, which claims that Colonel Eanes and his troops were acting to save 'democracy' from a Communist/leftist coup. The evidence, however, points to a carefully planned series of provocations by the Right designed to induce a false step by the progressive forces (as finally occurred with the paratroops) and thus justify its own coup (Clemente 1976; Faye 1976). It also seems probable that there were actually two coups in preparation, one by the extreme Right (which wanted a Pinochet-style repression and a new Fascism) and one by the moderates (who succeeded). In this it also seems probable that European Social Democracy played a key role, backing Mário Soares and the Socialist Party in order to avert the explosive situation that would have followed a Fascist coup. The solution was indeed very elegant, worthy of a chess grand master: it neutralised the revolutionary Left not only in Portugal but in Europe as a whole for many years to come, and made possible peaceful and controlled transition in Spain (which in other circumstances might well have exploded).

For our purposes, however, the Portuguese process has very different lessons. Even if geo-politics made the prospects for true revolutionary victory in Portugal remote, there were other factors which are linked to the process itself and are more relevant for our general analysis. One has to do with the internal regional imbalance: if the strength of the Right in the north and the islands was in part a result of social structure (predominance of smallholding peasants who lacked the class consciousness of the landless workers of the Alentejo and were much more dominated by the Catholic Church), this was not necessarily a fixed reality that could never be overcome. The Left did have a presence in Oporto, the country's second city and industrial capital of the north, and in a few other industrial towns such as Braga, and in the Machico area of Madeira where the Marxist-Leninist UDP managed to organise local women employed as home-workers in the embroidery trade. The MFA did make an effort to penetrate the rural north with its 'cultural dynamisation' programme, in which teams of soldiers and civilian professionals toured the villages offering practical instruction in productive crafts, cooperative organisation and other skills and proselytising for the concept of the MFA as popular liberation movement. But this effort was too little and too late (it only began in the spring of 1975).

Secondly, the Portuguese experience confirms the divisive and dampening effect on the popular movement all too often caused by political parties. The PCP, solidly anchored in the most class-conscious sectors of the working class in Lisbon and the surrounding industrial belt and among the rural proletariat of the Alentejo, and with the prestige derived from its prominence in the clandestine resistance to the dictatorship, naturally aspired to a leading role. But true to the typical practice of Communist parties, its behaviour in the unions and in government ministries and agencies which it came to control in the second to the fifth provisional governments (July 1974–August 1975) tended to be sectarian and exclusive. Also, once it had achieved a share of power in these governments it tried to control and dampen down spontaneous popular struggles in the name of stability, discouraging strikes in order to promote 'the battle of production' – a policy which only makes sense when, as in Cuba after 1961, for example, popular power has been well and truly established, not when the struggle for power is still in full flux.

If the PCP's role is open to criticism, much worse was that of the PS (Socialist Party). Successor to a variety of Socialist groupings that had existed under the dictatorship, the PS was only formed in 1973 in exile, with strong support from the West German SPD. Its leader Mário Soares had been in the Communist Youth for a few years in the 1940s, but his position and that of most of the PS leadership was clearly Social Democratic. In the heady atmosphere of 1974 they adopted vaguely Marxist language, but their practice was strictly parliamentary and reformist, and when the revolutionary process intensified in the early summer of 1975 they broke with the fourth provisional government and allied with the Right on the pretext of stopping a Communist takeover. Soares' role may well have been crucial in preventing unity of the different MFA tendencies on a revolutionary basis in July–August 1975, and it is highly significant that the issues on which the PS took its stand were the *República* and Rádio Renascença affairs: disputes which posed the question of workers' power against private property, and where despite Soares' allegations, it was not the PCP but the revolutionary Left and the independent popular movement which had gained control of these media outlets and which he chose to attack. From this point onwards, until 25 November and beyond, the PS aligned itself with the right-wing parties, the Catholic hierarchy, the European Community and the US against not just the PCP but the popular revolutionary movement as a whole. It was, at a crucial moment, the spearhead of reaction: without the PS the counter-revolutionaries would have been much more isolated and the November coup might never have occurred.

The PS would object that the alternative would have been to allow the PCP to complete its domination of state institutions and turn Portugal into a Soviet satellite, but this was in fact highly unlikely. Given Portugal's geographical situation and its NATO membership, and Soviet caution on geo-political issues, the PCP and the Gonçalvist tendency of the MFA would almost certainly have been content with non-alignment in international affairs and a sui generis form of Socialism domestically, necessarily based on some kind of compromise with both the PS and the revolutionary Left represented by Otelo and COPCON. This in turn might have made it possible (although far from easy) to negotiate a modus vivendi with the Catholic Church, Spain and the European Community, which the US would then have been obliged to accept. All of this is hypothetical and would have been very difficult, but the tragedy is that it was never given a chance because of the pro-Western and objectively counter-revolutionary stance of Mário Soares and the PS.

Finally, we must address the issue of leadership and populism in relation to the Portuguese process. Portugal had already had an experience of progressive populism ten to 15 years earlier with Humberto Delgado, a flamboyant air force general who went into opposition to Salazar in the 1950s and ran as opposition candidate in the regime's sham presidential elections in 1958. Because of his bold stand and charismatic style Delgado caused a bigger upheaval for the regime than the underground and semi-legal opposition ever managed to do; he was subsequently disgraced and forced into exile, but continued to plot against the regime until he was murdered by the secret police (PIDE) in 1965, becoming a martyr and a legendary figure in Portugal down to the present.

The anti-Fascist resistance – the PCP and other underground revolutionaries, and also the semi-legal 'democratic opposition' – waged a valiant struggle against the regime for decades, but it was only Delgado, and then in 1974 the MFA, who really undermined Portuguese Fascism. With the MFA it was also the case that these junior officers, who succeeded where others had failed for nearly 50 years, immediately acquired a heroic charisma for the popular classes who had been subdued for so long that many of them no longer dared to believe that freedom might ever come. In particular Otelo Saraiva de Carvalho, the young major who led the liberating coup of 25 April, and Vasco Gonçalves, the colonel who as prime minister of four of the provisional governments clung steadfastly to the goal of Socialism based on the Aliança Povo-MFA, the People-MFA Alliance – these two captured the imagination of the people more than any of the politicians. The veteran Communist leader Álvaro Cunhal and Mário Soares as undisputed leader of the PS had an appeal for their respective followers, but Otelo and the *companheiro Vasco* (they were both known mainly by their forenames) had a charismatic and non-partisan attraction which transcended that of the politicians. In the end Vasco Gonçalves became too closely identified with the PCP for his own good; although he was not – as claimed by his opponents – simply a PCP stooge, his political line became very closely associated with that of the party. Otelo, on the other hand, was clearly independent, and as time went on he became identified with the popular movement and with the most revolutionary tendencies, but never with any particular party. He was therefore in a strong position to promote a truly original solution of popular power, as conceived in the DG (the MFA 'Guiding Document' of July 1975) and the COPCON document. But he was too inconsistent, allowing himself at times to be drawn into a tactical alliance with the PS which was fatal for the process.

But perhaps Otelo's biggest weakness was a naïve reluctance to assume leadership at all; at heart he was an autonomist, almost a precursor of Holloway, believing in popular power not only without parties but without structured leadership of any kind. At one point he declared, 'I could have been the Fidel Castro of Europe'; one is tempted to say that if this is the case, he should have done so rather than talking about it after the event. But the reason he did not was precisely his belief in autonomous mass action, evading the issue of leadership. On the basis of our analysis in this book it can therefore be affirmed that Otelo's renunciation of responsibility when the popular movement was crying out for effective non-partisan leadership was a significant factor in the failure of the Portuguese revolution.

An effective alliance between Otelo and Vasco Gonçalves and the forces they represented might have saved the Portuguese revolution, especially if Otelo had been able to draw the Socialists away from their pro-Western stance. The People–MFA Alliance, with Otelo and Vasco Gonçalves at the helm, might have created an unprecedented form of democratic popular power on the banks of the Tagus, with dramatic consequences for the rest of Europe; but it was not to be. Europe now has to look, no doubt appropriately, to its former colonies in Latin America for democratic and revolutionary inspiration. As for Portugal, it is now firmly anchored in the European Union as an elitist neo-liberal 'democracy', with a political establishment that pours scorn on the memory of what it labels the PREC, the 'Revolutionary-Process-Under-Way' of 1974–75. But as economic stagnation and unemployment grow, Portuguese workers are beginning to revive the memory of that brief moment when all things seemed possible; the more recent (February 2005) electoral victory of the Left, but more particularly the rise of the Bloco de Esquerda, the anti-capitalist Left bloc which in six years has risen from almost nothing to 6.5 per cent of the vote and eight deputies, is a sign that things are beginning to change on the banks of the Tagus.

## CONCLUSION

This brief analysis of three other revolutionary processes – revolutions which in the end were aborted, but in which popular democratic governments did achieve power at least for a short time – confirms the overwhelming importance of non-partisan popular unity on as broad a base as possible. Without a clear popular majority, but also one which is united and transcends conventional political parties, popular power can never be consolidated. But also these examples confirm the need to transcend liberal parliamentarism: although ideological pluralism is essential, it must not be allowed to create organisational and ultimately antagonistic divisions in the popular movement. Political parties have a role to play, but not if they become divisionist or if they claim to monopolise political representation. Furthermore, popular power must be based on autonomous community organisations which cannot be partisan in character and which must have institutionalised representation at the highest level of the state: only this can guarantee genuine participatory democracy and prevent either economic or bureaucratic elites from expropriating the popular will. Finally, despite the need for popular autonomy, leadership is also necessary; without leadership the popular movement can never acquire the political efficacy to achieve power and transform society. There is of course a tension between autonomy and leadership, but this is an inevitable tension and one which will never disappear, if at all, until an eventual worldwide final defeat of capitalism: an ideal which may or may not be realisable some time in the future, but which certainly cannot be allowed to paralyse the quest for effective popular political alternatives in the here and now.

# 7
# Leadership, Movement and Representation: Populism and Revolutionary Strategy

If the main purpose of this book has been, through an examination of key revolutionary processes such as those in Cuba and Venezuela, to reconsider the way ahead for the Left and the anti-capitalist movement in today's world, then one major issue remains to be examined: that of political leadership, its genesis and its relationship to the movement. We have considered the question of democracy (liberal versus direct and participatory) and that of Socialism (bureaucratic state Socialism versus popular power and workers' democracy). We have seen how revolutionary movements developed and achieved power in Cuba and Venezuela, and how they reached at least a share of power for a while in Chile, Nicaragua and Portugal. We have also seen that in the most successful cases victory was achieved by a broad, united popular movement transcending political parties and rooted in national popular culture and traditions, and with a flexible and dynamic leadership closely identified with the mass movement. But it remains to examine just how such a leadership develops and how it relates to the movement.

As we have seen, parties organised along standard Marxist-Leninist lines – Communist parties, but also most of their Maoist or Trotskyist variants – have not succeeded in leading successful popular revolutionary processes except in conditions of virtual state collapse through defeat in war (as in Russia in 1917) or in national liberation movements against foreign occupiers (China, Korea, Vietnam, Yugoslavia and Albania). In other cases (as in the rest of Eastern Europe) they came to power with the assistance of the Soviet Red Army through processes that were neither truly revolutionary nor entirely popular. In a number of other cases they have shared power in what were essentially reformist governments, and in many countries they have played an important part in working-class and popular struggles. But nowhere have they succeeded in making or leading revolution except in the aforementioned conditions of wartime defeat or national liberation struggles; and once in power, they have invariably ended up by installing centralised bureaucratic Socialist regimes which expropriate popular democratic power.

Communist parties have also been criticised for their sectarianism, hegemonism and dogmatism, and certainly they have often been characterised by these defects. They have also frequently been guilty of errors of class analysis or political alliances, but these are understandable conjunctural mistakes. In my view their fundamental error, shared in most cases by the Maoists and Trotskyists and lying at the root of all their defects, has been a lack of confidence in popular instincts and in the autonomous dynamics of popular movements. This is most apparent in their strategy of building a revolutionary mass party on the basis of the doctrinaire imposition of complex theories, as if the complexities of Marx, Engels and Lenin, which have caused endless debate among many of the world's finest intellectuals, could be reduced to trite formulae rather than serving as a source of creative (and therefore variable) inspiration. Coupled with this is their tendency to impose control by a bureaucratic group which is neither democratic nor in many cases capable of effective leadership. The problem with Holloway (2002), or with other autonomists like Hardt and Negri (2000), is not their emphasis on popular autonomy and protagonism but their refusal to consider the need for organisation and leadership.

Leadership is thus necessary, indeed essential, but it must be intimately linked to the popular movement and must respect its autonomy. The task of leadership is to synthesise and express the will of the movement and to develop an effective strategy for its implementation; and to contribute to the movement's further development by generating a revolutionary consciousness through praxis (that is, conscious self-critical political practice). Above all, it must actually lead, demonstrating its capacity in the course of struggle. Fidel and his comrades in the M-26-7 (even before the movement had a name) began by taking up arms against Batista, building on popular repudiation of the dictatorship and traditional Cuban popular values derived from Martí and the *mambises*: racial equality, national independence, agricultural self-sufficiency and integrity in public life (*vergüenza contra dinero*). Similarly, Chávez and the MBR-200 responded to the *caracazo* by taking up arms and appealing to the memory of Bolívar, the 'Tree of the Three Roots', the ideal of participatory democracy and hatred of the 'oligarchy'. Socialism, Marxism, open and conscious confrontation with imperialism – these things did not feature in the initial ideology of the movement in either case, but would come later, as and when the dynamic of the struggle and the development of popular consciousness demanded them. Thus in both Cuba and Venezuela determined leadership was accepted by the popular movement and was able to develop and lead that movement to a qualitatively new level – but only because the leaders began by accepting popular consciousness and culture.

This does not mean that identification with popular culture is sufficient by itself: even where a spontaneous 'organic' leadership emerges from the heart of the movement, there is no guarantee that it will have the necessary political capacity. Perhaps the clearest example of such organic leadership of a major political movement in recent times is Lula in Brazil, a grass-roots activist who emerged as spokesman of the São Paulo metallurgical workers in the late 1970s and went on to become undisputed leader of the PT and now president of the country. While Lula personally is still highly respected by the mass of Brazilian workers, his government is widely regarded as having sold out to capitalist interests and Lula himself is considered by many to have become a prisoner of a Social Democratic PT elite; 'organic' working-class leadership is no guarantee that a popular anti-capitalist agenda will be implemented. The contrast between the Brazilian case and those of Cuba and Venezuela is at least in part one of revolutionary vision and strategy: Lula and the PT have allowed themselves to be entrapped by the existing power structure. The task of the leadership, while accepting and indeed obeying the popular will for revolutionary change, is to develop and implement an effective strategy for implementing that change.

The question of leadership is connected to another, even less fashionable concept, that of vanguard. At least since the time of Lenin, revolutionary parties have claimed to be vanguard parties, and this is one of the issues that the debate about the renewal of the Left in recent years has had to address: what form the vanguard should take or whether it is necessary at all. The problem with classic Marxist-Leninist parties is that they proclaim themselves to be the vanguard, on the basis of ideological consciousness and political/organisational dedication; but this begs the question of whether the mass of the working class and/or people recognise them as the vanguard. It has to be recognised that the vanguard, like leadership in general, cannot be decreed, and neither can it be imposed bureaucratically. A vanguard party, like an individual leader, gains recognition through action, by demonstrating a decisive capacity to lead in a critical situation.

Lenin and the Bolshevik Party became the vanguard of the Russian revolutionary movement in practice through their demonstrated capacity for clandestine organisation and agitation from the early 1900s to 1917, their success in seizing power in 1917, and on through the civil war. Mao and the Chinese Communist Party showed a similar capacity in the Long March and the anti-Japanese resistance, and the Vietnamese Communists under Ho Chi Minh in the epic struggle against the Japanese, French and Americans. Similarly with Tito and the League of Yugoslav Communists and with Enver Hoxha and the Albanians: whatever their subsequent defects when in power, they showed a genuine popular leadership capacity during the revolutionary insurgency. But with rare exceptions, other Communist parties have not shown the same capacity, and neither have other self-proclaimed revolutionary parties; they have either wallowed in sectarian isolation or become resigned to militant reformism.

Thus in Cuba the original Communist Party, the PSP, gained the support of a sector of the Cuban working class by its success in organising effective class-based trade unionism, but over the years proved incapable of acting as revolutionary vanguard, despite its Leninist rhetoric; in contrast, Fidel Castro and the M-26–7 became such a vanguard in practice through the Moncada assault, the Granma expedition, the success of the rebel army in the Sierra Maestra, and the capacity to unite the broadest possible coalition in resistance against Batista and imperialism. In Venezuela Hugo Chávez and the MBR-200 became the vanguard of the popular movement through the uprising of 4 February 1992, the 1998 elections, the process of the Constituent Assembly, the creation of the Bolivarian circles, the defeat of the April coup and the *paro*, while the MAS, the PPT, the PCV and other parties of the Venezuelan Left could only tag along supporting Chávez (in the best of cases, since various 'left' parties joined the opposition) and clearly lost any claim to a vanguard role.

## PERSONAL LEADERSHIP AND POPULISM

Our analysis of Cuba and Venezuela has shown that a highly successful popular revolutionary strategy is possible without the leadership of a Communist or Socialist party but impossible through pure spontaneity or autonomism. Both cases were characterised by mass movements independent of political parties, broad popular unity, ideologies derived from national democratic culture, and charismatic personal leadership. However, the form taken by the revolutionary movements in these countries, both before and after attaining power, raises other fundamental questions. The exceptional prominence in both cases of individual charismatic leaders – Fidel and Chávez – inevitably poses the issue of populism. Compelling oratory, mass adulation, personal protagonism: these characteristics fuel the accusations of demagogy, manipulation and even dictatorship frequently directed at both leaders. In my view such accusations are profoundly mistaken, but they cannot be refuted by pretending that the issue does not exist: some ardent admirers try to dismiss the problem by declaring that 'the Cuban revolution is not just Fidel' or 'the Bolivarian revolution is not just Chávez', but that they are the Cuban and Venezuelan peoples respectively. Of course: but this does not alter the fact that neither revolution would be what it is, indeed might not even have succeeded at all, without these two extraordinary leaders.

To insist on the crucial importance of Fidel in the Cuban revolution, or of Chávez in contemporary Venezuela, is not to deny the role of their comrades in the M-26–7 or the MBR-200 and MVR, or indeed of millions of Cubans and Venezuelans participating in different ways in these two processes. Of course no leader makes a revolution single-handed, and indeed not even the several thousand active militants of the respective movements make the revolution unaided. The more genuine and profound the revolutionary process, the more it will involve actions by millions of anonymous citizens. But these millions of anonymous actors do not participate with a common purpose, and certainly not in a sustained way, without leadership. The leadership represents them, reflects their aspirations and responds to them, but it also guides them, stimulates them, takes decisions and directs them – in a word, it leads. A poor or ineffective leadership will sooner or later lose popular support and fail – or will become dependent on anti-popular vested interests and change its allegiance. But a successful leadership which is in tune with the popular will grows stronger and increases its capacity for decisive action, and has the ability and indeed the obligation to take the initiative in further crucial decisions which only a central executive power can take. It may be a governmental team or the central committee of a party which takes these decisions, but frequently it will be an individual leader; and it will be the leader in direct communication with the people, in the public square or on television, in the language of the people, without bureaucratic mediation and with direct feedback.

In the case of Cuba there can be no doubt that the mass of the people wanted agrarian reform in 1959, but without the decisions, which were above all Fidel's decisions, to issue the Agrarian Reform Law in May and to take measures to implement it swiftly, it would not have occurred so rapidly or so thoroughly. Undoubtedly the Cuban people wanted economic independence from the United States, but it is very doubtful that they would have achieved it to anything like the same degree were it not for the dramatic decisions, which were above all Fidel's decisions, to expropriate the foreign oil companies in July 1960, to expropriate US-owned sugar estates and mills the next month, and the remaining US-owned industries in October of that year. Undoubtedly the people wanted free universal education, but without the decision – which again was above all Fidel's – to launch the extraordinary and unprecedented literacy campaign, they would not have had it anything like so quickly or so completely. To say therefore, as some Socialists do, that it was the Cuban people and not Fidel who did these things, is factually incorrect and dangerously misleading. It was Fidel *with* the Cuban people; of course he could not have done so without the active support and participation of the people; but if it had not been for his extraordinary political will and vision, it is safe to say that the Cuban revolution would not have gone nearly as far or as fast as it did, and it could quite possibly have degenerated into a pattern of division and confusion reminiscent of 1933.

Much the same can be said of Venezuela today; without the leadership of Hugo Chávez Frías, it is very unlikely that there would be a revolutionary government in power. There would be a situation of crisis, of intense social conflict, possibly the emergence of armed insurgent organisations, but no revolutionary power giving direction to the process. Certainly the discontent and rebellious disposition of the people of the *cerros* created the conditions for such a process; the popular uprising of the *caracazo* (and its brutal suppression) sounded the death-knell of the corrupt Punto Fijo system and showed that conditions were ripe for a dramatic change. The people were looking for leadership, but no party provided it, and it was Chávez and the MBR-200 who took the initiative, albeit with three years' delay, in the February 1992 uprising. Despite its failure the 4 February uprising showed that there was an organised group in the military who were in tune with the popular mood and who were willing to risk all. The subsequent amnesty campaign for Chávez and his comrades was indeed the work of the people (and of a few left-wing politicians who got the message), but it was in itself a response to the leadership shown by the Bolivarian revolutionaries. In the 1998 elections it was clearly understood that Chávez was the people's candidate, and throughout the twists and turns of the political process that followed the protagonist was the Venezuelan people, but with Chávez at the head. In the defeat of the April 2002 coup it was the people with the revolutionary military who took the lead, but it is no accident that their key demand was for the return not only of democracy, but also specifically of Chávez. Again in the *paro* it was Chávez who took the key decisions, announced to and ratified by the sovereign people in the great rally of 7 December 2002 outside Miraflores, to dismiss the PDVSA management and send in the military to take control of the oil industry.

During the hardships of the *paro* Chávez knew that he could rely on the people to resist and not to be provoked; that much-abused term 'dialectical' applies perfectly to the relationship between Hugo Chávez and the Venezuelan people, a mutually reinforcing partnership in which both terms of the equation are indispensable. The Venezuelan people acquired a collective identity and were constituted as a political subject through the actions of Hugo Chávez and the Bolivarian Movement; to speak of one without the other is, in the present historical phase, meaningless. This is also why in recent years Chávez, like Fidel before him, has become the object of enthusiastic popular rallies whenever he goes abroad (at least in Latin America); he projects internationally the revolutionary spirit of the Venezuelan people. When crowds in Lima or Buenos Aires or Santo Domingo gather to greet Chávez, it is not some irrational media-created frenzy, but popular recognition that this man represents an authentic revolutionary process which offers the greatest hope for progressive change in Latin America since the Sandinista victory in Nicaragua a quarter-century ago.

In order to understand both Fidel and Chávez it is necessary to recognise that their political origins had little to do with leftist orthodoxy but a great deal to do with Latin American popular tradition. We have already seen that both the content and style of Fidel's discourse – until at least April 1961 – and of Chávez' discourse until at least December 2004, was populist rather than Socialist. It was only after these dates that they began to talk explicitly of Socialism, and even then there was (is) much about their oratorical style which conforms to the classic image of the populist leader. It is worth returning to key aspects of their discourse to remind ourselves of just how unorthodox they are in terms of conventional Marxist politics.

In Fidel's case the flexible, inclusive and anti-dogmatic content of his speeches – combined, for sure, with anti-imperialist and anti-oligarchic passion – was the most noticeable characteristic of his discourse during 1959. It is impossible to ignore his famous 'humanist' speech in New York in April of that year: 'Neither bread without liberty, nor liberty without bread; neither dictatorships of men, nor class dictatorships; government of the people, with neither dictatorship nor oligarchy. Freedom with bread and bread without terror: that is humanism' (in *Bohemia* 3 May 1959, 67, 93). In fact Fidel returned to the concept of humanism in several speeches of April and May 1959; it seems to have summed up his political and philosophical vision at that time. To some extent it might be seen as a tactical reaction to accusations of Communism which were already being levelled at the revolution in reactionary circles; thus when questioned on the subject in a television interview on 2 April, he replied:

What's the reason for wanting to arouse the spectre of Communism on the grounds that we do not persecute Communists, when here we don't persecute anyone ... Those who are most demanding about freedom and democracy don't like to talk about the right of people to eat or to work, and the unfortunate people who are dying of hunger can't eat democratic theory ... The ideal politico-philosophical theory is that which gives man all freedoms and also provides him with material satisfaction. That is our revolutionary doctrine. Everything else, shall I tell you what it is? Excuses ... . (in *Revolución* 3 April 1959)

But there is much to suggest that Fidel's arguments here were more than simply a tactical device to avoid the 'Communist' label; his insistence on philosophical flexibility and broadness of vision was such as to cause genuine confusion for many listeners (and will surely astound many of today's dogmatic leftists). In a speech on 8 May 1959, having just returned from a long trip to several Latin American countries, Fidel declared:

We respect all ideas; we respect all beliefs ... we are not going to place ourselves on the Right nor are we going to place ourselves on the Left, neither are we going to place ourselves in the Centre ... We are going to put ourselves a bit further forward than the Right or the Left ... a step beyond the Right and a step beyond the Left. Or do men have to remain tied to ideas which others want to impose on them? (in *Revolución* 9 May 1959)

Not surprisingly this caused a good deal of discussion, and when questioned about it in a television interview a fortnight later Fidel insisted: 'Our revolution is not capitalist because it has broken many rules of capitalism which had been laid down for years. Our revolution isn't Communist either, our revolution has a position which is neither the one nor the other and which with all its characteristics is an original revolution ... ' (in *Revolución* 22 May 1959).

These declarations, which to many undoubtedly appeared completely incoherent and self-contradictory, reflect a desire to transcend conventional political definitions and to achieve a new synthesis, a unitary and innovative position. What we have here is an anti-schematic discourse which suggests the idea that the Left has failed because of its identification with rigid doctrinal formulae, and that there are elements of revolutionary thought with which even the Right may agree. This is moreover a classic populist theme, formulated in remarkably similar terms by Perón when he tried to define his 'Justicialist' doctrine:

For us there is nothing fixed and nothing to deny. We are anti-communist because Communists are sectarians, and anti-capitalist because capitalists are sectarians. Our Third position is not a central position. It is an ideological position which is in the Centre, on the Right or on the Left, according to specific circumstances. (quoted in Pendle 1963, 127)

This might be seen as pure opportunism, but if such were the case Perón would have been unlikely to state it so explicitly; what we have here is also an attempt to formulate an anti-schematic position transcending conventional political divisions. *Justicialismo*, according to Perón, aimed to balance the 'four forces' at work in society: materialism and idealism, individualism and collectivism.

Now this is not to say that Fidel was (even in May 1959) the same as Perón nor that the M-26–7 was equivalent to the Partido Justicialista, but rather that the two movements had similar roots in the Latin American populist tradition, which was nationalist, anti-oligarchic and potentially revolutionary. The difference was that Fidel, because of his intellectual training and his experience of armed struggle, was much more consistent than Perón and capable of taking the movement to its ultimate consequences; and also that in Cuba, because of the country's extreme dependence and frustrated national development, the populist movement had a more pronounced popular character and was less open to bourgeois influence. But the symbolic roots of the two movements, their initial sources of ideological inspiration and the style of the discursive interaction between the leaders and the people were similar. It was with good reason that Fidel insisted on the importance for the revolution of the example set by Eduardo Chibás, the populist founder of the Ortodoxo Party, declaring that without the seeds sown and the ideas preached by *El Adalid* (the Guide), the Cuban revolution would not have been possible.

The insistence on ideological breadth and originality and on concepts like humanism should not be taken to mean that the Cuban revolution could have been led in a capitalist direction, at least not very easily. During the first year there were many observers who thought this, and some historians still take such a view. But the fact that the revolution was not Communist or Marxist at the beginning does not mean that it lacked clear goals of national emancipation and social transformation. Those who interpret these declarations of humanism and ideological pluralism as indications that the leadership was capable of wavering or temporising on essential issues are profoundly mistaken. For those who were willing to listen, this was made clear by several of Fidel's statements in the first few months. Thus on 9 April 1959 he declared: 'And here, listen carefully, the Cuban problem isn't an internal one. The Cuban problem is that quite possibly there are ranged against the Cuban Revolution the interests of the international oligarchy which is very powerful ... ' – and he concluded categorically: 'For the first time in our history the two camps are clearly demarcated. On one side the national interest; on the other side the enemies of the Nation. On one side the people; on the other side the people's enemies. On one side, justice; on the other side, crime ... ' (in *Revolución* 10 April 1959). Precisely when Fidel was talking about humanism and about not being on the Right, Left or Centre, he was insisting in practical terms on a radical commitment to national emancipation and social justice.

Equally in the case of Hugo Chávez, his insistence on the democratic and humanist character of the Bolivarian revolution has often led to misunderstanding. Repeatedly denying that the revolution is Communist or Marxist, he also refers frequently to Christ and to his Christian faith, but not in the dogmatic manner of a George W. Bush condemning abortion or proclaiming war on Islamic terrorism, rather in the style of a liberation theologian, citing the Gospel as inspiration for the salvation of the poor and to condemn the injustice of capitalism:

The world situation is terrible: and what we're doing here in Venezuela is to make a gigantic effort to change direction, to change from the road to hell to the road to life ... So that there can be equality, so that the Kingdom announced by Christ can become real, the Kingdom of Equality and the Kingdom of Justice, that is our struggle ... . (Chávez Frías 2004, 41–2)

And just like Fidel, while Chávez would ultimately recognise his identification with the Left and proclaim his goal as the 'Socialism of the twenty-first century', he has also on occasion claimed to be beyond the Right/Left divide, being 'Bolivarian' and revolutionary rather than a prisoner of conventional leftist ideas.

Critics of Chávez have repeatedly accused him of populism, singularly failing to understand why the accusation may ultimately be irrelevant since (as we shall see) it is possible, and perhaps even necessary, to be both populist *and* revolutionary. One of the more erudite critics is the Venezuelan scholar Alfredo Ramos Jiménez who edited a collection of essays published in 2002 by the Universidad de los Andes. Ramos Jiménez categorises *chavismo* as a case of neo-populism, comparing him to Presidents Menem of Argentina and Fujimori of Peru. He uses as theoretical references the classic texts of Max Weber on charismatic leadership and Michael Oakeshott on the 'politics of faith' as opposed to the 'politics of scepticism', but he also cites contemporary political scientists such as Bruce Ackerman of Yale on the concept of the 'triumphalist scenario' and the French scholar Guy Hermet on the 'mirage' of populism. Ramos Jiménez says that *chavismo* presents itself as an alternative based on a 'voluntarist "starting from scratch" ... necessary to put an end once and for all to the frustrations and disillusionments of the past', and that this 'starting from scratch' is presented as a reflection of the popular will, 'which thus arrives at what Ackerman has called the triumphalist scenario of a politics with self-evident cultural-religious roots' (Ramos Jiménez 2002, 19). A more superficial version of this critique can be found in the recent book by Michael McCaughan, *The Battle of Venezuela*: 'The second Venezuela [as opposed to the first, wealthy one] lives in the hillsides and survives on its wits, in constant search of a messiah with a magical formula to relieve them of their misery. As we know, the messiah strategy is a recipe for futile martyrdom' – but McCaughan provides no evidence that poor Venezuelans are 'in constant search of a messiah' or of 'a magical formula', when it could be argued that they have quite a realistic understanding of political reality and of the possible alternatives. In another passage he produces this gem: ' ... the real Chávez – if such a thing exists – is to be found in astrological circles' (McCaughan 2004, 158, 160).

It is undeniable that Chávez exhibits characteristics of charismatic leadership and that in the popular enthusiasm manifested at *chavista* rallies there is an element of 'triumphalism'. But the problem with this analysis lies in the tone of ironic scepticism which runs through it, with the implication – at times made explicit – that the country ought to adopt 'the politics of scepticism' and of moderate compromise prevalent in advanced countries. This scepticism is profoundly conservative and implies that conventional liberal pluralism is the only valid model for a modern society. It does not even admit the possibility that there really can be a new beginning, a 'starting from scratch' which will radically change the political, social and economic structure to the benefit of the popular classes. Similarly it refuses to consider the possibility that the charismatic leadership and chiliastic enthusiasm which it so despises may fulfil a necessary symbolic function in popular mobilisation and in the real, effective construction of a new and more just social system which will also be more democratic. One does not have to believe literally in the New Jerusalem to accept that such a myth may inspire people to create a far superior (although not perfect) society, *haciendo posible lo imposible* – 'making the impossible possible' – in the words of the Cuban revolutionaries quoted by Marta Harnecker (Harnecker 2000). It is also important to recognise – which these critics do not – that chiliastic enthusiasm may be associated with a perfectly rational political project, that Chávez and his movement emerged from 20 years of dialogue with all sections of the Venezuelan Left and that many of his passionate supporters also have a very clear understanding of the specifics of the Bolivarian project. The poor of the *cerros* may indeed identify passionately with Chávez' charisma, but they also perceive correctly that he represents a real and radically different alternative. The blind search for a Messiah, on the other hand, emerges when all rational hope is gone, as in today's Haiti where after the brutal destruction of Aristide and his *Lavalas* movement, the people are turning in desperation to *voudou* and Evangelical churches (and to crime). At root what is at stake here is a refusal by the critics to accept the legitimacy or feasibility of revolution.

## THE LATIN AMERICAN POPULIST TRADITION

But this recognition of the vital importance of charisma and of ideological flexibility in these, the two most profound popular revolutions of our times, does require us to examine much more carefully the entire issue of populism. There is after all a rich tradition of populism in Latin America, associated with leaders such as Perón in Argentina, Cárdenas in Mexico, Vargas in Brazil and Gaitán in Colombia, who played a key role in the emergence of mass politics and the formation of the modern state in these countries in the mid-twentieth century. The term 'neo-populist' has also been applied to a series of more superficial and demagogic politicians in recent times like Menem in Argentina, Fujimori in Peru, Collor in Brazil and Bucarám in Ecuador. Whereas the classic populists, those of the first generation, were associated with nationalist and reformist policies of state intervention and popular welfare, the 'neo-populists' have turned the phenomenon on its head, promoting neo-liberalism, free trade and fiscal austerity, albeit cultivating popular support with targeted welfare programmes. Elsewhere in the world the term 'populism' has been applied to everything from Russian nineteenth-century *narodniks* – aristocratic intellectuals with a romantic attachment to 'the people' – to US and Canadian farmers' protest movements and Fascists such as Hitler and Mussolini. The Left has generally dismissed populism as bourgeois reformism and as a deviation from the path of revolution, while at the other extreme in recent years neo-liberals have condemned any kind of non-selective public welfare programme as 'populist' and unsustainable. Does the term, then, have any real utility, and what does it have to do with the Cuban and Venezuelan revolutions?

The standard analyses of early Latin American populism identified it with the phase of 'import-substitution industrialisation' (ISI) from the 1930s to the 1960s, and with a multi-class developmental alliance of the national bourgeoisie, the urban working class and middle sectors (sometimes also extending to the peasantry) (Weffort 1968; Di Tella 1970; Ianni 1975). Others argued that it was a transitional phenomenon associated with urban-rural migration and the presence of a 'disposable mass' of migrants with little political consciousness (Germani 1962). This process and the political and economic strategy of ISI ran into serious obstacles in the 1960s and 1970s due to the restricted size of the national market, bottlenecks associated with the second phase of ISI (the attempt to develop capital-goods industries) and the unfavourable international context with the postwar industrial recovery of North America and Europe. This led to the abandonment of ISI and, after a period of intense social and political conflict and (in many countries) military dictatorship, to the rise of neo-liberalism, and most observers concluded that Latin American populism was a thing of the past. However from the late 1980s onwards the emergence of the 'neo-populists' led to a reconsideration of the question, and many specialists began to refer to populism as a recurrent phenomenon on the Latin American scene (although still associating it with opportunism and demagogy).

There is however a radically different interpretation of the phenomenon, first put forward in 1977 by the Argentine theorist Ernesto Laclau. For Laclau populism is a multi-class or supra-class political movement, emerging in critical conjunctures and characterised by charismatic leadership and a radical anti-establishment discourse. It has no inherent political orientation or programme: populism may be of the Right, Left or Centre depending on the balance of class forces existing in a specific country at a particular moment. It is a conjunctural phenomenon, but one which is both a symptom of and a factor in a critical moment leading to regime change if not social revolution. But the fulcrum of Laclau's theory is discourse analysis: taking Althusser's structuralist Marxism as his point of departure, Laclau examines the process of elaboration of a populist discourse through the combination of different 'interpellations'. An orator 'interpellates' (addresses) the audience as 'the people', as 'workers', 'patriots', 'Argentinians', or (Perón's trademark) *descamisados* (bare-chested, in other words, manual labourers). Through the systematic use of certain interpellations the audience is fashioned as a political subject and develops a political consciousness and identity. But the ideological themes expressed through this process of 'interpellation' cannot be purely arbitrary: they must be 'popular-democratic' interpellations, drawn from national popular culture and traditions and reflecting a particular social reality. Finally, in a populist discourse the interpellations are not class-specific but tend to have a broader appeal: 'the people', 'the nation', 'honest citizens' and the like.

One consequence of Laclau's analysis is that the process of formation of a populist movement is not qualitatively different from that of a proletarian revolutionary one, and that a successful popular revolutionary movement will necessarily have populist characteristics. The ideology of a proletarian revolutionary movement cannot be – as doctrinaire Marxist-Leninists assume – exclusively based on class, but must incorporate supra-class 'popular-democratic' interpellations; in order to be successful the movement must fuse an amalgam of diverse interpellations into a 'synthetic-antagonistic complex in relation to the dominant ideology' (Laclau 1977, 172–3). Laclau recognises that not all populist ideologies, and therefore not all populist movements, are revolutionary or even progressive; he distinguishes between 'populisms of the dominant classes' and those 'of the dominated classes'. The former will still appear very radical and will mobilise powerful mass movements capable of producing profound political upheavals, but their ideologies combine a gamut of popular-democratic interpellations with others that are profoundly reactionary: racist and imperialist values, for example. This accounts for the undeniable reality of reformist or even outright reactionary populisms, and Laclau does not flinch at recognising the existence of populisms of the extreme Right: Italian Fascism and German Nazism were clearly populist movements.

What this means, then, is that populism is neither (as is often assumed) a specific political ideology (generally assumed to be reformist), nor does it have an inherent political orientation. Rather, it is a political technique or phenomenon which may manifest itself at different times in movements of totally opposed ideology and significance. To say, therefore, that both Italian Fascism and the Cuban revolutionary movement had populist characteristics does not in any way imply that they are politically similar; it means only that both were based on massive popular mobilisation with charismatic leadership, emerging in situations of hegemonic crisis, and that there were similarities in their internal dynamics. These as it were technical similarities are what distinguish both of them from, say, the conventional political practice of the German Christian Democrat Party or the equally conventional practice of its Social Democrat opponents: two parties of quite contrary political ideology, class base and significance, but sharing a non-populist, non-charismatic and purely institutional political practice. The polar opposite of populism is not Socialism or any other specific ideology, but conventional institutional politics.

For Laclau, the key to a reactionary populism lies in the *manner of incorporation* of popular-democratic interpellations into the overall ideology, and in the control of the mass movement by an anti-oligarchic fraction of the bourgeoisie (Laclau 1977, 172–4). In effect, the autonomous popular movement, which in a progressive populism finds supreme expression in the discourse of the popular leader, in a reactionary populism is captured and manipulated by a demagogic leader and an apparatus at the service of bourgeois interests. For a 'populism of the dominant classes' to emerge, it is sufficient for a class or class fraction to require a substantial transformation in the power bloc, and hence to appeal directly to the people; but since this is potentially explosive, the bourgeois fraction concerned has to inject racist or other reactionary notions into the ideological mix in order to prevent the movement from fulfilling its liberating potential. This contradiction may also require a reactionary populism to assume very repressive characteristics at certain moments.

Most significant and relevant for our purposes, however, is Laclau's affirmation that a 'populism of the dominated classes' has revolutionary potential, and correspondingly, that any Socialist or revolutionary movement, if it is to be really successful, must become populist in form:

The struggle of the working class for its hegemony is an effort to achieve the maximum possible fusion between popular-democratic ideology and socialist ideology. In this sense a 'socialist populism' is not the most backward form of working class ideology but the most advanced – the moment when the working class has succeeded in condensing the ensemble of democratic ideology in a determinate social formation within its own ideology … . (Laclau 1977: 174)

– and at another point Laclau is even more explicit:

In socialism … coincide the highest form of 'populism' and the resolution of the ultimate and most radical of class conflicts. The dialectic between 'the people' and classes finds here the final moment of its unity: there is no socialism without populism, and the highest forms of populism can only be socialist. (Laclau 1977, 196–7; emphasis in original)

Class conflict is thus subsumed in political conflict between 'the people' and 'the power bloc' (and/or imperialism), in a dramatic expression of (in Marxist terms) the 'relative autonomy of the political' and a refutation of simplistic economic determinism.

So far, so good – and in my view Laclau must be credited with a brilliant insight into the dynamics of popular movements. However, there are some problems with his analysis, in particular his almost exclusive concentration on ideology. Laclau provides a devastating critique of the functionalists and the dogmatic Marxists, but he fails to analyse the political and organisational aspects of populism, and although he refers to 'class' it remains so vague and abstract as to be meaningless. This deficiency was identified by Nicos Mouzelis who argued that what identifies a movement as populist is not only its ideological discourse but also its style of leadership, the dynamics of its popular mobilisation and its organisational fluidity (Mouzelis 1978). Moreover, what determines the ultimate political orientation and significance of a specific populist movement is surely not just discourse but social reality: the constellation of class forces in a particular society at a given conjuncture.

An effective adaptation of Laclau's theory is provided by Paul Cammack, who agrees that populism can run the gamut of the political spectrum from Right to Left but insists that it must be defined in terms not only of discourse but of its genesis in a situation of hegemonic crisis: 'populist discourse may be ubiquitous, but it is of greatest significance in these relatively rare conjunctures [of a fundamental crisis of accumulation], (never defined discursively, but in terms of political economy, institutions, and the complex relations between them ...)' (Cammack 2000, 154). Many conventional politicians sometimes resort to populist discourse, but they do so only as a temporary tactical device. Those who are truly populist, however, operate outside established institutions or, if they emerge from within these institutions, threaten to subvert them completely. This is the crucial point about populism as a political movement: it has a dynamic force of mass mobilisation which easily displaces or overwhelms established political parties and institutions, and this is what gives it revolutionary potential. In Cammack's words, 'the emergence of a form of politics centred on a direct appeal to the people indicates a crisis of existing institutions, and itself constitutes and extends a crisis of political and institutional mediation.' The crucial words here are 'centred on' and 'direct'; all politicians appeal to the people, but a leader and a movement who make a direct appeal to the people their fundamental modus operandi are consciously or unconsciously undermining the entire existing regime. The principle of popular sovereignty is as we have seen the basis of true democracy, and if put into practice will inevitably lead to popular power in all spheres of life, which in turn implicitly tends towards Socialism.

## THE DIALECTIC OF POPULIST REPRESENTATION

The bond which is formed between the populist leader and the mass is of extraordinary intensity, bordering sometimes on the mystical. The leader develops a powerful charismatic appeal, and a key element in this is oratory: the capacity to speak passionately and often at great length, but in the language of the people, to such an extent that they feel that their own innermost thoughts and desires are being expressed. To some readers this will smack of demagogy and manipulation, but a close examination of the phenomenon suggests that what actually occurs is much more interesting: the orator is indeed expressing the thoughts and will of his audience. Such is the identification of the true populist leader with the audience that s/he assimilates the 'general will' and then expresses it more clearly and forcefully than the people themselves, and projects it on to a new plane, as a political programme for the realisation of these latent popular desires. What takes place is an implicit dialogue, a reciprocal process which contributes powerfully to the generation of a collective identity among the participants:

– in populist rallies the followers identify with each other. As in the Carnival analysed by Bakhtin, populist rallies are not spectacles which are observed but spectacles in which everyone participates. This participation 'celebrates a temporary liberation from the prevailing wisdom and the established order; it marks the suspension of all hierarchies of rank, privilege, norms and prohibitions' … Therefore it makes possible the creation of a new language among the participants … . (De la Torre 1994, 51–2)

It is necessary to take into account not only the speaker's oratory, symbols and actions, but also the expectations of the audience, their posters, banners, shouts and interjections. Moreover – and this is overlooked by almost all writers – it is important to recognise that many populist leaders do not limit their interaction with the people to mass rallies and broadcast or televised speeches, but engage in frequent personal dialogues with individual working people or small groups. Fidel constantly travels around Cuba talking and listening to all manner of people; Chávez' *Aló Presidente* programmes are far from being presidential monologues but involve frequent interaction with a studio audience and with 'phone-in' participants, who are clearly not hand-picked; and Chávez also is constantly conversing with people all over Venezuela. Similarly Lázaro Cárdenas in Mexico began his presidency by setting aside one day a week for receiving delegations of workers and peasants in his official residence.

We are dealing therefore with a genuine dialogue, a process which contributes to the forging of a collective identity among the participants and also to the ideological evolution and maturity of the leader. The latter, after all, assumes an extraordinary responsibility, and must be only too aware of how much rests on their shoulders; but at the same time this becomes a source of strength, at least in the most authentic leaders, who become popular tribunes whose proclamations and decisions are reinforced by the people and who are supported and protected by them. The more the leader identifies with the people, the more they identify with him or her, to such a point that betrayal becomes virtually unthinkable. It is for this reason also that the class origins of the individual leader are not particularly important: the populist leader has typically broken with the norms of his class background in the initial process of forging the charismatic bond with the people, and in moments of crisis is more likely to be guided by political instinct derived from this process of political socialisation than by family background. This is the meaning of the famous phrase of the great Colombian populist leader Jorge Eliécer Gaitán, *Yo no soy un Hombre, yo soy un Pueblo* – 'I am not a Man, I am the People': such apparent arrogance was tantamount to a statement of fact, an expression of how close had become the bond between Gaitán and the popular classes of Colombia. In this case, the Colombian oligarchy recognised the danger and assassinated Gaitán in April 1948 before it was too late (before he could come to power); they thus averted revolution, but at the price of plunging Colombia into a fratricidal conflict from which it has still not emerged. It is reported that when Perón heard of Gaitán's assassination he declared 'That country will not return to normality for 50 years', and never did he speak a truer word; to thwart popular aspirations in such a brutal fashion is to invite open revolt.

The Colombian example also illustrates tragically the most obvious weakness of populist movements, namely their dependence on the person of the leader. A great deal depends on just how far the consolidation of the process has advanced and to what extent the movement itself has matured in organisation and structure. *Gaitanismo* is seen by many as an extreme case of amorphous populist mobilisation which disintegrated as soon as the leader was gone, although Gaitán's daughter Gloria denies this, claiming that the movement was quite sophisticated but was systematically crushed by a well-planned campaign of repression (Gaitán 1985). Gloria Gaitán produces evidence, which has been supported by further research (Green 2003), that the oligarchy of both the Conservative and Liberal parties began to incite systematic violence against Gaitán's followers from late 1945 onwards, and that tens of thousands of *gaitanistas* were slaughtered in what was later distorted to become the partisan Liberal/Conservative strife which is often seen as the hallmark of the Colombian *violencia* of the 1940s and 1950s. Former *gaitanistas* were also prominent in the guerrilla resistance which subsequently emerged in the country's eastern plains and later contributed to the revolutionary FARC and ELN guerrilla movements. It is arguable therefore that Gaitán's movement was by no means as amorphous or directionless as has been suggested, neither was it so exclusively dependent on Gaitán; it was crushed by a vicious and systematic campaign of repression, which only an exceptionally well-structured movement organised and prepared for armed resistance could have withstood.

Unprepared for the assassination of their leader, *gaitanistas* responded by taking to the streets of Bogotá and other cities in a spontaneous revolt, and contrary to the prevailing interpretation which sees the *Bogotazo* as mindless and directionless rioting, they did initially try to seize power by assaulting the key government buildings; it was only when they were beaten back that the uprising in the capital lost direction. Moreover, in some provincial towns the revolt showed very clear political direction; in the oil port of Barrancabermeja on the River Magdalena the popular movement seized power and established a revolutionary commune for ten days before being crushed, and similar 'revolutionary juntas' also appeared briefly in Cali, Barranquilla, Cartagena, Ibagué and other cities (Sánchez 1985, 219). In other words, while it may be true that this movement of populist inspiration had not yet reached the degree of national organisation and strength to resist the savage repression to which it was subjected, it was far from being the amorphous and directionless mass which has been portrayed by some critics.

This discussion of the Colombian case is important in order to provide some perspective on the relationship between leader and mass in populist movements: it is by no means the simple manipulation of an ignorant multitude that is often implied. Despite the crucial role of the leader in galvanising and focussing popular discontent where established political parties have singularly failed to do so, the movement is not simply created by the leader and neither is it a passive tool in his or her hands. It is essential to insist on the autonomous development of the popular movement and on its dialectical relationship with the leader. In many ways the movement creates the leader; in conditions where there exists generalised popular discontent and uncoordinated mobilisations which lack national coordination and leadership, the appearance of a potential leader, an individual with the conviction, talent and disposition to fulfil this essential role, is recognised by the popular classes who then appropriate the individual and make him/her their tribune. However, for this to happen favourable conditions have to exist, namely a crisis of political representation and a powerful but disorganised popular movement. If the majority of the working class or of the popular classes in a broader sense are already organised in support of a Socialist, Communist or other party which they recognise as representing them, then there is no room for a populist movement to develop; would-be independent leaders may appear but their impact will be strictly limited. Equally, even where mass parties are weak, if there is little autonomous mobilisation then a potential leader, however capable, will have difficulty in generating an effective movement.

This latter situation was arguably the case in Brazil in the 1930s, where Getúlio Vargas (generally categorised as a populist leader) was able to come to power in 1930 with the support of the *tenentes* (progressive junior officers) and of a middle-class reform movement. Although Vargas remained in power for 15 years, first as provisional president, then through elections and finally as dictator, and carried out some progressive reforms, his popular support was limited and passive and his overthrow in 1945 in favour of a liberal constitutionalist regime was achieved without great upheaval. But with the incipient industrialisation which Vargas himself had promoted, the development of the working-class and urban popular sectors was such that by 1950 he was able to capitalise on popular discontent with the conservative President Dutra (1945–50) and return to power through elections with much greater popular appeal. He then governed for four years in a more radical and clearly populist manner, benefitting from and further stimulating a mass movement in favour of stronger anti-imperialist and pro-worker measures; this provoked intense opposition from Brazilian landlords and industrialists, precipitating a political crisis in which Vargas committed suicide, claiming in a dramatic letter to the Brazilian people that his popular programme had been sabotaged by the oligarchy and imperialism. In this case Vargas, an established politician with progressive but contradictory ideas, was able to become a genuine populist tribune in his final period only because of the development of the popular movement in the intervening period. In other words, before 1945 Vargas was a would-be populist without a movement (or with a weak and ineffective movement), but in 1950 the popular movement which had since developed to a new level accepted Vargas as leader and both enabled him and drove him on to take more radical measures.

In the case of Argentina and the emergence of the man generally regarded as the paradigmatic Latin American populist, Juan Domingo Perón, it is also clear that his rise was preceded by the development of a powerful autonomous movement and a crisis of representation. Argentina in the early twentieth century had the most powerful labour movement in Latin America, but despite a process of liberal constitutional development, the middle-class Radical Party (in power 1916–30) and a similarly petit bourgeois Socialist Party failed to provide effective representation for the working class. With repressive military-dominated governments after 1930, the labour movement evolved from anarchist to syndicalist/autonomist positions (albeit with a Communist minority), and by the early 1940s was displaying increasing militancy and politicisation without being effectively represented by any political party. It was in these circumstances that Colonel Perón was appointed Secretary of Labour and Social Welfare in the reformist junta that seized power in 1943, and proceeded to cultivate popular support with a series of progressive welfare measures and by using his powers of arbitration in labour disputes in favour of the workers. He also began to address mass rallies with his powerful rhetoric against the oligarchy and for the *descamisados*. It was this which led to Perón's arrest and removal from the government followed by his dramatic return – in response to mass demonstrations – on 17 October 1945, and his victory in presidential elections four months later.

It is of course true that Perón represented only a reformist populism which was ultimately controlled by the bourgeoisie, but a careful look at his movement tells us much about the dynamics of populism. Perón undoubtedly emerged in response to the strength of the existing labour movement, and with the express intention of winning over the workers, both in order to carry out a nationalist and welfarist transformation of the Argentine state and in order to avert what many bosses and military leaders in Argentina saw as a threat of Communism (Fayt 1967, 92). Once firmly established as president, he took measures to purge the unions of independent militants, and took control of the Labour Party (Partido Laborista, spontaneously created by union activists in 1945 and pro-Perón but independent), turning it into the Partido Justicialista (also known as the Partido Peronista). However, such was the strength of the labour movement, which he himself had helped to increase by his pro-labour measures and inflammatory rhetoric, that Perón became in many ways a prisoner of the movement:

... if Peronism made a vital contribution to the self-identification of the workers, for their part the workers also left an indelible mark on Peronism ... In fact, a large part of Perón's efforts after 1946 were directed to bringing under control the social force he had brought into action in order to win power. (Torre 1994, 108)

Perón's wife Evita, who although loyal to her husband acquired a charismatic appeal of her own which threatened to transcend his, gained a reputation (which may have been justified) for being more radical than he, and the *Montoneros*, the radicalised Peronist/Marxist youth of the 1970s, cultivated above all the memory of Evita.

Perón's overthrow by the conservative military in 1955 came just in time to save his reputation with the workers; and despite his political failure when he returned from exile in 1973 to be president again for one year before his death, the movement he created has remained hegemonic in Argentine labour down to the present. The corrupt politicians who surrounded Perón in the 1970s and most of those who claim his mantle today have not been able to extinguish the belief of Argentine workers, including most of the militants of today's autonomous *piquetero* movement, that the original Peronism – represented above all by Evita – was the true expression of a movement for revolutionary popular power in their country.

Peronism, and in particular the rise of Perón over the period 1943–46, also illustrates very well a crucial point which tends to get lost in Laclau's emphasis on discourse, namely that the charismatic appeal of the populist leader does not derive only from oratory but also from decisive *actions* demonstrating his or her leadership capacity and commitment. The *descamisados* marched to demand the release of Perón in October 1945 not only because of his incendiary anti-oligarchic rhetoric, but also because of the remarkable body of progressive legislation he had decreed in the previous two years. Similarly in Mexico in 1936 workers and peasants rallied to the defence of President Lázaro Cárdenas in his confrontation with the reactionary strongman Calles because of Cárdenas' promotion of agrarian reform and assault on corruption since his inauguration in December 1934. In Colombia over the period 1945–48 the people identified with Gaitán not only because of his passionate denunciations of the oligarchy, but also because of his defence of workers and peasants as a lawyer in the courts, as a parliamentary deputy and then senator. Progressive populism, we must insist, is not demagogy: this is why the so-called 'neo-populists' like Bucarám in Ecuador, Collor in Brazil and Menem in Argentina are so insignificant compared with their predecessors of the first wave. To compare Menem with Perón is like comparing Napoleon III with the great

Napoleon, the comparison which produced Marx's celebrated remark that History does indeed repeat itself, the first time as tragedy and the second time as farce (Marx and Engels 1968, 97).

There is however another aspect to the forging of charisma which creates a populist leader. The actions contributing to the emergent leader's prestige are not only practical measures like those mentioned above (Perón's welfare measures, Cárdenas' agrarian reforms and so on). Typically there is also a highly symbolic gesture (and possibly more than one), a feat which takes on heroic significance: 'To have carried out an extraordinary or unusual act is one of the elements which generates a relationship of charismatic leadership' (De la Torre 1994, 45). Perón's captivity and triumphal return in October 1945 falls into this category, as does Cárdenas' expulsion of Calles and his associates from Mexico in April 1936, Gaitán's defence of the massacred Colombian banana workers in 1928, Fidel's leadership of the Moncada attack in July 1953 and Chávez' uprising of February 1992. All of these events rapidly acquired symbolic status in their respective countries and contributed decisively to the charismatic aura of their protagonists.

The career of the most outstanding charismatic leaders is punctuated by further such symbolic events: in Fidel's case, his leadership of the *Granma* expedition in November 1956, the survival of the guerrillas in the Sierra Maestra and the subsequent victory, the defeat of the Bay of Pigs invasion in April 1961 and the successful resolution of the Missile Crisis of October 1962. Of course in all of these Fidel was accompanied by other revolutionary comrades, and in the last two events the protagonist was the Cuban people as a whole, what María del Pilar Díaz Castañón describes as the 'collective protagonist', the unity 'Homeland-Nation-Revolution'; but this only underlines how far Fidel had come to symbolise the Cuban people. Similarly with Chávez, the February 1992 uprising was followed by the election victory of December 1998, the defeat of the coup in April 2002, the defeat of the *paro* in December 2002–February 2003, and the recall referendum victory of August 2004. Here too the Venezuelan people were an ever more active protagonist, in a relationship of intense symbiosis with Chávez.

### THE LEADER AS A PRODUCT OF THE MOVEMENT

At this point it is necessary to return to the question of the autonomy of the popular movement and its relationship with the leader. A fundamental issue here is the process of construction of a collective identity: 'the people' is not simply a given, an objective social category; rather, as E.P. Thompson argued with regard to class and class-consciousness, it is something that *happens*, and that happens in a particular context (Thompson 1966, 11–12), when a large group of people come to feel an identity in relation to another group which they see as antagonistic. This identity may be constituted in part through collective acts and experiences – strikes, demonstrations, a common response to repression by police or the military. It may also be generated in part by a party or movement which helps to organise such acts of resistance. But the process may also be furthered by a leader who summons the people to come together and act, who in Laclau's terms 'interpellates' them, thereby helping to constitute them as a collective entity. In the words of Jean Grugel, 'the people' is not simply a social category but rather a group of people with a shared experience who feel themselves to be part of a common universe: 'the consciousness of forming part of the people is not a constant and gathers strength at times of crisis or of political rupture ... ' (Grugel 1994, 201). If the working class emerges as a 'class for itself' in opposition to the bourgeoisie, the people emerges as a conscious entity in opposition to 'the oligarchy' and imperialism. But in both cases, this constitution of a collective subject is a supremely political act or process; and in this process leadership is an essential element.

Certainly in this process of formation of a collective subject the leader's oratory can play a powerful role. An atomised mass of workers, peasants, the poor and marginalised, become aware of their common oppression and interests when addressed as 'the people', 'the poor', the *descamisados*, and called upon to unite against the rich, the oligarchy, the *escuálidos*. The appearance of a leader who not only appeals to them but who looks and sounds like them gives them a collective voice as never before. But here again, it is necessary to go beyond the limitations of Laclau: it is not only the 'interpellation' of the people which constitutes them as a conscious entity. Quite apart from what has already been said about the importance of both practical and symbolic actions, even on the level of discourse analysis there is an essential factor which Laclau fails to consider: as Carlos de la Torre points out, not all discourses are accepted, at any one moment a number of political discourses are in competition, and it is necessary to consider not only the conditions of production of a given discourse but also its circulation and reception (De la Torre 1994, 47). And the conditions of reception are determined above all by the predisposition of the audience, in other words by the latent consciousness of the popular classes whom the leader is addressing.

The implication here is that when the leader first bursts upon the scene, the masses s/he addresses are by no means entirely atomised, dispersed or passive; the common image of a histrionic orator arousing an ignorant and pliable mob is a complete caricature. In fact, in almost all cases the people are already quite highly mobilised and have a latent collective consciousness which only lacks effective leadership in order to become a revolutionary force. When Perón arrived on the scene the Argentine working class was already mobilised to an extent which scared the more conservative members of the oligarchy – one of the leading generals is quoted as saying how the May Day labour rally of 1943, with 'an enormous multitude, with red flags in front, their fists raised and singing the Internationale, presaged really tragic days for the Republic' (Fayt 1967, 92) – and they had a strong sense of their autonomous class interests as expressed in the predominant syndicalist ideology with its rejection of all existing parties. All they lacked was political leadership, which Perón provided. Similarly in Cuba, the people had already demonstrated their repudiation of the corrupt politicians of the Auténtico era (1944–52) and of Batista's tyranny, and when leadership was provided by Fidel and the M-26–7 they showed their support in the clandestine struggle and above all in the huge mass rallies after victory in 1959. In Venezuela the poor of the *cerros* of Caracas and other cities showed their combative disposition in no uncertain terms in the *caracazo* of February 1989, and Chávez and the MBR-200 simply provided the guidance which they lacked with the armed revolt three years later. In all three cases – and in others where the phenomenon of radical populism has manifested itself – it is the lamentable failure of left-wing and supposedly revolutionary parties which has opened the way for courageous and charismatic leaders who have taken up the banner of revolt and provided the orientation which the people were crying out for. In the case of Perón, as we have seen, the leadership was ultimately inadequate and the *caudillo* tried (with only limited success) to put the genie back in the bottle; but the movement continued without either him or Evita, leading to the paradox of Maoist and Trotskyist Peronism on the one hand and Fascist Peronism on the other.

It is clear from this analysis that however magnetic the leader's personality and however remarkable his or her capacity for communication, s/he can ultimately only lead the people where they are disposed to go. This does not exclude the possibility that the dynamic momentum of the dialectic between leader and mass may take both to places which neither consciously envisaged at the beginning; but those destinations were nevertheless implicit (as possibilities at least) in the existing social structure and in the cultural heritage of the original movement. Thus in Cuba, the extreme dependence of the Cuban bourgeoisie, the radical proletarianisation of the great majority of the peasantry, and the egalitarianism and anti-imperialism of the *cubanía radical* analysed by Kapcia, all predisposed the movement to evolve in a Socialist direction although this was not the original vision of Fidel and the M-26–7 nor the consciousness of the mass of the people before late 1960 at least. By contrast in Argentina, the much greater strength of the Argentine bourgeoisie and its relative autonomy in the 1930s and 1940s, as it worked itself free of the clutches of a declining British imperialism yet was still far from being completely dominated by the US; this combined with a much more contradictory cultural and ideological heritage in which large sectors of the popular classes were far from immune to European Fascist and corporatist ideas; all of these factors made it much easier for a reformist fraction of the bourgeoisie represented by Perón to first appropriate and then limit or distort the revolutionary potential of the popular movement.

In view of the negative implications of the term 'populism' and the bad reputation it has acquired among both scholars and activists, there is a strong case for avoiding its use with regard to what I have thus far designated as 'revolutionary' or 'progressive' populism. The term could then be confined to reformist or bourgeois leaders like Perón or Vargas, or demagogic opportunists like Menem, Collor or Bucarám; and genuinely revolutionary leaders like Fidel and Chávez could be described as popular tribunes or *caudillos*. Some such term really cannot be avoided, however much the leaders themselves might dislike it; their exceptional leadership role has to be recognised both for analytical purposes and to achieve political clarity with regard to revolutionary strategy. Simón Bolívar was the supreme popular *caudillo* of the independence era, and Ezequiel Zamora, the Venezuelan liberal leader of the mid-nineteenth century whom Chávez also reveres, was a popular *caudillo* of that period; it seems only logical to recognise Chávez as their legitimate successor and thus as the popular *caudillo* of contemporary Venezuela. What must be clear, however, is the intimate symbiosis between the leader and the popular movement and the fact that the leader is in many ways a creation of the movement. It is not a question of the people looking to a 'Messiah' to save them – a notion rightly repudiated by most activists – but of a genuine popular leader emerging in response to the needs and demands of the popular movement.

In this context it is necessary to look once again at the classic populist leaders of the first phase: Perón, Vargas, Cárdenas and Gaitán, for example. They and the movements they led had undeniable populist characteristics, but their achievements and significance far exceed those of the demagogic neo-populists. Surely what really happened here was that they began to transcend populism and to become true popular revolutionary leaders, although the circumstances of the time prevented this transformation from being consummated. Subsequently, in Cuba and Venezuela, movements and leaders which originally had characteristics of progressive populism have been able to complete this transformation, with dramatic consequences. This is the key to the paradoxical nature of the phenomenon which has caused so much confusion: progressive populism has the potential to evolve and mutate into a popular revolutionary movement, and the individual leader (depending no doubt on personal origins and characteristics) has the potential to undergo a similar transformation. Thus Fidel Castro and the Cuban revolution did initially have progressive populist characteristics but are no longer populist, having been transformed into a genuine social revolution led by a popular *caudillo* or tribune; and Venezuela and Chávez are in the process of undergoing a similar transformation. Nevertheless, just as with the accusations of Communism which Fidel denied so often, only to say eventually, 'Yes, this is a Socialist revolution and I am a Marxist-Leninist'; and just as Perón, also accused by oligarchic spokesmen of Communist tendencies, declared in July 1945, 'We have been calumnied; we have been insulted; what an honour this is for us, because it has been for taking up a most noble cause, the defence of the humble and of the men who work daily with the sweat of their brow for the greatness of this Homeland' (quoted in Fayt 1967, 109–11); similarly one wonders if the time has not come, in reply to constant reactionary and dogmatic Marxist accusations of populism, for revolutionary leaders to respond 'Yes, alright, we are populists! And so what?'. Indeed, it seems that in this I am in the excellent company of the Brazilian writer Emir Sader, who comments on how neo-liberals become apoplectic when condemning populism:

What are they referring to when they talk about the 'exaltation of the charismatic leader'? To the panic they feel when faced with the emergence of popular leaders, of leaders who unite the people, who translate popular needs into a political movement. They want to keep the people fragmented, passively subjected, through the influence of their infernal media machine, to brutalising conditions of exploitation. They need people to remain separated from politics and to entrust it to professional 'politicians' who govern society in the name of the prevailing interests … . (Sader 2005)

To paraphrase a classic author, 'A spectre is haunting the world: the spectre of populism … '.

In analytical terms however, there is here another substantive point which needs to be made. Paul Cammack makes the interesting argument that if, as he suggests, populism emerges in conjunctures of hegemonic crisis, and if it extends and deepens that crisis with potentially revolutionary consequences, then a populist regime can only succeed if it promotes a resolution of the crisis by acting as midwife of a new political system: 'the "populist moment" is a brief one, reflective of a conjunctural crisis, and its fortunes will depend on its ability to move on to a "foundational project" and create a new institutional order' (Cammack 2000, 152). This is surely what happened in Cuba between 1961 and 1965, and it could be said that with the consolidation and institutionalisation of Cuban Socialism the process lost its revolutionary-populist characteristics. Alternatively, one could say that the revolutionary mass movement with Fidel as charismatic popular tribune, having swept aside all domestic and foreign opposition, became institutionalised in Socialist form.

When the populist movement fails to move on to a 'foundational project', Cammack hypothesises that it will either 'collapse into incoherence' or 'revert to neo-liberalism' (here he is thinking of recent neo-populisms, but with reference to an earlier age preceding the concept of neo-liberalism we could formulate it as 'revert to the status quo'). This is essentially what happened with Peronism: after the dramatic advances of the 1943–49 period, Perón's regime 'collapsed into incoherence', which is why it was overthrown with relative ease by the conservative military in 1955. Perhaps the best example in Latin America of a populist regime producing a successful non-Socialist 'foundational project' was Mexico under Cárdenas: the stability of the corporatist PRI regime, often traced back to the creation of the official party (under another name) in 1929, in fact resulted from the major popular reforms of Cárdenas over the period

1934–40 which ended a period of chronic instability. But the Mexican solution occurred in a very different era from our own, and in today's world it is doubtful whether a national-corporatist 'foundational project' is viable; and in discussing the 'neo-populisms', Cammack suggests that their only conceivable positive outcome would be to 'radicalise and transmute into a genuinely socialist project' (Cammack 2000, 157–8). I would submit that with most of the neo-populisms mentioned – those of Bucarám, Menem, Collor and Fujimori – this is (or was, since they have already come and gone) inconceivable; they were not based on movements with revolutionary potential and their ideological orientation, in each case, combined 'democratic-popular interpellations' with others of bourgeois and authoritarian characteristics. The one exception to date, of course, is Chávez, and as we have seen both he and his movement, despite the superficial comparisons sometimes made, are light-years away from the other cases just mentioned. The Bolivarian revolution in Venezuela is still very much a dynamic and unfinished process, but already we can see in Chávez' discourse the emergence of a coherent 'foundational project', the 'Socialism of the twenty-first century' of which he has been speaking since December 2004. This further confirms our analysis, that a movement with populist characteristics can be revolutionary; but only when its social base is an autonomous movement of the dominated classes and where its leader is a true representative of that movement, not necessarily in terms of his/her class origins but in terms of cultural and ideological identification and political practice.

What, then, are the implications of all this for political organisation and strategy? Obviously socialists and progressives in other countries cannot just sit around waiting for a charismatic leader to appear. But it should be clear from the above analysis that charismatic leadership does not emerge in isolation from the popular movement; indeed, in many ways the movement creates the leader. Also, such exceptional individual leadership is much less necessary if there is an organised political structure (party or movement) which adequately represents the popular movement, as was the case (at least in the initial period) with the Sandinistas in Nicaragua. The problem has been precisely that in so many cases, progressive political parties have become bureaucratic, sectarian or dogmatic – or a combination of all of these – and have failed to provide adequate leadership and representation.

So what – apart from charismatic leadership – are the essential characteristics of the movements we have analysed? First of all, that they are firmly rooted in popular culture. Parties based on abstract principles or bureaucratic organisational structures will never arouse passionate allegiance unless they can also relate to, and give expression to, popular cultural practices and traditions. Secondly, they must be democratic both in political practice and internal structure, and in the true, popular sense of the term, not the liberal, elitist sense. Thirdly, they must be ideologically pluralist (although within the limits implied by a firm commitment to popular interests), permitting and indeed encouraging the free discussion of all ideas except those clearly contrary to the class interests of the popular sectors (such as racism and imperialism). Finally, they must be firmly committed to fundamental (and ultimately revolutionary) change, although with the flexibility necessary to participate in electoral politics and tactical agreements. These are indeed very much the characteristics already exhibited by the anti-globalisation movement and autonomous social movements in many countries; but the one characteristic that these movements generally lack, and which is also essential, is a vocation for winning power and an acceptance of the need for leadership, without which dispersal and frustration are inevitable. As Tariq Ali proclaimed recently in Venezuela, we must 'change the world *by* taking power', quite contrary to Holloway's illusory dream and following the example set by another dreamer – but one whose dreams are firmly anchored in political praxis – Hugo Chávez. Leadership must be intimately linked to the popular movement, indeed must as far as possible be the ultimate political expression of that movement; but leadership, and the achievement of state power, are absolutely essential if the movement's gains are to endure.

# 8
# The Way Forward:
# Democracy, Popular Power
# and Revolution

If the Left was in crisis after 1989, it is now in a position to take the initiative again. It is now Western neo-imperialism and neo-liberalism that are in crisis, and with the revival of popular anti-capitalist and anti-war movements in the West, the Iraqi and Palestinian resistance, and above all the resurgence of popular movements with a clear political agenda all over Latin America, with the Bolivarian revolution in Venezuela at the head, the way forward is at last becoming clear. The 'Socialism of the twenty-first century' will be different in many ways, and it does not offer the formulaic certainties of the previous orthodoxy, but it promises to be more creative, more dynamic and ultimately more resilient.

The survival of the Cuban revolution and its original character, to which it is now endeavouring to return after nearly three decades of distortions caused by excessive Soviet influence, is a beacon of hope which demonstrates the extraordinary capacity of a revolutionary people with a committed leadership to resist imperialism, even if its Socialist system is in the travails of a difficult adjustment to the new conditions of globalisation and the need to further democratise the structures of popular power. But equally inspiring is the totally unanticipated example of the Bolivarian revolution in Venezuela, continuing to advance seven years after Chávez was first elected, with its experiment in participatory democracy, endogenous development and now 'Socialism of the twenty-first century'. Although both Cubans and Venezuelans are the first to insist that their revolutions cannot be copied, they clearly provide inspiration for other countries in Latin America, and Venezuela in particular suggests new forms of political action and of social and economic organisation which are already having an influence elsewhere in the region. A successful revolution is a subversive example, which is (even more than oil) the biggest reason for Washington's hostility.

For us in Europe all of this, however inspiring, may seem very remote. But if the Zapatero government in Spain has been supporting Venezuela through commercial deals including the sale of arms, and if even the conservative French government has welcomed Chávez' initiatives in pushing for a multi-polar international order, then its relevance to Europe cannot be dismissed. Here in Britain the Trades Union Congress has voted to support Venezuela and sent a top-level delegation there in November 2005, as trade unionists begin to realise that however exotic it may seem, this is the first new attempt to construct Socialism since the collapse of the Soviet bloc and in fact since the Sandinista victory in Nicaragua. Moreover the advance of the Left and of the popular forces throughout Latin America suggests that at last – and not before time – the global right-wing tide that began with Pinochet, Thatcher and Reagan is beginning to ebb.

So far the signs of change in Europe are small, but nevertheless real. The anti-globalisation movement merged with the anti-war movement which in the run-up to the Iraq war in early 2003 reached truly massive proportions in Britain, Spain and Italy, Washington's three principal European allies. Although the movement has inevitably diminished somewhat from its immediate prewar peak, it remains strong and has had a significant impact on politics in several countries. More importantly for our purposes, a new Left is beginning to emerge with both parliamentary and extraparliamentary tactics. In Italy the Rifondazione Comunista has established a solid basis with 6 to 8 per cent of the vote, and while identifying with the Communist heritage in a broad sense, it is internally pluralist and democratic with three quite distinct tendencies. In Portugal the Left bloc, a coalition of three anti-capitalist parties, has gone from one to three to eight deputies in the last three general elections. In Germany the new Left Party has made an immediate impact with 8.7 per cent of the vote, and in Britain the emergence of Respect, winning one parliamentary seat and coming second in three others, together with the growth of the Green Party, marks the best showing for 50 years for parties to the left of Labour.

None of these parties is sufficient by itself to revolutionise the politics of these countries, but they can serve as the foundation for a new, dynamic and independent popular movement with a clear political perspective. In Europe of course the extreme Right is also mobilising, and the way forward is much less straightforward than in Latin America; but for the first time in decades the anti-capitalist Left has begun to acquire a mass base and a clear political direction. The crisis of neo-liberalism could not be more evident, with stagnation and unemployment spreading across the Continent and the British boom (based in any case on a speculative service economy with drastic suppression of labour rights) showing signs of coming to an end. The political crisis of the liberal establishment is even more acute, with abstention reaching record levels in Britain, the dominant parties losing voting share in several countries including Britain and Germany, and France rocked by riots in immigrant *banlieues*. The responsibility of the new Left parties is therefore all the greater: they must not repeat the errors of the past but must learn from the social movements and from Latin American examples (bearing in mind contextual differences) how to develop a new politics of popular democratic power.

This is where the lessons of Cuba and Venezuela, but also of Chile, Nicaragua and Portugal, and for that matter of Brazil and other countries, are relevant despite the enormous cultural, social and economic differences. The first lesson is that of democracy: that any new party or movement must be democratic and must fight for democracy in society, not merely in conventional liberal terms but in substantial protagonistic terms, in other words for direct popular participation in decision-making at all levels, and not merely in the formal structures of government but at the workplace and in all forms of social activity. *It is essential to reclaim democracy from the liberal elites* and to insist that pluralist elections are only one form of democracy, and a very limited form at that. The second lesson is that of unity: any political expression of working-class or popular movements must strive for unity in action, not for unanimity or uniformity but for the effective unity of a broad movement engaging in political action for the benefit of the popular sectors as a whole. Political parties therefore must accept their limitations: they have a role to play in terms of political debate, mobilisation and electoral participation, but they cannot monopolise political expression and representation and must be prepared to subordinate party interests to the broader unity of the movement when necessary. If a truly representative party emerges which combines these characteristics within itself, then so much the better, but otherwise all progressive parties must strive to promote the interests of the entire movement and accept their place as part of a larger whole.

The third lesson is that of ideological pluralism: not the competitive party pluralism of liberal convention, but pluralism of ideas and debate within the party and/or movement. The days of orthodoxy are gone, and while unity in action is an essential goal it can never preclude debate and accountability. Class consciousness does not emerge purely spontaneously from within the movement, but neither can it be imposed on the movement by an enlightened elite: Lenin's unfortunate phrase about the workers on their own only achieving 'trade union consciousness' and needing to have revolutionary ideas brought to them by Communist intellectuals (Lenin 1936, 53) has caused enormous damage in this respect. The real process, which was much better understood (or at least expressed) by Gramsci, is that revolutionary class consciousness emerges in a dialectical process between the mass movement and the leadership, in which both terms of the equation are essential: intellectuals and leaders perform an essential function but can only do so properly to the extent that they are inspired by, answerable to and indeed part of the movement.

The dialectical process of ideological development is also directly related to the fourth lesson of the processes examined, which is the need for revolutionary ideology to fuse with the popular culture of each nation or society if it is ever to achieve hegemony. In this book I have frequently criticised Marxists, but this does not imply rejection of Marxism either as a scientific analysis of society or as a revolutionary ideology. It does however mean that dogmatism is dead, and more than that, even creative undogmatic Marxists must recognise that universal revolutionary ideas can never become effective unless they are genuinely fused with national popular culture and traditions; indeed, a specific revolutionary movement must develop *first* on the basis of national popular and democratic culture *before* going on to fuse with universal revolutionary ideology. This does not mean accepting uncritically all elements of national culture: here the terms 'popular' and 'democratic' are crucial. Any revolutionary or progressive movement must strive to develop a *national-popular* ideology which is *all-inclusive*, in other words it must include all sectors except those which are clearly part of the dominant social and economic class bloc. It is in this sense that class is indeed decisive: it is not a question of building a pure working-class movement in the sense of strict conventional Marxist analyses, but a movement of the popular classes in the broadest sense, encompassing ethnic minorities, immigrants, women, sexual minorities, students, pensioners, and small and medium businesspeople: the whole gamut of oppressed and excluded groups. But the line of division is nevertheless ultimately a class one, and very clearly so: nowhere is this clearer than in Venezuela, where mass support for Chávez goes way beyond the conventionally defined proletariat but is very much based on the poor and the popular sectors, and the opposition *escuálidos* consist overwhelmingly of the rich and middle classes.

The importance of Venezuela lies in having demonstrated that it is possible to build a mass anti-capitalist movement with a national political agenda, and to do so democratically, with a national-popular discourse that encompasses the broadest sectors and many different ideological tendencies. It also demonstrates that once in power, such a movement can take effective measures not only to improve popular welfare but also to confront national and transnational capital, yet without provoking a catastrophic rupture and consequent international isolation. Finally, Venezuela has shown that the long-term dynamic of such a movement is indeed Socialist, in terms of the only meaning which Socialism can have in today's world: that of *a state of revolutionary popular power in permanent tension with capitalism and imperialism*, but never fossilising into a fixed bureaucratic system which would inevitably lose its popular democratic character and lead eventually to capitalist restoration.

This brings us to the fifth and final lesson of these revolutionary processes, which is the crucial importance of organisation and leadership. While flexibility, democracy and internal pluralism are fundamental, unified organisation and effective leadership are also essential if popular democratic and anti-capitalist movements are not to remain trapped in a permanent cycle of struggle, partial triumphs, defeats and decline, without ever dealing decisive blows to the world capitalist system. Lack of effective leadership was a significant factor in the defeats in both Chile and Portugal, and may well be a serious deficiency endangering the current process in Brazil as well. Moreover the Venezuelan process confirms the need, once popular power with a solid democratic majority has been achieved, to take bold and decisive action to transform all aspects of the state; in this respect Lenin (and the Jacobins) were right. All the caveats in the world about the dangers of centralism and authoritarianism cannot alter the reality that without effective leadership, popular movements are doomed to failure, and that the establishment will resort to all the dirty tricks in the book to preserve its privileges. Yes, leadership must be flexible, democratic and must always remain intimately linked to the mass movement from which it springs, but without it we are doomed to remain spectators of the headlong genocidal and ecocidal career of late capitalism. Here again Hugo Chávez is the most far-sighted leader in the world today: as he declared at the closing session of the Sixteenth World Festival of Youth and Students in August 2005, the terrible dilemma posed by Rosa Luxemburg, that the world faced 'Socialism or Barbarism', has become worse still: the dilemma now is 'Socialism or Destruction of the Planet'. The task could not be more urgent: to build in each country an effective anti-capitalist alternative capable of attaining power in order to save humanity through the development of a just and sustainable world order. As this book goes to press, this analysis of the way forward has been spectacularly confirmed by the great electoral victory of Evo Morales and the MAS in Bolivia. Also encouraging (although less spectacular because representing a less radical line) is the victory of the Socialist Michelle Bachelet in Chile, and the prospect of further electoral victories for the Left elsewhere in Latin America. The prospect of another revolutionary popular regime in Bolivia, and of reformist governments in neighbouring countries which will at least provide a more favourable environment for the trio of Cuba, Venezuela and Bolivia, suggests that a new era for popular anti-capitalist politics is indeed at hand.

# Bibliography

Aguilar, Luis E. (1972), *Cuba 1933: Prologue to Revolution* (New York: W.W. Norton).

Alavéz, Elena (1994), *Eduardo Chibás en la hora de la Ortodoxia* (Havana: Editorial de Ciencias Sociales).

Alonso, Aurelio (2004), 'Notas sobre la hegemonía, los mitos y las alternativas al orden neoliberal', *Pasos* 114 (July–August), pp. 4–13 (San José, Costa Rica: Departamento Ecuménico de Investigaciones).

Álvarez Béjar et al. (1994), *Amérique latine: démocratie et exclusion* (Paris: Éditions L'Harmattan).

Ameringer, Charles D. (2000), *The Cuban Democratic Experience: the Auténtico Years,1944–1952* (Tampa, FL: University Press of Florida).

Amin, Samir and Herrera, Rémy (2005), '¿Hacia una solidaridad renovada de los pueblos del sur? Entrevista a Samir Amin, en el 50 aniversario de la Conferencia de Bandung', *Pasos* 119, May–June, pp. 1–13 (San José, Costa Rica: Departamento Ecuménico de Investigaciones).

Aporrea 63341: www.aporrea.org/dameverbo.php?docid=63341, 17 July 2005.

Aporrea 63345: www.aporrea.org/dameverbo.php?docid=63345, 17 July 2005.

Aporrea 67532: www.aporrea.org/dameverbo.php?docid=67532, 20 October 2005.

Asamblea Nacional Constituyente (1999), *Constitución de la República Bolivariana de Venezuela* (Caracas).

August, Arnold (1999), *Democracy in Cuba and the 1997–98 Elections* (Havana: Editorial José Martí).

Bartley, Kim and O'Briain, Donnacha (2003), *The Revolution Will Not Be Televised*, video available from Power Pictures – Screen Scene, 41 Upper Mount Street, Dublin 2, Ireland.

Beckett, Andy (2002), *Pinochet in Piccadilly: Britain and Chile's Hidden History* (London: Faber & Faber).

Black, George (1981), *Triumph of the People: The Sandinista Revolution in Nicaragua* (London: Zed).

Blanco, Juan Antonio (1994), *Cuba: Talking About Revolution. Conversations with Juan Antonio Blanco by Medea Benjamin* (Melbourne: Ocean).

Blanco Muñoz, Agustín (1998), *Habla El Comandante (testimonios violentos)* (Caracas: UCV).

Bobbio, Norberto (1996), *El futuro de la democracia* (México: Fondo de Cultura Económica).

Bonachea, Ramón and San Martín, Marta (1974), *The Cuban Insurrection, 1952–1959* (New Brunswick, NJ: Transaction Books).

Boron, Atilio (2005), in 'Forum on John Holloway', *Capital and Class* 85, Spring.

Branford, Sue and Kucinski, Bernardo (with Hilary Wainwright) (2003), *Politics Transformed: Lula and the Workers' Party in Brazil* (London: Latin America Bureau).
Buch Rodríguez, Luis M. (1999), *Gobierno Revolucionario Cubano: Génesis y Primeros Pasos* (Havana: Editorial de Ciencias Sociales).
Buxton, Julia (2001), *The Failure of Political Reform in Venezuela* (Aldershot: Ashgate).
Cabrera, Olga (1977), *Guiteras: El Programa de la Jóven Cuba* (Havana: Editorial de Ciencias Sociales).
Cammack, Paul (1994), 'Démocratie et citoyenneté en Amérique latine', in A. Álvarez Béjar et al. (eds), *Amérique Latine: Démocratie et Exclusion* (Paris: Éditions L'Harmattan), pp. 101–20.
Cammack, Paul (2000), 'The resurgence of populism in Latin America', *Bulletin of Latin American Research* 19:2 (April), pp. 149–61.
Cantón Navarro, José (1998), *History of Cuba: the Challenge of the Yoke and the Star* (Havana: Editorial Si-Mar).
Cardoso, Fernando Henrique and Faletto, Enzo (1969), *Dependencia y Desarrollo en América Latina* (México: Siglo XXI).
Carmona Báez, Antonio (2004), *State Resistance to Globalisation in Cuba* (London: Pluto).
Carranza Valdés, Julio, Gutiérrez Urdaneta, Luis and Monreal González, Pedro (1996), *Cuba: Restructuring the Economy – A Contribution to the Debate* (translated with Foreword by Ruth Pearson) (London: Institute of Latin American Studies).
Casanueva Valencia, Fernando and Fernández Canque, Manuel (1973), *El Partido Socialista y la Lucha de Clases en Chile* (Santiago, Chile: Editora Nacional Quimantu).
Castañeda, Jorge G. (1994), *Utopia Unarmed: The Latin American Left after the Cold War* (New York: Vintage). First published in Spanish in 1993.
Chávez Frías, Hugo (2004), *¡Venezuela se Respeta! Acto de concentración contra la intervención* (Caracas: República Bolivariana de Venezuela, Ministerio de Energía y Minas).
Clemente, Capitão Duran (1976), *Elementos para a Compreensão do 25 de Novembro* (Lisbon: Edições Sociais).
Cole, Ken (1998), *Cuba: From Revolution to Development* (London: Pinter).
Collazo, Enrique (1972), *Los Americanos en Cuba* (Havana: Editorial de Ciencias Sociales).
Colletti, Lucio (1972), *From Rousseau to Lenin: Studies in Ideology and Society* (London: New Left Books).
Coronil, Fernando and Skurski, Julie (2004), 'Dismembering and remembering the national: the semantics of political violence in Venezuela', in Jo-Marie Burt and Philip Mauceri (eds), *Politics in the Andes: Identity, Conflict, Reform* (Pittsburgh, PA: University of Pittsburgh Press), pp. 81–106.
Cuesta Braniella, José M. (1997), *La Resistencia Cívica en la Guerra de Liberación de Cuba* (Havana: Editorial de Ciencias Sociales).
Cunhal, Álvaro (2003), 'O Mundo de Hoje', *Avante!* (Lisbon), 1664, 6 November.
De la Torre, Carlos (1994), 'Los significados ambiguos de los populismos latinoamericanos', in José Álvarez Junco y Ricardo González Leandri (eds), *El Populismo en España y América* (Madrid: Editorial Catriel), pp. 39–60.

Debray, Régis (1967), *¿Revolución en la Revolución?* (Havana: Casa de las Américas).

Derham, Michael (2002), 'Undemocratic democracy: Venezuela and the distorting of history', *Bulletin of Latin American Research* 21:2 (April 2002), pp. 270–89.

Di Tella, Torcuato (1970), 'Populism and reform in Latin America', in Claudio Véliz (ed.), *Obstacles to Change in Latin America* (London: Oxford University Press).

Díaz Castañón, María del Pilar (2001), *Ideología y Revolución: Cuba, 1959–1962* (Havana: Editorial de Ciencias Sociales).

Dos Santos, Theotônio (1973), 'The crisis of development theory and the problem of dependence in Latin America', in H. Bernstein (ed.), *Underdevelopment and Development: The Third World Today* (Harmondsworth: Penguin).

Elizalde, Rosa Miriam and Báez, Luis (2004), *Chávez Nuestro* (Havana: Abril).

Ellsworth, Brian (2005), 'Venezuela ensaya la gerencia de obreros', *New York Times* article reproduced in *El Nacional* (Caracas), 13 August 2005, p. 4.

Ewell, Judith (1984), *Venezuela: A Century of Change* (London: Hurst).

Faye, Jean-Pierre (1976), *Le Portugal d'Otelo: La Révolution dans le Labyrinthe* (Paris: Lattès).

Fayt, Carlos S. (1967), *La Naturaleza del Peronismo* (Buenos Aires: Viracocha).

FIDES (Fondo Intergubernamental para la Descentralización) (2003), *Ley de los Consejos Locales de Planificación Pública* (Caracas).

Foner, Philip S. (1972), *The Spanish–Cuban–American War and the Birth of American Imperialism*, two vols (New York: Monthly Review).

Frank, André Gunder (1967), *Capitalism and Underdevelopment in Latin America: Historical Studies of Chile and Brazil* (New York: Monthly Review).

Frank, André Gunder (1969), *Latin America: Underdevelopment or Revolution* (New York: Monthly Review).

Fukuyama, Francis (1992), *The End of History and the Last Man* (London: Hamish Hamilton).

Furci, Carmelo (1984), *The Chilean Communist Party and the Road to Socialism* (London: Zed).

Furtado, Celso (1970), *Economic Development of Latin America: A Survey from Colonial Times to the Cuban Revolution* (Cambridge: Cambridge University Press).

Furtado, Celso (1974), *Teoría y Política del Desarrollo Económico* (México: Siglo XXI).

Gaitán, Gloria (1985), 'Orígenes de la violencia de los años 40', in G. Gonzalo Sánchez (ed.), *Once Ensayos sobre la Violencia* (Bogotá: CEREC/Centro Gaitán), pp. 325–60.

García Naranjo, Francisco (1996), *Historias Derrotadas: Opción y obstinación de la guerrilla chilena (1965–1988)* (Morelia, México: Universidad Michoacana de San Nicolás de Hidalgo).

García-Pérez, Gladys Mariel (1998), *Insurrection and Revolution: Armed Struggle in Cuba, 1952–1959* (Boulder, CO: Lynne Rienner).

Germani, Gino (1962), *Política y Sociedad en una Época de Transición* (Buenos Aires: Paidós).

Gilbert, Dennis (1988), *Sandinistas: The Party and the Revolution* (Oxford: Basil Blackwell).

Gills, Barry, Rocamora, Joel and Wilson, Richard (1993), *Low Intensity Democracy: Political Power in the New World Order* (London: Pluto).

Golding, Sue (1992), *Gramsci's Democratic Theory: Contributions to a Post-Liberal Democracy* (Toronto: University of Toronto Press).

Gott, Richard (1973), *Rural Guerrillas in Latin America* (Harmondsworth: Penguin).

Gott, Richard (2000), *In the Shadow of the Liberator: Hugo Chávez and the Transformation of Venezuela* (London: Verso).

Gott, Richard (2004), *Cuba: A New History* (New Haven, CT: Yale University Press).

Grass, Gunter (2005), 'The high price of freedom', *Guardian*, Weekend Review, 7 May 2005, pp. 4–5.

Green, W. John (2003), *Gaitanism, Left Liberalism, and Popular Mobilization in Colombia* (Gainesville, FL: University Press of Florida).

Grugel, Jean (1994), 'El populismo en Chile', in José Álvarez Junco and Ricardo González Leandri (eds), *El populismo en España y América* (Madrid: Catriel), pp. 199–214.

Guevara, Ernesto 'Che' (1963), *Pasajes de la Guerra Revolucionaria* (Havana: Ediciones Unión).

Guevara, Ernesto 'Che' (1968), *Reminiscences of the Cuban Revolutionary War* (London: George Allen & Unwin).

Guevara, Ernesto 'Che' (1996), *Episodes of the Cuban Revolutionary War, 1956–58*, Mary-Alice Waters (ed.) (New York: Pathfinder).

Halebsky, S. and Kirk, J. (eds) (1985), *Cuba: Twenty-Five Years of Revolution, 1959–1984* (New York: Praeger).

Hardt, Michael and Negri, Antonio (2000), *Empire* (Cambridge, MA: Harvard University Press).

Harnecker, Marta (1986), *La estrategia política de Fidel* (México: Nuestro Tiempo).

Harnecker, Marta (2000), *La Izquierda en el Umbral del Siglo XXI: Haciendo Posible lo Imposible* (Madrid: Siglo XXI).

Harnecker, Marta (2002), *Hugo Chávez Frías: Un Hombre, un Pueblo* (Caracas: Desde Abajo).

Harris, Richard and Vilas, Carlos M. (1985), *Nicaragua: A Revolution under Siege* (London: Zed).

Hart Dávalos, Armando (1997), *Aldabonazo* (Havana: Letras Cubanas).

Hellinger, Daniel C. (1991), *Venezuela: Tarnished Democracy* (Boulder, CO: Westview).

Henfrey, Colin and Sorj, Bernardo (1977), *Chilean Voices: Activists Describe their Experiences of the Popular Unity Period* (Brighton: Harvester).

Hinkelammert, Franz J. (1990), *Democracia y totalitarismo* (San José, Costa Rica: Departamento Ecuménico de Investigaciones).

Holloway, John (2002), *Change the World Without Taking Power* (London: Pluto).

Hoyt, Katherine (1997), *The Many Faces of Sandinista Democracy* (Athens, OH: Ohio University Press).

Huntington, Samuel (1991), *The Third Wave* (Norman, OK: University of Oklahoma Press).

Ianni, Octavio (1975), *La Formación del Estado Populista en América Latina* (México: Era).

Ibarra Guitart, José Renato (2000), *El Fracaso de los Moderados en Cuba: Las Alternativas Reformistas de 1957 a 1958* (Havana: Editora Política).

INTI (2004), *Tiempo de Zamora* 8 (January) (Republica Bolivariana de Venezuela, Instituto Nacional de Tierras), p. 3.

Jacques, Martin (2004), 'The only show in town', *Guardian*, 20 November 2004.

Kapcia, Antoni (2000), *Cuba: Island of Dreams* (Oxford: Berg).

Kay, Cristóbal (1989), *Latin American Theories of Development and Underdevelopment* (London: Routledge).

Kayman, Martin (1987), *Revolution and Counter-Revolution in Portugal* (London: Merlin).

Kohan, Néstor (1997), 'El Che Guevara y la filosofía de la praxis', *América Libre* (July), special number: 'Ernesto Che Guevara, 30 Aniversario' (Havana: Abril), pp. 59–75.

Labrousse, Alain (1972), *L'Expérience Chilienne: Réformisme ou Révolution?* (Paris: Seuil).

Laclau, Ernesto (1977), *Politics and Ideology in Marxist Theory* (London: New Left Books).

Lanz Rodríguez, Carlos (2004), *El Desarrollo Endógeno y la Misión 'Vuelvan Caras'* (Caracas: Alcaldía de Caracas).

Laughland, John (2004), 'The revolution televised', *Guardian*, 27 November.

Lebowitz, Michael (2005), *Lecciones de la Autogestión Yugoslava* (Caracas: La Burbuja, Instituto Municipal de Publicaciones de la Alcaldía de Caracas).

Lenin, V.I. (1936), 'What Is To Be Done?', in *Selected Works*, Vol. II (London: Lawrence & Wishart).

Lenin, V.I. (1965), *The State and Revolution* (Peking: Foreign Languages Press).

Levine, Daniel (2003), 'Undemocratic Venezuela', *Bulletin of Latin American Research* 22:3 (April), pp. 231–6.

Linz, Juan J. and Stepan, Albert (1996), *Problems of Democratic Transition and Consolidation* (Baltimore, MD: Johns Hopkins University Press).

Macpherson, C.B. (1962), *The Political Theory of Possessive Individualism: Hobbes to Locke* (Oxford: Oxford University Press).

Mariátegui, José Carlos (1969), *Siete Ensayos de Interpretación de la Realidad Peruana* (México: Solidaridad).

Marini, Ruy Mauro (1973), *Dialéctica de la dependencia* (México: Era).

Martí, José (1975), *Inside the Monster: Writings on the United States and American Imperialism*, Philip S. Foner (ed.) (New York: Monthly Review).

Marx, Karl and Engels, Frederick (1968), *Selected Works in One Volume* (London: Lawrence & Wishart).

Mason, Patricio (1986), *El Movimiento Obrero Chileno y la República Socialista de 1932: Breve Síntesis Histórica* (Santiago: Cambio).

Matthews, Herbert L. (1975), *Revolution in Cuba: An Essay in Understanding* (New York: Charles Scribner's Sons).

McCaughan, Michael (2004), *The Battle of Venezuela* (London: Latin America Bureau).

Mencía, Mario (1993), *The Fertile Prison: Fidel Castro in Batista's Jails* (Melbourne: Ocean).

Méndez, Ana Irene (2004), *Democracia y Discurso Político: Caldera, Pérez y Chávez* (Caracas: Monte Ávila).

Méndez, Juan E., O'Donnell, Guillermo and Pinheiro, Paulo Sérgio (eds) (1999), *The (Un)Rule of Law and the Underprivileged in Latin America* (Notre Dame, IN: University of Notre Dame Press).

Mercedes Cobo, Maria (2005), 'Antídoto contra el hambre y la pobreza', *Patria Grande* 5 (June), (Caracas: Ministerio de Comercio Internacional), pp. 10–12.

Ministry of Science & Technology (2004), 'Reporte: Cifras (para finales marzo 2004) de las misiones del gobierno reflejan grandes avances en materia social', www.aporrea.org, 28 May 2004.

Molina V., José E. (2002), 'The presidential and parliamentary elections of the Bolivarian Revolution in Venezuela: change and continuity (1998–2000)', *Bulletin of Latin American Research* 21:2 (April), pp. 219–47.

Mouzelis, Nicos (1978), 'Ideology and Class Politics: a Critique of Ernesto Laclau', *New Left Review* 112 (November–December), pp. 45–61.

Norden, Deborah L. (2003), 'Democracy in uniform: Chávez and the Venezuelan armed forces', in Steve Ellner and Daniel Hellinger (eds), *Venezuelan Politics in the Chávez Era: Class, Polarization and Conflict* (Boulder, CO: Lynne Rienner), pp. 93–112.

North, Liisa (2004), 'State building, state dismantling, and financial crises in Ecuador', in Jo-Marie Burt and Philip Mauceri (eds), *Politics in the Andes: Identity, Conflict, Reform* (Pittsburgh, PA: University of Pittsburgh Press), pp. 187–206.

Nun, José (2003), *Democracy: Government of the People or Government of the Politicians?* (Lanham, MD: Rowman & Littlefield).

O'Donnell, Guillermo (1994), 'Delegative democracy', *Journal of Democracy* 5:1, pp. 55–69.

O'Donnell, Guillermo, Schmitter, Philippe and Whitehead, Lawrence (eds) (1986), *Transitions from Authoritarian Rule: Comparative Perspectives* (Baltimore, MD: Johns Hopkins University Press).

Oltuski, Enrique (2000), *Gente del Llano* (Havana: Imagen Contemporánea).

Palacios, Angel (2004), *Puente Llaguno: Imágenes de una Masacre*, documentary produced by Venezuelan public television (Channel 8) and directed by Palacios.

Palacios Cerezales, Diego (2003), *O Poder Caiú na Rúa: Crise de Estado e Acções Colectivas na Revolução Portuguesa, 1974–1975* (Lisbon: Imprensa de Ciências Sociais).

Pendle, George (1963), *Argentina* (London: Oxford University Press).

Pérez, Louis A. (1988), *Cuba: Between Reform and Revolution* (New York: Oxford University Press).

Philip, George (2003), *Democracy in Latin America: Surviving Conflict and Crisis?* (Cambridge: Polity).

Przeworski, Adam (1986), 'Some problems in the study of the transition to democracy', in Guillermo O'Donnell, Philippe C. Schmitter and Lawrence

Whitehead (eds), *Transitions from Authoritarian Rule: Comparative Perspectives* (Baltimore, MD: Johns Hopkins University Press), pp. 47–63.

Qathafi, Muammar Al (n.d.), *O Livro Verde* (Tripoli: Empresa Pública de Edição, Publicidade e Edição).

Raby, D.L. (1983), *Populism: A Marxist Analysis* (Montreal: Centre for Developing-Area Studies, McGill University).

Raby, D.L. (1988), *Fascism and Resistance in Portugal: Communists, Liberals and Military Dissidents in the Opposition to Salazar, 1941–74* (Manchester: Manchester University Press).

Ramírez Rojas, Kléber (1998), *Historia Documental del 4 de Febrero* (Caracas: UCV/Asamblea Legislativa del Estado Miranda).

Ramos Jiménez, Alfredo (2002), 'Los límites del liderazgo plebiscitario: el fenómeno Chávez en perspectiva comparada', in Ramos Jiménez (ed.), *La Transición Venezolana: Aproximación al Fenómeno Chávez* (Mérida, Venezuela: Universidad de los Andes).

*Relatório do 25 de Novembro: Texto Integral* (1976), (Lisbon: Abril).

Rodrigues, Avelino, Borga, Cesário, and Cardoso, Mário (1974), *O Movimento dos Capitães e o 25 de Abril* (Lisbon: Moraes).

Rodrigues, Avelino, Borga, Cesário, and Cardoso, Mário (1976), *Portugal Depois de Abril* (Lisbon: António dos Reis/DIG).

Roig de Leuchsenring, Emilio (1973), *Historia de la Enmienda Platt* (Havana: Editorial de Ciencias Sociales).

Roman, Peter (2003), *People's Power: Cuba's Experience with Representative Government* (Lanham, MD: Rowman & Littlefield).

Rousseau, Jean-Jacques (2001), *Du contrat social (Présentation, notes, bibliographie et chronologie par Bruno Bernardi)* (Paris: Flammarion).

Roxborough, Ian, O'Brien, Phil and Roddick, Jackie (1977), *Chile: The State and Revolution* (London: Macmillan).

Ruchwarger, Gary (1987), *People in Power: Forging a Grassroots Democracy in Nicaragua* (South Hadley, MA: Bergin & Garvey).

Sader, Amir (2005), *El Populismo: Su más Completa Traducción* (Rio de Janeiro: Servicio Informativo ALAI-Amlatina, www.alai-amlatina.org).

Sánchez, Gonzalo (1985), 'La violencia y sus efectos en el sistema político colombiano', in Sánchez (ed.), *Once Ensayos sobre la Violencia* (Bogotá: CEREC/Centro Gaitán), pp. 209–58.

Sanoja Hernández, Jesús (1998), *Historia Electoral de Venezuela (1810–1998)* (Caracas: El Nacional).

Scheer, Robert and Zeitlin, Maurice (1964), *Cuba: An American Tragedy* (Harmondsworth: Penguin).

Schumpeter, Joseph (1942), *Capitalism, Socialism and Democracy* (New York: Harper & Row).

Silverman, Bertram (ed.) (1973), *Man and Socialism in Cuba: The Great Debate* (New York: Atheneum).

SIPC (Serviço de Intercâmbio Político e Cultural) (1976), *Portugal: Um Guia Para o Processo* (Lisbon: Editorial SLEMES).

Steele, Jonathan (2004), 'Ukraine's postmodern coup d'état', *Guardian*, 26 November.

Sunacoop (2005), www.sunacoop.gov.ve/estadisticas/cuadro1.htm.

Sunkel, Osvaldo (1973), 'The pattern of Latin American dependence', in V.L. Urquidi and R. Thorpe (eds), *Latin America and the International Economy* (London: Macmillan).

Sweig, Julia E. (2002), *Inside the Cuban Revolution: Fidel Castro and the Urban Underground* (Cambridge, MA.: Harvard University Press).

Tabares del Real, José A. (1973), *Guiteras* (Havana: Editorial de Ciencias Sociales).

Tamargo, Agustín (1959) 'Contra esto y aquello', *Bohemia* 31 May, p. 65.

Thomas, Hugh (1971), *Cuba: or, The Pursuit of Freedom* (London: Eyre & Spottiswoode).

Thompson, E.P. (1966), *The Making of the English Working Class* (New York: Vintage).

Torre, Juan Carlos (1994), 'La formación del sindicalismo peronista en Argentina', in José Álvarez Junco and Ricardo González Leandri (eds), *El Populismo en España y América* (Madrid: Catriel), pp. 91–108.

Traynor, Ian (2004), 'US campaign behind the turmoil in Kiev', *Guardian*, 26 November.

Tulchin, Joseph S. and Romero, Bernice (eds) (1995), *The Consolidation of Democracy in Latin America* (Boulder, CO: Lynne Rienner).

Valdés, Juan Gabriel (1995), 'Changing paradigms in Latin America: from dependency to neoliberalism in the international context', in Joseph S. Tulchin with Bernice Romero (eds), *The Consolidation of Democracy in Latin America* (Boulder, CO: Lynne Rienner), pp. 127–38.

Vanden, Harry E. and Prevost, Gary (1993), *Democracy and Socialism in Sandinista Nicaragua* (Boulder, CO: Lynne Rienner).

Vitale, Luis et al. (1999), *Para Recuperar la Memoria Histórica: Frei, Allende y Pinochet* (Santiago: ChileAmérica – CESOC).

Wainwright, Hilary (2003), *Reclaim the State: Experiments in Popular Democracy* (London: Verso).

Walker, Thomas W. (1991), *Nicaragua: The Land of Sandino* (Boulder, CO: Westview).

Wallerstein, Immanuel (1980), *The Modern World-System I: Capitalist Agriculture and the Origins of the European World-Economy in the Sixteenth Century* (New York: Academic Press).

Wallerstein, Immanuel (1982), *The Modern World-System II: Mercantilism and the Consolidation of the European World-Economy 1600–1750* (New York: Academic Press).

Weffort, Francisco (1968), 'El populismo en la política brasileira', in Celso Furtado (ed.), *Brasil: Hoy* (México: Siglo XXI).

Wright, Bruce E. (1995), *Theory in the Practice of the Nicaraguan Revolution* (Athens, OH: Ohio University Press).

Zago, Ángela (1998), *La Rebelión de los Ángeles*, 4th edition (Caracas: WARP).

# Index